GLASGOW TERCENTENARY ESSAYS

300 Years of the School of Law

Publication of this volume
has been supported by the
University of Glasgow

GLASGOW TERCENTENARY ESSAYS

300 Years of the School of Law

Edited by

Ross G Anderson LLB (Hons), PhD, Dip LP
Advocate; Honorary Research Fellow, University of Glasgow

James Chalmers LLB (Hons), LLM, Dip LP
Regius Professor of Law, University of Glasgow

John MacLeod LLB (Hons)
Lecturer in Commercial Law, University of Glasgow

Avizandum Publishing Ltd
Edinburgh
2014

Published by
Avizandum Publishing Ltd
25 Candlemaker Row
Edinburgh EH1 2QG

First published 2014

ISBN 978-1-904968-13-9

British Library Cataloguing in Publication Data
A catalogue entry for this book is available from the British Library

Typeset by Waverley Typesetters, Warham
Printed and bound by Martin's the Printers, Berwick upon Tweed

Contents

Foreword

Rt Hon Sir Menzies Campbell CH, CBE, QC, MP

It seems presumptuous of me to write a foreword to a series of essays from such a distinguished group of lawyers. They all display intellectual rigour and academic discipline, both of which are traits which every lawyer should cultivate but are not necessarily found in politicians. I am only slightly encouraged to do so by the fact that I have appeared with, against, and before several of them.

I represent that rapidly declining hybrid species: the lawyer cum politician. Where once the Westminster Parliament's hours were fixed to suit lawyers who practised in the morning and early afternoons at the Royal Courts of Justice, but did not have to vote until 10 pm, now all is changed with the House of Commons sitting in the morning and, as I write, a non-lawyer in the office of Lord Chancellor. What must those two distinguished Lord Chancellors from Scotland, James Mackay and Alexander Irvine, think of that?

I am among the last of those Scots lawyers who were not allowed into the Law Faculty of Glasgow University unless we were able to provide proof of prior education in the form of a first degree (in my case a very ordinary MA) before being admitted to the mysteries of conveyancing, jurisprudence, and delict. We would not be recognised as students today: our business suits, stiff collars and – in some brave cases – bowler hats would be the objects of mirth and puzzlement. We were the last generation to be simultaneously both students and apprentices. Formal dress and classes in the early morning and late afternoons coupled with a few hours in a solicitor's office in between were soon replaced by a cohort of young men and women who studied full-time and who more closely resembled the popular idea of a student.

Ours was a fraught existence. The partners to whom we were apprenticed expected more of us than we had time to give and lecturers and professors simply expected to see more of us! We were part-time students often taught by part-time lecturers. Something had to give and so the full-time LLB was created. The consequences seem to have been entirely beneficial, save for one group of lawyers – aspiring politicians. The reason John Smith and Donald Dewar were able to hone their debating skills to the point that made them powerful candidates for selection as candidates and election as

MPs was that they, like many others under the part-time system, spent up to seven years at the University and, equally importantly, in the Union. By the time they left the University their skills had been finely honed in a noisy and rumbustious union debating chamber.

The law is a useful preparation for Parliament. New MPs who are lawyers at least know one end of a statute from another, a long title from a schedule, an Order in Council from a statutory instrument. But in the adversarial political system at Westminster, the qualities of analysis and logical argument that legal education is designed to engender are often subordinated to noisy opinion, as is reason to vehemence. And just as some lawyers never adjust to the challenge of advocacy, some legally-qualified MPs never adjust to the House of Commons. The rational (and occasionally didactic) style which is often necessary with an unsympathetic judge is not suited to a chamber which can be irreverent, noisy and intimidating. Good law and good lawyers should have reason as a handmaiden; but in the passion of political debate it can be a hindrance.

Nor does the style of contemporary politics lend itself to the rational legal approach. The advent of 24-hour news channels; the need to comment almost before an event has taken place; and the sheer pace of political discourse under the influence of the information revolution, do not sit easily with the measured legal analysis which is the hallmark of the good lawyer.

So in the face of the limitation on effectiveness placed upon legal aptitude and training is there any particular contribution the legally qualified can make to politics? In one major respect I would say, yes: that is the quality of good judgment which the legally-qualified mind should acquire by reason of learning and experience.

Politics is a world of relative, not absolute, values. Take, for example, the need to balance the budget against the need to protect the poor and needy, or the desirability of the free market against the risk of monopoly. Major decision-making, particularly for Ministers, involves the weighing up of competing solutions or courses of action. This is precisely the skill which the legal mind is able to provide. An American judge put it well when he said good lawyers should be problem solvers. Politicians daily have to solve problems either in their constituencies, in Parliament or their ministries. Good judgment is essential.

Will any of this limit the attraction for lawyers of the House of Commons? There are nearly a hundred MPs in the present House of Commons whose profession has been, and in some cases continues to be, the law. But the days when John Mortimer's Rumpole could inveigh against the style and gilded career available to Sir Guthrie Featherstone are long since gone. As the respect of the public for MPs has dwindled so too has the respect of MPs for the lawyers.

The exhortation expressed in Henry VI, Part II "The first thing we do, let's kill all the lawyers" was written in 1592. It has proved more easily said than done not least in the political life of the United Kingdom. But the days when solicitors or advocates, or barristers such as my predecessor in Fife, Asquith, could simply use their legal training to achieve high political office are passed. Legal competence and experience are no longer enough. All this having been said, however, none of the distinguished contributors to this volume is or has been a politician.

The essays which are reproduced here are a credit to the study of law at Glasgow University.

MENZIES CAMPBELL
House of Commons
30 April 2014

Contributors

J Craig Barker is a graduate (LLB (Hons), PhD, Dip LP) of the University of Glasgow, a solicitor, and Professor of Law at the University of Sussex.

Gillian Black is a graduate (LLB (Hons)) and former member of staff in the School of Law of the University of Glasgow. She is a solicitor and Senior Lecturer in Law at the University of Edinburgh.

Kenneth Campbell QC is a graduate (LLB (Hons), Dip LP) of the University of Glasgow and member of the Faculty of Advocates.

James Chalmers is Regius Professor of Law at the University of Glasgow.

Maksymilian Del Mar is Senior Lecturer in Law and Philosophy at Queen Mary, University of London.

William W McBryde is a graduate (PhD) and former Lecturer in Private Law at the University of Glasgow. He is a solicitor and Emeritus Professor of Commercial Law at the University of Edinburgh.

Stan Naismith is a graduate (LLB (Hons), PhD) of the University of Glasgow, a solicitor, and presently Registrar, Second Section, European Court of Human Rights.

Robert Reed is a Justice of the Supreme Court of the United Kingdom, an honorary graduate of the University of Glasgow (LLD) and a member of the School of Law's Advisory Panel.

O F Robinson is Douglas Professor Emeritus of Roman Law at the University of Glasgow.

J Irvine Smith QC is a graduate (MA (Hons), LLB) and former Lecturer in the History of Scots Law at the University of Glasgow. A member of the Faculty of Advocates, he was Sheriff at Glasgow and thereafter at Greenock, Rothesay and Dunoon.

S J Summers is a graduate of the University of Glasgow (LLB (Hons)) and is SNSF Professor of Criminal Law and Criminal Procedural Law at the University of Zurich.

The Teaching of International Law: Fragmentation or Cohesion?

J Craig Barker

I am deeply honoured to have been asked to contribute to this volume. The eight years I spent studying at the University of Glasgow, School of Law, completing my LLB, PhD and Diploma in Legal Practice, were certainly among the best of my life and provided a wonderful foundation for my career as a teacher of international law. As well as marking the three-hundredth anniversary of the Regius Chair, 2013 also marks the thirtieth year since I commenced my legal studies at Glasgow, the twentieth anniversary of my taking up my first lecturing position at the University of Reading and the tenth anniversary of my securing a Chair in International Law at the University of Sussex and so there is a great deal for me to celebrate. Writing this essay has given me a wonderful opportunity to reflect on my teaching and research and especially on what I owe to my time at Glasgow.

I have been pondering the issue of the coherence of international law for some years and saw the invitation to contribute to this volume as an opportunity, finally, to contribute something to the debate. As I will show, international law has changed significantly in the last thirty years. It has become more pervasive, more mature and more complex. It has moved considerably beyond the basic existential question that used always to precede its formal study: the "Is international law really law?" question, into what has been described as a post-ontological period.[1] International law now covers a wide range of sometimes unrelated issues and topics. As a result concern has been raised in the academic literature and beyond about the apparent fragmentation of international law and its division into unrelated sub-systems resulting, potentially, in a loss of universality and coherence. The academic literature addressing the question of the fragmentation of international law is vast and will not be explored fully in this essay. However, I will suggest that the fragmentation literature has not addressed what I consider to be one very important element of the response to the fragmentation argument; that is, the issue of the teaching of international law.

---

[1] T Franck, *Fairness in International Law and Institutions* (1995) p 6. See further below.

This essay will begin with a brief description and personal analysis of the history of international law teaching at the University of Glasgow. It will then turn to consider the growing maturity and complexity of international law, before introducing the fragmentation debate. Drawing on my own teaching and research in the field of international immunities from jurisdiction, the essay will then consider one of the most controversial examples of the fragmentation debate, that is, the conflict between state immunity and human rights, particularly as exemplified in the recent decision of the International Court of Justice in *Jurisdictional Immunities of the State (Germany v Italy).*[2] Having highlighted the problems inherent in the process of fragmentation, the final section of the essay will argue that teachers of international law have a central role to play in avoiding further fragmentation of international law.

THE TEACHING OF INTERNATIONAL LAW AT GLASGOW: AN INSTITUTIONAL AND PERSONAL JOURNEY

The teaching of law at Glasgow appears always to have had an international element. When the former Regius Professor of Law, David M Walker, wrote *A History of the School of Law, The University of Glasgow* he noted that: "until the fifteenth century the thorough study of law could only be pursued abroad, and there is ample evidence of young Scots, nearly all clerics, seeking leave of their bishops or abbots to go to Paris, Orleans, Toulouse, sometimes even Bologna, to study law. A few went to Oxford".[3] Latterly, international scholars were welcomed to Glasgow in so far as the establishment, by papal bull, of a *stadium generalium* at Glasgow in 1451 was for a place of study "attended by scholars from all parts" where students from everywhere were welcome and not merely those from the local district or region.[4]

The *lingua franca* of legal studies in medieval times was Latin and the law was thoroughly based on religious and Roman foundations. Thus, the establishment of the Scottish universities of St Andrews, Glasgow and Aberdeen in the fifteenth century was "for the study *inter alia* of canon and civil law",[5] and these universities welcomed scholars from around the world. However, the years 1451–1712, described by Walker in his book as a period of "Foundation and Frustration",[6] saw the teaching of law removed from the

---

[2] *Case Concerning Jurisdictional Immunities of the State (Germany v Italy)* ICJ Judgment, 3 February 2012.

[3] D M Walker, *A History of the School of Law, The University of Glasgow* (1990) p 9.

[4] See H Rashdall, *The Universities of Europe in the Middle Ages*, vol II (1895) p 3.

[5] Walker, *History* (n 3) p 9.

[6] At p 11.

University of Glasgow,[7] only to be finally reinstated by the establishment of the Regius Chair of Law in 1713. Once re-established, the teaching of law at Glasgow continued to attract scholars from around the world.[8]

Nevertheless, by the eighteenth century the teaching and study of law had developed from a single "science" into a multiplicity of different legal "sciences" based on national legal systems. As Reinhard Zimmermann has pointed out, "[t]here is no such subject as German chemistry or French medicine. But for the past hundred years or so there have been, in principle, as many legal systems (and consequently, legal sciences) in Europe as there are nation states".[9] In Glasgow this resulted, for example, in John Millar, Glasgow's fourth Regius Chair, having to teach Scots law and English law in alternate years.[10] To the extent that there was any international law teaching at Glasgow after the establishment of the Regius Chair, it was probably focused around the work of the moral philosophers such as Hugo Grotius, Samuel Puffendorf and Emmerich de Vattel, individuals whom we now recognise as among the classical writers on international law. In addition, the moral philosophy of Adam Smith, who was himself Professor of Moral Philosophy at Glasgow University from 1752–64, contributed to the development of the discipline.[11] It was not until the late nineteenth century, after the most noted Scottish international lawyer, Professor James Lorimer of the University of Edinburgh, delivered a course on public law at Glasgow in 1877, that there was established at Glasgow a lectureship in public law, including jurisprudence and international law, a position filled in 1878 by William Galbraith Miller. The teaching of both public and private international law were separated from the teaching of jurisprudence in 1894 and both have remained on the Glasgow law syllabus since that date.[12]

Although international law had featured independently on the Glasgow syllabus since the end of the nineteenth century, it was not until the early 1960s that the study of international law at honours level emerged. At this time, the need to expand international law teaching beyond merely

---

[7] Walker refers (at p 15) to the decision of John Mair (or Major) to divert revenues of the readership in canon law to the teaching of Arts. He notes also, nevertheless (at pp 16–17) that this lack of legal education did not prevent Viscount Stair from teaching himself law and developing his *Institutions of the Law of Scotland* (1681).

[8] Walker, *History* (n 3) p 26. Walker refers specifically to the reputation of John Millar who was appointed to the Regius Chair in 1781 and who "attracted students from England, and even two from Russia".

[9] R Zimmermann, "Civil Code and Civil Law: the 'Europeanization' of private law within the European Community and the re-emergence of a European legal science" (1994) 1 Columbia Journal of European Law 63 at 65.

[10] Walker, *History* (n 3) p 26.

[11] At pp 27–28.

[12] See generally Walker, *History* (n 3).

the ordinary course necessitated the development of a range of honours courses and the appointment of additional international law staff. The most significant appointment, from my perspective, was that of John P Grant who was appointed as a senior lecturer in 1974 and was elevated to a titular chair in 1988, serving as Dean of the Faculty of Law at Glasgow from 1985 to 1989 and from 1992 to 1996. My own passion and understanding of international law owes a great deal to this individual who became my mentor, co-author and friend.[13] The teaching of international law at Glasgow has benefited from the work of *inter alia* Professor Tony Carty, Professor Iain Scobbie and now Professor Christian Tams, ably assisted by Dr Akbar Rasulov and Dr James Sloan (with apologies to the many experts whom I have not mentioned).

My personal involvement with public international law at Glasgow began in 1983, the year I began my legal studies. I was allowed in my first year to choose between civil law and public international law and I readily chose the latter, having failed to progress my Latin studies beyond merely rudimentary level at school. I vividly remember my first PIL lecture at the University of Glasgow, which was delivered by John Grant. Rather than begin with the standard ontological question referred to above, John began his course with an analysis of the recently concluded conflict between the United Kingdom and Argentina over the Falkland/Malvinas Islands introducing his students to key issues of title to territory, the law of armed conflict, and the laws of war. I, for one, was immediately hooked. The course then proceeded to cover the traditional core issues of international law including the sources of international law, the subjects of international law, the relationship between international law and municipal law as well as issues of state responsibility and the peaceful settlement of disputes. In the second term, the course moved to consider the use of force in more depth as well as the law of the sea, human rights and some of the emerging topics of international law including international environmental law. As the course progressed I became more and more enamoured of the subject, reflecting on many of the subject's myriad of conceptual problems and practical questions.

As an aside I feel compelled to mention how much I benefited from pursuing an honours degree at a Scottish university. Having now taught in England for twenty years, I cannot question the level of achievement of my English-based students. However, that additional year of honours study that I was "required" to take in Glasgow provided a stronger foundation in

---

[13] John and I have co-authored three books: *Deskbook of International Criminal Law* (2005); *The Harvard Research in International Law: Contemporary Analysis and Appraisal* (2007); and *Encyclopaedic Dictionary of International Law* (3rd edn, 2009).

international law than I would have achieved elsewhere. Having completed my "introduction" to public international law in my first year of study at Glasgow, I could not wait to submit my application to complete my honours in that subject. During my third and fourth years of study I completed courses in the law of the sea, contemporary issues in international law, the law of international institutions, private international law, and took the opportunity to complete a dissertation on "The Legality of the Strategic Defence Initiative" or "Star Wars". During this time I was introduced to many of the key theories of international law, including New Haven Scholarship and Critical Legal Studies. I had the opportunity to analyse in detail some of the key judgments of the International Court of Justice, including, most notably, the decision of the Court in *Military and Paramilitary Activities in and against Nicaragua (Nicaragua v United States of America)*.[14] Additionally, I had the opportunity to participate in a new optional course in foreign relations law, which introduced me to the study of the law of international immunities, including diplomatic and state immunity, which subsequently formed the basis of my PhD and much of my published work.

Having spent eight years of study developing my interest in, and knowledge of, international law, I was singularly disappointed after securing my first teaching job at the University of Reading that, as there was only one international law course – a final year option that was being taught by another member of staff – I was required to teach business law, employment law and, latterly, company law. This situation was not unusual in provincial English law schools in the early 1990s. It was only the major university law schools in England that taught a broader range of international law subjects. Even at Masters level, the opportunities were limited and it was only through working with colleagues in the Department of Politics and International Relations that I was finally able to develop an MA in Diplomacy and an MA/LLM in International Law and World Order in order to allow me to teach international law. However, this situation was quickly to change.

THE MATURITY AND COMPLEXITY
OF INTERNATIONAL LAW[15]

In the relatively short time since the 1990s opportunities for teaching and learning international law have increased significantly, not only in the United Kingdom, but also around the world. This is due, in part at least, to the increasing maturity and complexity of international law. The

---

[14] 1984 ICJ Rep 392.
[15] I readily admit to having borrowed this heading from the work of Franck, *Fairness in International Law and Institutions* (n 1) pp 4–6.

School of Law at the University of Glasgow, like many other law schools in the United Kingdom, including my own, now offers, in addition to an undergraduate law degree, a number of Masters programmes in law. In addition to recruiting international students to Glasgow, an astonishing 65 per cent of the School of Law's honours students now take the opportunity to spend some or all of their third year studying abroad. This internationalisation of the study of law and of the Law School itself must be a significant part of why Glasgow is currently ranked as the top law school in Scotland.[16]

This "brave new world" of internationalised law schools in the United Kingdom has developed not on the back of the desire of foreign students to learn about different domestic legal systems, although there will certainly be some comparativitists among them. Nor is it being driven by conflict of laws concerns. It has, rather, flourished on the back of the teaching of public international law and its various sub-systems. Many of the readers of this essay will be surprised at this very broad assertion about the extent of public international law's apparent reach. Those who did not study public international law will probably have deliberately avoided an interesting looking but ultimately not very "legal" optional subject. Even those who enjoyed the opportunity to take a break from the rigorous black letter of their more doctrinal subjects to take the PIL option will no doubt also question how such an ephemeral subject might now be seen as so important. Even the few of us who were, in my view, fortunate enough to take the study of international law to honours level and beyond will, like me, be constantly surprised at the size and content of the subject of public international law as it continues to develop today.

Undoubtedly Professor Franck's assertion referred to earlier that international law has entered its post-ontological era is correct. According to Franck:[17]

> [International lawyers] need no longer defend the very existence of international law. Thus emancipated from the constraints of defensive ontology, international lawyers are now free to undertake a critical assessment of its content.

The analysis of the content of the law must also take account of the broader focus of the law in terms of its "subjects". In 1994, the then Professor Rosalyn Higgins, in her seminal Hague Lectures, identified the subject/object dichotomy as "an intellectual prison of our own choosing".[18] She preferred instead to speak of "participants" in the international legal

---

[16] In 2013, Glasgow was ranked first in Scotland in league tables published by *The Guardian*, *The Times* and *The Sunday Times*.

[17] Franck, *Fairness in International Law and Institutions* (n 1) p 6.

[18] R Higgins, *Problems and Process: International Law and How We Use It* (1994) p 49.

process.[19] Today's participants include not only states but international governmental and non-governmental organisations, multilateral corporations and also individuals, among others.

A critical assessment of the content of international law must also recognise the vast array of topics that international law now purports to cover. This is perhaps best illustrated by reference to another of Franck's assertions to the effect that "international law has entered the stage of practitioner-specialist".[20] He notes that: "Specialization [sic] is a tribute which the profession pays to the maturity of the legal system."[21] It is certainly the case that the legal profession in the UK, and in many other states, is increasingly concerned not only with matters of international commerce, trade and investment, but also with human rights, with the protection of the environment and with international criminal law. The interface between international and domestic law has always given rise to interesting legal questions, many of which have been argued before the British courts. However, recently, the significance of issues such as immunities from jurisdiction, immigration, and the ex-territorial application of domestic and regional human rights obligations have come more and more to the fore in the actual practice of the law.

Twenty years ago when I was considering how I might use my interest in (and passion for) international law in practice, and taking the step after completing my PhD of actually qualifying as a solicitor, I searched around in vain for solicitors' practices that had more than simply a couple of enthusiasts who professed to being international law specialists, and most of those I did find were located in only a very few large commercial firms based in London. Furthermore, the barristers who took instruction in international law matters were essentially professors of international law who had qualified at the bar. My only options at that time appeared to be to become an academic, go and work for the United Nations or one of a very small number of international institutions, or to secure a job in the Foreign and Commonwealth Office as a legal adviser (hence the decision to complete my solicitor qualifications).[22] Ultimately I chose the academic route and have never looked back.

A student who is enthusiastic about international law today has a wealth of opportunities available to him or her. Most large commercial firms now practise international (or perhaps more properly transnational)

---

[19] Higgins, *Problems and Process*, p 49. See also R Higgins, "Conceptual thinking about the individual in international law" (1978) 4 British Journal of International Studies 1 at 5.

[20] Franck, *Fairness in International Law and Institutions* (n 1) p 4.

[21] Franck, p 4.

[22] Glasgow has historically been very successful in placing alumni in the legal adviser's department at the FCO, due in no small measure to the work of Professor Grant.

commercial law to a greater or lesser extent,[23] and many have significant international practices.[24] Outside the commercial world, many law firms offer specialisms in areas such as human rights, immigration, the environment and international criminal law. Indeed, one firm, Volterra Fietta, has recently set itself up in London as "the Public International Law Firm" and specialises only in matters of public international law. Many barristers' chambers in London are similarly focused on matters of international law including, most notably, Matrix Chambers in international human rights and 39 Bedford Row in international criminal law. The extraordinary growth in international governmental institutions and non-governmental organisations offers significant opportunities for students of international law to develop their skills. Having taught international criminal law (ICL) for the last ten years I have seen a significant number of students undertake internships in the primary ICL institutions in The Hague, including not only the International Criminal Court (ICC) but also the International Criminal Tribunal for the Former Yugoslavia (ICTY), the Special Court for Sierra Leone (SCSL) and the Special Tribunal for the Lebanon (STL). A number have gone on to secure full-time positions in these and other international organisations.

Having had the opportunity of teaching across a variety of sub-disciplines of international law, including, in particular, international criminal law and, most recently, international commercial law, I have become aware of the need for students to have a grounding in the fundamental principles of international law. In the context of international criminal law, for example, although the jurisprudence of the *ad hoc* and hybrid tribunals, as well as the emerging jurisprudence of the International Criminal Court itself, are creating a wealth of material that is increasingly demanding of specialist analysis, the foundations of the sub-discipline are firmly grounded in general international legal scholarship. Thus, the Nuremberg Tribunals were products of a desire

---

[23] In spite of the significant number of LLM programmes in international commercial law taught in the UK and around the world, the term transnational commercial law is probably the more correct term to use, particularly in the context of international or trans-boundary commercial transactions, and refers to "that set of private law principles and rules, from whatever source, which governs international commercial transactions and is common to legal systems generally or to a significant number of legal systems" (R Goode, H Kronke and E McKendrick, *Transnational Commercial Law: Text, Cases and Materials* (2007) p 4).

[24] The leading City law firm Clifford Chance, for example, only took on its current form in 1987 with the merger of two City firms and operated primarily in Europe until 2000 when it merged with German firm Pünder Volhard Weber & Axster and New York firm Rogers & Wells to create an international law firm which is currently based in twenty-seven countries around the world (see *www.cliffordchance.com*). Other major City firms boast similar, if not greater, international networks of offices and partnerships.

to punish those responsible for serious violations of international law; and the core crimes of genocide, crimes against humanity and war crimes themselves were developed by international lawyers rather than by domestic criminal lawyers.[25] The *ad hoc* tribunals were created by the United Nations Security Council and demand an understanding of Chapter VII of the UN Charter in order to fully comprehend both their historical provenance and their current importance.[26] Finally, the International Criminal Court is founded on an international treaty and many of its current problems relate to the consensual nature of its statute and to questions of jurisdiction that have been the concern of international law for many centuries.[27]

My recent "forced" introduction into the teaching of international commercial law has caused me further to realise the reach of international law as a discipline. As well as providing the historical context for the development of transnational commercial law, public international law is increasingly important in the development of a harmonised system of rules that might, in due course, lead to the creation of a truly harmonised system of international commercial relations that might properly be called an international legal system.[28] Thus, although writers have frequently tried to draw parallels between *lex mercatoria* and customary international law, and between the general principles of commercial law and the general principles of international law, it is, more particularly, the international treaty that is at the heart of the on-going harmonisation of international commercial law.[29] Furthermore, the importance of the development of soft law processes is as important in the field of international commercial law as it is in the field of international environmental law.

All of this positivity about international law presents exciting opportunities but also problems to the teacher of the general subject of international law. While it is, of course, possible and, indeed, necessary to provide a general survey of the nature, subjects, and sources of international law it is becoming increasingly difficult even to attempt to do justice to this wide array of substantive topics. The result is that students and teachers are increasingly becoming specialists in one or two specific sub-systems of the law. They are, if you like, delivering a fragmented syllabus.

---

[25] See further R Cryer, H Friman, and E Wilmshurst, *An Introduction to International Criminal Law and Procedure* (2010) p 8.

[26] See *Prosecutor v Duško Tadić, Decision on the Defence Motion for Interlocutory Appeal on Jurisdiction*, decision of 2 October 1995.

[27] See Rome Statute of the International Criminal Court 1998, 2187 UNTS 90; 37 ILM 1002 (1998).

[28] See further Goode et al, *Transnational Commercial Law* (n 23) ch 3.

[29] Goode et al, ch 5. See, in particular the Vienna Convention on the International Sale of Goods 1980, 1489 UNTS 3; 19 ILM 668 (1980).

THE FRAGMENTATION OF INTERNATIONAL LAW

The suggested fragmentation of the teaching of international law mirrors a broader debate at the heart of international legal discourse concerning the fragmentation of international law itself. This concern recently gave rise to the creation of a special study group within the International Law Commission aimed at addressing this perceived problem. The Report of the International Law Commission's Working Group on "Fragmentation of International Law",[30] published in 2006, has noted that one of the features of "late international modernity" is "functional differentiation"; that is, "the increasing specialisation of parts of society and the related autonomization of those parts".[31] According to the Report: "It is a well-known paradox of globalisation that while it has led to increasing uniformization of social life around the world, it has also led to its increasing fragmentation – that is, to the emergence of specialised and relatively autonomous spheres of social action and structure."[32] This apparent fragmentation has been no more apparent than in the field of international law. Thus, according to the Report:[33]

> The fragmentation of the international social world has attained legal significance especially as it has been accompanied by the emergence of specialized and (relatively) autonomous rules or rule-complexes, legal institutions and spheres of legal practice. What once appeared to be governed by "general international law" has become the field of operations for such specialist systems as "trade law", "human rights law", "environmental law", "law of the sea", "European law" and even such exotic and highly specialised knowledges as "investment law" or "international refugee law" etc – each possessing their own principles and institutions. The problem, as lawyers have seen it, is that such specialised law-making and institution-building tends to take place with relative ignorance of legislative and institutional activities in the adjoining fields and of the general principles and practices of international law. The result is conflicts between rules or rule-systems, deviating international practices and, possibly, the loss of an overall perspective on the law.

Portrayed in this way, the fragmentation of international law is a problematic and negative process. As one commentator has suggested, use of the notion of fragmentation implies that "something is splitting up, falling apart, or worse. ... In international legal parlance the term has gained ... prominence out of the fear that international law might lose its universal applicability, as well as its unity and coherence".[34] On the other hand, the fragmentation

---

[30] UN Doc A/CN.4/L.682. The Report was authored by Professor Martti Koskenniemi.
[31] Report, para 7.
[32] Report, para 7.
[33] Report, para 8.
[34] B Simma, "Universality of international law from the perspective of a practitioner" (2009) 20 EJIL 265 at 270.

analysis is intended both to explain the phenomenon (of fragmentation) and to identify various legal techniques, such as *lex specialis* and *lex posterior*, or normative hierarchy, that might be used to avoid conflict between different regimes. The response to fragmentation becomes a process of developing relationships between rules and systems, seeking harmonisation through systemic integration, and clarifying jurisdictions and applicable law.

Until recently my own thinking on the fragmentation debate was initially rather dismissive. I tended to agree with the views of Judge Simma of the International Court of Justice to the effect that "the phenomenon described as 'fragmentation' of international law is nothing but the result of a transposition of functional differentiations of governance from the national to the international plane ... international law has developed, and is still developing, its own more or less complete regulatory regimes which may at times compete with one another".[35] In other words, I believed, in so far as the post-ontological era has begun and we should not be put off course by overly technical concerns about *lex specialis*, *lex posterior*, normative hierarchy and self-contained regimes. Unfortunately, these technical issues are not easily dismissed.

COMPETING DISCOURSES OF INTERNATIONAL IMMUNITIES AND HUMAN RIGHTS

As a result of this realisation, my views on the problem of fragmentation have changed somewhat in recent years, particularly as a result of my struggle to balance the competing normative frameworks of immunities from jurisdiction and human rights. Having routinely ignored the problem of fragmentation, its full extent came crashing to the fore as a result of the recent decision of the International Court of Justice in *The Case Concerning the Jurisdictional Immunity of the State (Germany v Italy)* of 3 February 2012, a decision that fell squarely within my area of research expertise. In my early work on immunity from jurisdiction I had confronted the potential conflict between immunity and human rights in a variety of articles and case reviews, most notably in relation to the decision(s) of the House of Lords in the *Pinochet* litigation.[36] In that case, former Chilean President Augusto Pinochet was arrested in London in execution of a warrant for his extradition to Spain to face charges of, amongst other things, torture. Ultimately, any possible conflict between international legal rules pertaining to what was an issue of head of state immunity and questions of human rights and

---

[35] Simma at 270.
[36] See, in particular, *R v Bow Street Metropolitan Stipendiary Magistrate and others, ex p Pinochet Ugarte (No 3)* [2000] 1 AC 147. See further J C Barker, "The future of head of State immunity after *ex parte Pinochet*" (1999) 48 ICLQ 937.

international criminal law were avoided as a result of a technical decision involving an analysis of the impact of the incorporation of the relevant international treaty on torture into UK domestic law. Although subject to criticism, I felt comfortable with my analysis of what was a particularly difficult case. Others, however, proclaimed the so-called *Pinochet* precedent as the basis for future challenges to jurisdictional immunities on human rights grounds which resulted in a plethora of cases emerging in primarily domestic and international courts around the world.[37]

A particularly important case for present purposes was brought in the Italian courts by Mr Luigi Ferrini, an Italian national who had been arrested and deported to Germany during the Second World War. Mr Ferrini and many of his compatriots had been forced to work in munitions factories in Germany and had been subjected to gross violations of their human rights and were seeking compensation in respect of that treatment. The Italian courts at first instance, and on appeal, dismissed Ferrini's case due to the jurisdictional immunity of Germany.[38] However, at the Italian Court of Cassation on 11 March 2004, it was held that the immunity of Germany did not apply as the act complained of constituted an international crime.[39] The case was returned to the original court which held, nevertheless, that the claim was time barred. This decision was, however, reversed by the Court of Appeal of Florence, and Germany was held liable to pay damages.[40] After the initial Court of Cassation decision in *Ferrini*, subsequent cases were brought by further claimants in Turin and Sciacca. These led to the filing of an interlocutory appeal by Germany before the Italian Court of Cassation requesting a declaration of lack of jurisdiction. By two orders of 29 May 2008, "the Italian Court of Cassation confirmed that the Italian courts had jurisdiction over the claims against Germany".[41] Ultimately, Germany brought the case to the International Court of Justice alleging *inter alia* that by allowing civil claims to be brought against it, Italy had failed to respect the jurisdictional immunity that Germany enjoyed under international

---

[37] There is insufficient space to develop an analysis of all of these cases but some of them certainly deserve mention here. Reference can be made to the *Case concerning the Arrest Warrant of 11 April 2000, 2002* ICJ Reports 3 before the International Court of Justice; *Al-Adsani v United Kingdom* (2002) 34 EHRR 237 before the European Court of Human Rights; *Filártiga v Peña-Irala* 630 F2d 876 (2d Cir 1980); *Siderman de Blake v Republic of Argentina* 965 F2d 699 (9th Cir 1992) before the US courts; and *Jones v Saudi Arabia* [2006] 2 WLR 1424 in the UK as examples.

[38] See *Germany v Italy* (n 2) para 27.

[39] *Ferrini v Federal Republic of Germany*, Decision No 5044/2004 (2004) 87 Rivista di diritto internazionale 539; 128 ILR 658.

[40] See *Germany v Italy* (n 2) para 27.

[41] *Giovanni Mantelli and others* (Italian Court of Cassation, Order No 14201) (2009) 134 Foro italiano I, 1568); *Liberato Maietta* (Order No 14209) (2008) 91 Rivisita di dritto internazionale 86. See *Germany v Italy* (n 2) para 28.

law.[42] It is not intended here to provide a detailed analysis of the court's decision, something that has been done elsewhere by others as well as by the present author.[43] The purpose here, rather, is to highlight, very briefly, the two very different approaches to the case taken first by the majority and, secondly, by the minority, judges, including, in particular, that of Judge Cançado Trindade.

The court, in its majority decision, pursued an essentially positivist analysis. First, it acknowledged the illegality of the various acts committed by German forces during the requisite period. It proceeded then to examine the relevant law of state immunity asserting that states have a right to claim immunity before the courts of foreign states on the basis of established state practice, particularly in light of the, as yet inoperative, United Nations Convention on the Jurisdictional Immunities of States and Their Property 2004.[44] In relation to the specific circumstances of the case, based on an analysis of a limited number of domestic cases and legislation, the court found that the so-called territorial tort exception to immunity did not apply in the case of the activities of the armed forces of a state during an armed conflict, effectively asserting thereby the negative proposition that, in so far as there was no exception to immunity in such cases, Germany was entitled to immunity.[45]

The court then specifically rejected Italy's assertion that the nature of the acts in question, as international crimes, required that immunity should be removed. Again the court drew on a limited number of international and municipal cases in which the so-called *jus cogens* argument had been rejected.[46] Crucially, the court did not deny that certain substantive rules of the law of armed conflict could be considered as *jus cogens*.[47] However, it did not see a conflict between those rules and the rules on state immunity. In the circumstances of the present case, the court was clear that the violations of the law of armed conflict were openly recognised as illegal by all parties,

---

[42] See further *Germany v Italy* (n 2) paras 15, 16, 17 and 37.

[43] For my own analysis of the case see J C Barker, "Jurisdictional Immunities of the State (*Germany v Italy*) Judgment of 3 February 2012" (2013) 62 ICLQ 741; J C Barker, "Negotiating the complex interface between State immunity and human rights: an analysis of the International Court of Justice decision in *Germany v Italy*" (2013) 15 ICLR 415.

[44] *Germany v Italy* (n 2) paras 53-56.

[45] *Germany v Italy* (n 2) paras 62-77.

[46] The *jus cogens* (or normative hierarchy) argument, briefly stated, asserts that certain norms, including specifically certain international criminal prohibitions are hierarchically superior to other international law rules, specifically rules relating to state immunity, and therefore the rules of immunity are "trumped" and made ineffective when argued alongside the hierarchically superior human rights and international criminal norms.

[47] The court specifically referred to the prohibition of "the murder of civilians in occupied territory, the deportation of civilian inhabitants to slave labour and the deportation of prisoners of war to slave labour".

but that did not involve any conflict with the question as to whether or not the Italian courts had jurisdiction to hear claims arising out of the violations.[48]

The decision of the majority in this case should be clearly contrasted with the position taken by the minority and, in particular, by Judge Trindade. Trindade premised his dissent on his fundamental rejection of the "State-centred distorted outlook" approach to international law,[49] in favour of an approach based on fundamental human values.[50] Trindade did not explicitly acknowledge the existence of two different systems of international law. Rather, he argued that recent doctrinal developments in international law have changed the law from being exclusively state-centric into one in which individuals are "subjects" and not simply "actors".[51] Trindade's analysis is worthy of significantly more analysis than is possible here. But that is not the purpose of this article. The purpose here is to highlight a potential schism at the heart of international legal discourse and that is perhaps best encapsulated in the following quote from Trindade's dissenting opinion. In a direct and undisguised critique of the majority's positivist analysis, Trindade challenged the court's methodological framework:[52]

> As to national legislations, pieces of sparse legislation in a handful of States, in my view, cannot withhold the lifting of State immunity in cases of grave violations of human rights and of international humanitarian law. Such positivist exercises are leading to the fossilization of international law, and disclosing its persistent underdevelopment, rather than its progressive development, as one would expect. Such undue methodology is coupled with inadequate and unpersuasive conceptualizations, of the kind so widespread in the legal profession, such as, *inter alia*, the counterpositions of "primary" to "secondary" rules, or of "procedural" to "substantive" rules, or of obligations of "conduct" to those of "result". Words, words, words. ... Where are the values?

In the context of the present discussion I find these words both troubling and challenging. They appear to suggest something greater than "mere" fragmentation. To this extent the debate around the relationship between state immunity and human rights may be one debate too far in terms of the progress of international law and may eventually result in a schism at the heart of international law.[53] Far from evidencing shared understandings

---

[48] *Germany v Italy* (n 2) para 94.
[49] *Germany v Italy* (n 2), Judge Conçado Trindade dissenting opinion to the judgment of the court, paras 172–76.
[50] Dissenting opinion, paras 32–40.
[51] Dissenting opinion, para 180.
[52] Dissenting opinion, para 294.
[53] A schism constitutes more than just a split or separation. In theological terms, it is a "rupture of ecclesiastical union and unity" (Catholic Encyclopaedia *http://www.newadvent. org/cathen/13529a.htm, sub nom* Schism). Within an intellectual community, schisms may be

and co-operative analysis of the nature and language of international law, the discourse, as evidenced in the judgment and dissents in *Germany v Italy*, is moving towards what has been described as an "epistemic trap" whereby different autopoietic systems[54] produce reality constructions of their own but struggle to interrelate.[55]

BEYOND FRAGMENTATION: THE ROLE OF THE TEACHER OF INTERNATIONAL LAW

Given the apparent fragmentation of international law into separate and arguably unrelated sub-disciplines it seems inevitable that the cohesion of international law will, at some point, collapse. After all, given the clear differences of approach in *Germany v Italy* in relation to even the most fundamental of principles concerning, for example, the subjects and sources of international law, it is at least arguable that the existentialist debate that characterised international law until relatively recently served only to mask incoherence and disunity. It is certainly the case that the growing complexity and sophistication of international law has opened it up to greater and more intense critical analysis. However, this should not in and of itself be a bad thing. The study of international law should be a study not only of the successes and achievements of international law but also of its failures and its inconsistencies. Having moved beyond the "is international law really law" question, scholars and students can finally engage in that critical analysis that ought to be at the heart of learning about the law.

---

unavoidable. Thus St Paul's call to the people of the Church that he established in Corinth to "agree in what you say so that there will be no divisions among you. Be completely united, with only one thought and one purpose" (1 Corinthians 1, 10) apparently fell on deaf ears.

[54] Autopoiesis is a biological concept developed by Humberto Maturana and Francisco Vaturela (see Maturana and Vaturela, *Autopoiesis and Cognition* (1980)) that defines a closed system that is capable of creating itself. The term has been used in systems theory and sociology, primarily by Niklas Luhmann (see Luhmann, *Soziale Systeme: Grundriß einer allgemeinen Theorie* (1984)), and has been applied to legal analysis by Luhmann himself and by Gunther Teubner (see G Teubner, "How the law thinks: toward a constructivist epistemology of law" (1989) 23 Law and Society Review 727). Teubner's analysis identifies law in its entirety as an autopoietic system that struggles to interrelate with other autopoietic systems. Thus, he argues (at 742) that

In the dynamics of social evolution, self-referential relations are multiplying within the legal process, culminating in a hypercyclical linkage of the law's components. The law becomes autonomous from general social communications. It develops into a closed communicative network that produces not only legal acts as its elements and legal rules as its structures, but legal constructions of reality as well. The autonomy of modern law refers primarily to its normative operations that become independent from moral and political normativity.

[55] Teubner (n 54) 742.

Perhaps I can best illustrate this by undertaking a critical analysis of the *Germany v Italy* case in the context of the fragmentation debate. My time at Glasgow instilled in me a belief in the importance of legal doctrine. In international law terms that locates me within the oft-disparaged "positivist" intellectual camp. From this perspective, although engaged by the emotion of Trindade's position and, perhaps, a belief in the justice of his cause, I find it difficult to accept his reasoning. Trindade summarily rejects and criticises the accepted sources of international law, including both treaty and customary international law, in favour of the moral discourse of normative hierarchy based on the rather esoteric and malleable concepts of humanity and human dignity.[56] The normative hierarchy discourse undoubtedly has validity when understood alongside the recognised sources of international law. However, when states have explicitly rejected any and all human rights exceptions to state immunity, as they certainly have in the context of the relationship between state immunity and human rights,[57] it is difficult to accept an analysis that ignores this "positive" law in favour of a moral assertion of human dignity.

On the other hand, while the decision of the majority in *Germany v Italy* may be technically "correct", it is also troubling and problematic. Trindade's allegation that the majority decision is excessively state-centric is undoubtedly correct. The court's condemnation of the acts of German forces during the Second World War and its contention that Germany could have done more to compensate those affected,[58] appears rather hollow when set alongside the court's overt reliance on a peace treaty that Italy had been effectively forced to sign in 1947,[59] and on the United Nations Convention on the Jurisdictional Immunities of States and Their Property 2004,[60] a treaty that has secured only sixteen states parties and twenty-eight signatories in the decade since its conclusion.[61] Furthermore, the process of identification of customary international law was equally problematic. In so far as the evidence of state practice relied on by the majority consisted only of the legislation of and judicial decisions in a very limited number of

---

[56] *Germany v Italy* (n 2), dissenting opinion, para 292.

[57] On this point see further below.

[58] The court expressed this as a "matter of surprise – and regret": *Germany v Italy* (n 2) para 99.

[59] 1 UNTS 747.

[60] GA Res 59/38 (2 December 2004), hereafter referred to as the 2004 United Nations Convention. On the Convention see further R O'Keefe, C J Tams and A Tzanakopoulos, *The United Nations Convention on the Jurisdictional Immunities of States and Their Property: A Commentary* (2013)

[61] As at 20 February 2014. For up-to-date information on the current status of the Convention and a list of parties see *https://treaties.un.org/*.

western states,[62] the bold, although very narrow, assertion that there is no exception to state immunity in the case of a tort committed by armed forces on the territory of another state during an armed conflict seems rather unproven. The fact that the court tried to limit the extent of its decision as much as it could suggests that the majority were themselves at least a little bit uncomfortable with the effect of their decision in the context of the extent and level of Nazi atrocities.

However, the decision is particularly problematic when examined in the context of the recent development of the law of state immunity. Until the middle of the twentieth century state immunity was regarded as absolute.[63] A process of development within domestic law, primarily in western states,[64] led to the development of the so-called restrictive doctrine of state immunity, which limits the immunity of states in the case of commercial transactions. Had that process been challenged before the International Court of Justice during the 1960s or 1970s the ICJ would, most likely, have asserted the pre-eminence of the absolute theory, which remained dominant in state practice at that time. The effect would have been to block the development of the restrictive doctrine. However, that did not happen and the restrictive doctrine is now fully accepted within state practice and reflected in the 2004 United Nations Convention.

As noted previously, since the 1990s similar challenges to the extent of state immunity in the context of human rights violations have been raised in domestic and international courts.[65] These challenges have given rise to important domestic decisions purporting to limit state immunity and analogous sovereign rights,[66] in a variety of circumstances. However, these decisions have not yet crystallised a change in the international law of state immunity. In fact they may never do so. What is clear is that the decision of the International Court of Justice in *Germany v Italy*, particularly when set alongside the failure of state representatives negotiating the 2004 United Nations Convention to include a human rights protocol to the Convention,[67] will constitute a significant, if not insurmountable, obstacle to the future development of a human rights exception to state immunity.

---

[62] On legislation see *Germany v Italy* (n 2) paras 70–71 covering the legislation of only seven states and on national judgments see paras 72–75, covering the state practice of fourteen states.

[63] See, eg, the decision of the House of Lords in *The Cristina* [1938] AC 495.

[64] See, eg, the Tate Letter (1952) 26 State Dept Bull 984; (1953) 47 AJIL 93 in the US and *Trendtex v Central Bank of Nigeria* [1977] QB 529 in the UK.

[65] See n 37 above.

[66] Including the immunity of former heads of state and of high-ranking state officials.

[67] On attempts by Amnesty International and Human Rights Watch to have included as an annex to the Convention a human rights protocol see C K Hall, "UN Convention on State Immunity: the need for a human rights protocol" (2006) 55 ICLQ 411.

All of this is speculation. For the purposes of the present discussion, the question is not about the future development of the law of state immunity. Rather, it concerns the fragmentation of international law of which the *Germany v Italy* case is a recent example. More particularly, my analysis concerns the role of teachers of international law in light of fragmentation and the almost inevitable conflicts that will arise between different sub-systems of the law. One response is for traditional, positivist international lawyers to assert the correctness of the decision and to disparage the claims of human rights lawyers. Human rights lawyers, on the other hand, will undoubtedly condemn the decision and hold up the dissenting opinion of Judge Trindade as the "correct" interpretation of state immunity and human rights. This divisive reaction is already apparent in the published literature on the case. However, this is the path to further fragmentation.

The teacher of international law ought to avoid such extreme discourse. On the other hand, the *Germany v Italy* case, and other examples of regime conflict within international law, should not be avoided by teachers. They reflect the type of complex legal question that is apparent in many branches of domestic law and European law. They provide an excellent framework for the critical analysis of the law. Students can be challenged to consider the different approaches from a critical perspective through questions such as: if states are the primary subjects of international law, what is the role of human rights organisations such as Amnesty International and Human Rights Watch? If international law is based upon the fundamental concept of human dignity, how do we conceptualise and implement that concept? If states have enacted a treaty that ignores human rights concerns, is that treaty valid? Can the treaty be interpreted in such a way that it would, nevertheless, give rise to the application of human rights concerns? All of these are legitimate and interesting questions and only a very few of many that arise.

It is my firm view that the international law of state immunity does need further development in order to reflect human rights concerns but this cannot be done simply by ignoring or deconstructing the existing law. We cannot simply assert, for example, that human rights law and the law of state immunity are different regimes and that one is legally, or morally, superior to the other. Both "regimes" are forms of international law. The same applies, for example, to international criminal law, to international environmental law and international trade law. Each of these specialisms requires its own analysis and, indeed, its own experts. But each requires a core understanding of the fundamental principles of international law, its sources, its subjects and its implementation. Each specialism will develop its own processes, its own substantive law and, in many cases, its own organisational structures. These organisational structures themselves reflect the growing sophistication of international law and include, for example, the World Trade Organisation in the context of international trade, and the International Criminal Court in the context of international criminal law. However, at some point students of these specialist areas need to understand that the foundations of their specialisms are to be found in traditional, general international law. In this more complex international law world a key role for the teacher is to look across the various specialisms in order to identify the lessons that might be learned from one sub-discipline to another particularly in relation to the constitutional framework of international law. Finally the teacher of international law is ideally placed to consider, analyse and assess some "constitutional" principles, such as fairness.[68]

CONCLUSIONS

The international law I learned at Glasgow thirty years ago did not address all of the different areas of international law that now abound. One could not have expected it to do so, given the exponential growth in the importance and reach of international law that has occurred during that period and that has been described above. Nevertheless, there was recognition, even then, of the interrelationship of different aspects of international law. The ways in which the law relating to armed conflict, which I was introduced to in my first ever lecture, interrelated with the law of human rights and the law of the sea was recognised. I have had the opportunity over twenty years to teach elements of the law of armed conflict, the law of international immunities, international criminal law, international trade law and international commercial law and I could not have done so without the understanding built from my time in Glasgow, of the cohesion of international law. Now, more than ever, when faced with the challenge of fragmentation, teachers of international law, whatever their specialism, must make a conscious effort to assert the coherence of international law.

---

[68] See Franck, *Fairness in International Law and Institutions* (n 1).

Exclusive Privilege: Adam Smith, John Millar, and the Creation of a New Right?

*Gillian Black**

INTRODUCTION

Historical background

The contribution of Glasgow scholars to Scots law is well established, thanks in no small part to the work of holders of the Regius chair since its inception in 1713. This paper sets out for the first time the role of one of the earlier holders of this chair, Professor John Millar,[1] together with his near contemporary in the Chair of Moral Philosophy at Glasgow University, Adam Smith,[2] in relation to the right of exclusive privilege. This right was first identified and delineated as a discrete real right in the lectures they delivered to their students – yet it has so far been under-explored and potentially under-utilised in Scots law. By setting out the history and context of exclusive privilege, this paper charts the emergence of the right in the eighteenth century and its subsequent subsidence in the course of the nineteenth century. This historical review also uncovers important evidence of the direct impact that Millar had on Baron Hume in this field. The final section then analyses the coherence of the doctrine to determine what future, if any, it has in Scots law in the twenty-first century. This review is therefore essential in order to provide a critical analysis of exclusive privilege in Scots law for the first time.

Legal background

As Smith and Millar identified exclusive privilege as a real right, it is instructive to start with the leading academic work on property and real rights in the twentieth century: Professor Kenneth Reid's title on *Property* in the *Stair Memorial Encyclopedia*, first published in 1993. Reid identifies

* The author would like to thank a number of colleagues for their very helpful comments on previous drafts of this paper, especially Professor Kenneth Reid, Professor John Cairns, and Dr Dan Carr. The staff of the University libraries at Edinburgh and Glasgow were also very helpful in assisting with access to historical material.

[1] Holder of the Regius Chair of Law from 1761–1801.
[2] In post from 1752–63.

eight real rights in Scots law: ownership (*dominium*); rights in security; proper liferent; servitude; lease; possession; rights held by the public; and exclusive privilege.[3] Of these, ownership is the "main real right"[4] and the others are subordinate real rights or "*jura in re aliena*, that is to say, property in the rights of another".[5] Thus, ownership is the primary real right and the other real rights typically exist in relation to a thing owned by another, as limitations on the other's right of ownership.

The exception to this is the eighth real right listed: the right of exclusive privilege. This is not a *jus in re aliena*, but appears to be a real right of a different type. Reid defines it as "an exclusive, and valuable, right to do something and, hence, to stop others from doing the same thing".[6] From this definition, exclusive privilege would appear to be a very broad right, capable of widespread application and therefore worthy of extensive academic treatment and practical application – yet in fact this has not been the case. Until discussed by Reid in 1993, the real right of exclusive privilege had all but vanished from the legal scene by the middle of the nineteenth century. Only by setting out the history of this right, from its first appearance, and examining its intellectual basis, can we understand why this happened.

ORIGINS OF EXCLUSIVE PRIVILEGE AS A REAL RIGHT

Smith's lectures

In listing exclusive privilege as one of eight real rights, Reid was drawing on the work of (Baron) David Hume in the early nineteenth century, with reference to Adam Smith before him.[7] The earliest mention I have been

---

[3] See Kenneth Reid writing in *The Laws of Scotland: Stair Memorial Encyclopaedia* vol 18 "Property" (1993), republished as K G C Reid, *The Law of Property in Scotland* (1996), paras 4 and 5. See also Roderick Paisley who adopts these eight, with reference to Reid: R R M Paisley, "Real rights: practical problems and dogmatic rigidity" (2005) 8 Edin LR 267, 268. Note, however, that not all eight have always been recognised in Scots law or by Civilian jurists: Reid, *Property*, paras 4 and 5; see also discussion of the thesis by Heinrich Hahn (n 52) below. Although the category of real rights is not irrevocably closed, the principle of *numerus clausus* applies in Scots law, as in the Civilian tradition: H L MacQueen and Lord Eassie, *Gloag and Henderson, The Law of Scotland* (13th edn, 2012) para 30.01.

[4] According to Stair, *Inst* II.1.28; see also Reid, *Property* (n 3) para 5.

[5] Reid, *Property* (n 3), para 6.

[6] Reid, *Property* (n 3), para 5. While acknowledging exclusive privilege as the eighth real right in Scots law, Reid does note that it "cannot be accepted without a certain amount of damage to the core idea of real rights". Nonetheless, he accepts that there are "points of resemblance" between the right of exclusive privilege (specifically intellectual property) and the real rights "in the traditional sense", and therefore suggests that it may be that this classification (as adopted by Hume) ought to be adopted.

[7] Reid, *Property* (n 3), para 5.

able to uncover of exclusive privilege as a unified real right is in Adam Smith's *Lectures on Jurisprudence*, from 1762-63,[8] delivered while he held the Chair of Moral Philosophy at the University of Glasgow. Although these lectures were never prepared for publication by Smith, two versions of student lecture notes, from 1762-63 and from (apparently) 1763-64[9] were eventually published, most notably in the Glasgow Edition, edited by Professors R L Meek, D D Raphael and P G Stein.[10] While an invaluable record of Smith's lectures, they must be treated with some caution: "these lecture notes cannot be an entirely faithful record of what was said, [although] they were based on painstaking collation and revision, whether for personal use or for sale".[11]

Smith's lectures at Glasgow were delivered under four headings – natural theology, ethics, justice, and political regulation[12] – and the third heading comprised his *Lectures on Jurisprudence*. These lectures provide a detailed treatment of jurisprudence, from persons to property and to government, yet it is critical to note at the outset that Smith was not a lawyer either by training or by profession. His education as a student at Glasgow and thereafter Balliol College, Oxford had not apparently included any legal education.[13] Instead, Smith's philosophical and economic interests, as evidenced most prominently in *The Theory of Moral Sentiments* and *Wealth of Nations* (the only two volumes he published),[14] must be borne in mind during any consideration of his legal analysis. Moreover, Smith does not explicitly restrict his *Lectures on Jurisprudence* to

---

[8] See R L Meek, D D Raphael and P G Stein, *Adam Smith, Lectures on Jurisprudence* (1978; reprinted, 1982). The coverage of exclusive privilege in Smith's 1762–63 lectures is considerably more detailed – or at least, it was reported in the student notes in considerably more detail – than that found in the subsequent lecture notes from 1763-64 (dated 1766). In the latter set of notes, exclusive privilege is covered in little more than a page, divided between *Part 1ˢᵗ*, paras 9–10 (at 400), and *Private Law*, paras 174–75 (at 471-72). Moreover, the focus here is more prominently on monopolies and the economic consequences of them. This paper will draw on the 1762-63 notes, unless otherwise indicated.

[9] The second set of notes is actually dated 1766, and appears to be a copy made by a professional copyist in that year – for a detailed discussion of the two sets of notes, see Smith, *Lectures* (n 8) pp 5-13 (*Introduction*).

[10] First published by OUP in 1978. The edition referred to in this paper is the Liberty Fund edition of 1982 (Indianapolis). An earlier edition of Smith's *Lectures on Jurisprudence* was published in 1896, edited by Professor Edwin Cannan.

[11] D Winch "Smith, Adam (bap. 1723, d. 1790)" *Oxford Dictionary of National Biography* (2004-).

[12] *ODNB* "Smith" (n 11) with reference to John Millar.

[13] *ODNB* "Smith" (n 11) lists his studies at Glasgow as comprising Latin, Greek, logic, moral philosophy, mathematics and natural philosophy, while at Balliol he studied ancient philosophy, and English, French and Italian literature.

[14] The implication being that he did not consider his other work sufficiently developed to merit wider distribution. He was, however, working on a manuscript for publication on *Jurisprudence* towards the end of his life, but this was destroyed, on his instructions, at his death.

Scots law, but rather draws on the civil law and the jurisprudence of civil governments more generally.[15]

In his treatment of real rights, Smith stated "they are four of them as they are enumerated in the civill law. *Dominium, Servitus, Pignus, Haereditas*".[16] These can be mapped onto the four rights of ownership, servitude, pledge, and inheritance. The last of these he defined as: [17]

> 4th *If we consider the right which an heir has before his accession to the estate of his father we shall find that it is a real right, tho different from that of property. The heir has the exclusive right to the inheritance. No one can meddle with it in any shape untill he has refused it, and he can obtain restitution for anything that it may have suffered from others as well as [to the] all the accessions that may have been added to it. And as soon as he has consented to enter to the inheritance he becomes full and complete proprietor of it.*

The legal question to be resolved was how to classify the interim period, being the gap between the ancestor's death and the heir's full ownership. As Smith posited:[18]

> It can be in no other case than during the time betwixt the death of the last proprietor and the entrance of the heir that the inheritance can be considered as giving a **new** species of real right. Now what right is it that the heir has before his entrance? No other but that of excluding all others from the possession untill he determine in whether he will enter heir or not.

While admitting that the right of the heir is "different from that of property", Smith nevertheless argued that it carried the characteristics of a real right, since no one can "meddle" with it: it is good against the world.[19] Reid suggests that the classification of the right of the heir as a real right is "doubtful" in Scots law.[20] Nevertheless, by asserting the right of the heir as a real right, Smith was thereafter able to extend by analogy the scope of *haereditas* or inheritance to encompass exclusive privileges more broadly:

---

[15] As per the opening words of his first lecture: Smith, *Lectures* (n 8) i.I (at p 5).

[16] Smith, *Lectures* (n 8) i.16 (at p 10).

[17] Smith, *Lectures* (n 8) i.19 (at p 11), emphasis added.

[18] Smith, *Lectures* (n 8) ii.27 (at p 81), bold added.

[19] See for example U Mattei, *Basic Principles of Property Law* (2000) p 9: "a real action protecting the thing (*res*) can be exercised against everybody, since a property right imposes duties of abstention to everybody in the world. In contrast, a personal action protecting the person can be exercised only against the particular person that is subject to the obligation ... Therefore, real actions have an *erga omnes* (against everybody) characteristic when contrasted with personal actions". This approach can be found in the *jus commune*: see S van Erp and B Akkermans (eds), *Cases, Materials and Text on Property Law* (2012), pp 51–53.

[20] Reid, *Property* (n 3), para 5, footnote 2, where he also notes that the analogy used by Hume here, following Smith, is "forced and unconvincing".

"[i]f therefore we account the right of inheritance to be a real right, as it certainly is, all other exclusive priviledges will for the same reason be accounted real rights".[21]

With this sleight of hand, Smith established exclusive privilege – and not merely inheritance – as a category of real right, and explicitly acknowledged that it was a new right, founded on the apparent real right of the heir in the period between the death of the ancestor and taking entry, ie *haereditas*. Having done so, he was able to proceed (in a subsequent lecture) to expand on the nature of this right of exclusive privilege.

Exclusive pursuit

However, if the right of the heir as a real right of exclusive privilege is "doubtful" according to Reid, then matters surely do not improve markedly with the next right judged by Smith to be a real right of exclusive privilege:

> Thus if one who has the right to hunt starts a deer, and when he is in pursuit another comes in and takes this deer before he has given over hopes of catching him, this 2d person appears evidently to have acted *contrary to good manners and may accordingly be punished* by the forest laws. It can not however be accounted a breach of property, as that can not begin till the beast is actually brought into the possession of the pursuer ... The trespass here is plainly against the exclusive priviledge the hunter has to the chase or pursuit of the beast he has started.[22]

There cannot be many real rights which owe their origin to good manners.[23] Smith was correct to note, however, that the right infringed cannot be one of ownership (or even possession) until the deer is actually caught. If, before that moment, it is to give rise to a *jus in re* then, on this analysis, that right must be exclusive privilege. A similar situation arises where an enemy ship is spotted and chase is given: should another ship intercede and take the enemy ship, then this would breach the exclusive privilege of the captain of the original chasing ship. Again, this cannot amount to an invasion of a right of ownership or possession, since the enemy ship is not yet caught. Smith included this example with reference to a decision of the Scots Privy Council from 1677 – a decision which the court, according to Smith, got right, but on the wrong legal basis:

> The captain of the man of war [the original ship] sued the privateer [the interceptor] before the Scots Privy Council ... The Privy Council ... adjudged

---

[21] Smith, *Lectures* (n 8) i.20 (at p 11) – a point he repeats at ii.28 (at p 82).

[22] Smith, *Lectures* (n 8) at ii.28 (at p 82), emphasis added. Note that this example is derived from the forest laws.

[23] Interestingly, Stair also comments on the "uncivility" of intercepting the chase, albeit to different legal effect: see Stair, *Inst* II.1.33, and discussion below.

the privateer to restore them, specifying that he had been guilty of a breach of property. *But if they had spoke properly, they would have said that he had been guilty of a breach of an exclusive priviledge* ... The breach was of the exclusive priviledge one has to pursue and take the ships he spies and chases.[24]

In fact, a reading of this case, *King's Advocate v Rankin*, does not assist much on either analysis. There is certainly no mention of the doctrine of exclusive privilege in the pleadings or judgment (as reported under the heading "Prize" in Morison's Dictionary, and in Gosford's report following). However, the pleadings for the defender referred to the equivalent situation of chasing a wild beast:[25]

The capture by the Scottish privateer ... established the property in him; ... it is not the expectation or prosecution, but the capture, that gives the right; for which there is a clear instance in the institutions of the Roman law, *De rerum dominio*, that he who pursues a wild beast, though he wound it, acquires not the property thereof, except he take it; and the law gives that reason, that many things may intervene that might hinder his actual occupation of it.

This passage would seem to suggest that the chase of neither the wild beast nor the ship gives rise to a right to complete the chase, and that the only enforceable right arises once the quarry has been captured. If so, this would rather undermine Smith's identification of an "interim" real right to exclude others, between the start of the chase and the eventual outcome. However, the defenders' pleadings did not succeed and the final decision by the Lords of the Privy Council was that the original frigate in pursuit of the prize "was in view and prosecution thereof", and the privateer's intervening capture of the prize was injurious.[26] While appearing to dismiss the defenders' submission that there is no right until the quarry is eventually captured, the legal basis for the decision is rather opaque[27] – leaving it enticingly open to interpretation. As a final note, Stair also discusses this case, but treats it within his material on acquiring ownership through possession rather than as an example of exclusive privilege.[28]

---

[24] Smith, *Lectures* (n 8), ii.30 (at p 82), emphasis added. See *King's Advocate v Rankin* (1677) Mor 11930. Curiously, the text of Smith's lecture refers to the year 1701, but the accompanying footnote cites this case (correctly) from 1677.

[25] *King's Advocate v Rankin* (n 24) 11932–3. See also discussion re the pursuit of whales in the later cases of *Addison v Row* (1794) 3 Paton 334 HL; and *Sutter v Aberdeen Arctic Co* (1861) 23 D 465.

[26] *King's Advocate v Rankin* (n 24) 11933.

[27] The report in Morison's Dictionary is then followed by a report from Gosford of the same case (at Mor 11934–11936), but there is nothing further to be gleaned from this second report.

[28] Stair, *Inst* II.1.33, and see also discussion below, at pp 27–28 below.

Other examples

Having set out these three examples of exclusive privilege (the heir, the deer and the ship) based on "natural reason and equity", Smith then moved on to consider other exclusive privileges regarding patents, copyright and corporations, including the Burgh guilds and trades. Here, however, he did not provide much detail as to the legal basis or implications of these rights (perhaps unsurprisingly, given his background), but rather lamented the adverse economic and social consequences which arose from granting such monopoly rights (equally unsurprisingly, in light of the subsequent focus of his work, for example in *Wealth of Nations*).[29]

Smith's treatment in context

Smith's analysis of this new right of exclusive privilege is therefore the starting point for any review of the doctrine in Scots law: it introduces the concept as a coherent whole and links together a number of different legal rights and privileges in one conceptual category. The main exclusive privileges covered are the right of the heir; of the hunter re the deer; the privateer re the enemy ship; the Burghs guilds and trades; patents; and literary property (or copyright).

If Smith was apparently the first scholar to expound the doctrine and unite these separate privileges, then it is instructive to review what had gone before. How did the leading Scottish jurists of the late seventeenth and early eighteenth centuries address the privileges covered by exclusive privilege?

THE LATE SEVENTEENTH AND
EARLY EIGHTEENTH CENTURIES

Institutional and other legal writers

A review of the works of Stair, Forbes, Bankton, Erskine and Kames shows that they typically recognised (almost all) the individual privileges Smith discussed, but treated them as separate rights: there was no attempt to unite them in one coherent category.

Stair

Stair identified three real rights: ownership, servitude and pledge,[30] with no mention of Smith's fourth right of exclusive privilege. Instead, Stair treated

---

[29] The regulation of trade through artificial means was clearly a key concern for Smith. In particular, Book IV of An *Inquiry into the Nature and Causes of Wealth of Nations* concerns "Of Systems of Political Economy" and discusses the artificial (and unreasonable) restraints upon imports and foreign trade, and the use of monopolies in relation to trade with colonies, especially those monopolies awarded to joint stock companies.

[30] Stair, *Inst* II.1.28.

a number of Smith's exclusive privileges simply as instances of acquiring ownership through occupation – notably the hunt of deer or fowl, and the prosecution of prizes at sea.[31] He did, however, concede that:

> Though the falling in upon another's game when he alone is in prosecution, may be uncivility or injury, yet it hindereth not the constitution of property; though it be a just ground to annul the right of the first possessor, and make him restore to the first prosecutor, if he continue his pursuit with a probability to reach his prey.[32]

On this account, intercepting the chase may affect the eventual ownership, but there is no exclusive privilege which has been impinged upon. In respect of the right of inheritance, Stair considered the rights of the heir in Book III, specifically in titles IV, V and VI,[33] and noted that the power of disposal of an estate "and succession thereby" was a real right.[34] While he provided considerable detail on this "most important title in law",[35] he did not name or otherwise identify the concept of *haereditas*.[36] Although Stair was more than willing to take account of Roman law, he did not claim that Roman law "is, or even ought to be, part of the law of Scotland. Where Stair thinks that a rule of Roman law ought to be adopted into Scots law, he says so".[37] Thus, it is not obvious that, in Stair's analysis at least, the Roman or Civil law concept of *jus haereditas* was recognised in the Scots law of succession – a significant point given that Smith's development of exclusive privilege is so firmly anchored to this concept.

Forbes

Forbes, as a fellow Glasgow scholar and the first holder of the Regius Chair in Civil Law, is also of considerable interest. In both his published *Institutes of the Law of Scotland* (1722 and 1730)[38] and his manuscript *Great Body of the Law of Scotland*,[39] he dealt with a range of the privileges but,

---

[31] Stair, *Inst* II.1.33, including a discussion of *King's Advocate v Rankin* (n 24).

[32] Stair, *Inst* II.1.33.

[33] Stair, *Inst* III.34.23 ff outlines the general principles of succession to immoveables, or heritable rights, and moveables.

[34] Stair, *Inst* III.4.2.

[35] Stair, *Inst* III.4.

[36] In discussing succession in the civil law, Stair noted that the order of succession varied greatly but that the "chief mean of succession, is the will or testament of the defunct": this express will of the owner was the first rule of succession in equity, and as a real right it trumped the deceased's personal obligation to provide for his family (derived from biblical authority). Although Stair considered the order of succession, there was no mention of the rights of the heir, however identified: Stair, *Inst* III.4.2, and 15–16.

[37] W M Gordon, "Roman Law as a Source", in D M Walker (ed), *Stair Tercentenary Studies* (1981) p 109.

[38] W Forbes, *Institutes of the Law of Scotland* ([1722–30], republished 2012).

[39] Available online at: *http://www.forbes.gla.ac.uk/contents/*.

again, these were treated as separate rights: there was no attempt to advance a single coherent doctrine of exclusive privilege. Thus, the privileges of trades and handicrafts and of fairs and markets were discussed in relation to Commerce,[40] while prize was covered under the broader heading of *The Law of Nations*.[41] Topics such as chasing deer, patents and copyright (or literary property) were apparently left untreated in his *Institutes*. In relation to heirs, Forbes introduced the rights of the heirs in succession and the differences between succession to heritage and succession to moveables, without introducing anything which resembles Smith's concept of *jus haereditas* or inheritance.[42]

Erskine

The work of John Erskine offers a very useful source of contemporary legal thinking, especially since the first edition of his *Principles of the Law of Scotland* was published in 1754 and would therefore have been current when Smith was writing and revising his *Lectures on Jurisprudence*. Moreover, by comparing the first edition of Erskine's *Principles* with later editions and with his subsequent *An Institute of the Law of Scotland*, we can determine whether his approach to exclusive privilege changed over that period. In fact, the short answer is that neither his first work of 1754, nor the last edition of the *Principles* published by Erskine himself, in 1769,[43] contains any account of exclusive privilege as a unified doctrine, and very little regarding any of the core privileges covered by Smith under this heading. The rights of those chasing deer or prizes at sea, the privileges of patents and literary property or copyright, and the privileges of burghs all go unexplored in the 1754 and 1769 editions. Erskine's *Institute*, published posthumously in 1773, also contains no account of exclusive privilege, indicating that Smith's thinking had not percolated to Erskine at any rate.

Bankton

As with Stair, Bankton identified three real rights: ownership, servitude and pledge.[44] He provided extensive discussion of the rules of succession and the rights of the heir. In Volume II of his *Institute* (published in 1752), Bankton treated succession in Book III, Title IV and the rights of heirs in Title V, but did not discuss *jus haereditas* in either. He did state that the heir

---

[40] Forbes, *Great Body*, Vol 3 Publick Law, Pt 1, Book 2, Chapters 2 and 3.

[41] Forbes (n 38) I.3.3 (at pp 25–26):

[42] See Forbes (n 39), Book II ("How property is transmitted to universal successors"), and especially chapters I and II, at pp 319-25.

[43] Erskine died in 1768, but this edition is described as being "The Fourth Edition, with the last Corrections of the Author".

[44] Bankton, *Inst* I, 503, 4 (Bankton is cited here by volume, page, paragraph).

has a year and a day to decide whether to take up the title,[45] and in this sense he discussed the privileges of the heir, but not in any way which can be meaningfully equated with Smith's approach to the right of inheritance. The closest Bankton came was in his reference to the heir having "a universal representation of the deceased, for *Haereditas in jure consistat*".[46] If this could be construed as providing the same opportunity that Smith used to build up the concept of exclusive privilege from inheritance, then Bankton certainly did not take it. The other privileges grouped together by Smith remained separate rights in Bankton's work, and were treated accordingly. For example, Bankton dealt with the right of chasing down enemy shipping but, as was usual, did so under the heading "Prize", rather than exclusive privilege, albeit he used the language of privilege in his discussion: "These privileges are regulated according to the statutes introducing them ... and continue only during the war to which they relate."[47]

Kames

Kames arguably merits more detailed treatment here: his patronage was instrumental at the start of Smith's academic career, as it was Kames who gave Smith his first opportunity to lecture by inviting him to deliver lectures on rhetoric and *belles-lettres* at the University of Edinburgh, from 1748 (where Smith continued until appointed to his first chair at the University of Glasgow in 1751). Critically, it was while at Edinburgh (and thus potentially in regular contact with Kames), that Smith extended his lectures on rhetoric and *belles-lettres* to include jurisprudence.[48] To what extent did Kames's work influence Smith?

While Kames did discuss a range of exclusive privileges, and accorded them some significance, he did not provide any unitary theory of the right. To provide a brief overview, he addressed the exclusive privilege of printing books in his *Principles of Equity*, from 1760; the rights of Burghs under a seal of cause in *Elucidations Respecting the Common and Statute Law of Scotland* (1777); and the exclusive privileges and jurisdiction of regalities in his *Historical Law Tracts*, first published in 1758.[49] Kames's

---

[45] Bankton, *Inst* II, 324, 7.

[46] Bankton, *Inst* II, 326, 14.

[47] Bankton, *Inst* II, 523, 11.

[48] *ODNB* "Smith" (n 11).

[49] Kames did, however, use the language of exclusive privilege in relation to one category of right which was not addressed by Smith or Hume, and which was potentially one of the earliest forms of exclusive privilege recognised in Scots law. In 1326, Robert I (the Bruce) and his parliament delegated the power of tax collection to the lords of regality: "[by indenture, they authorised] a tax to be levied for the King's use during his life, that many of the great Lords enjoyed the foresaid privilege ... And this exclusive privilege, in whatever manner introduced, came to be fully established in Lords of regality". See Kames, *Historical Law Tracts* (1758)

work is most relevant in relation to the privileges of the Burghs, granted to the Guilds and trades by a seal of cause, wherein he provided considerable detail on the rights and privileges enjoyed by the burgesses – and the limits thereon.[50] His emphasis on these rights demonstrates the changing commercial and political scene, when contrasted with the work of Stair, and reveals the irreversible changes to Scots life arising from the agricultural revolution and the increased opportunities for trade and commerce resulting from the Union with England in 1707. While his analysis of the scope of these privileges is interesting in its own right, it does not place them in the wider theoretical context later adopted by Smith.

It can be seen from this brief review that, in advancing exclusive privilege as a real right, Smith was uniting a range of privileges which were already well-established in Scots law – but which had not hitherto been classed together conceptually. As noted above, the foundation on which he built this doctrine was *jus haereditas*, the right of inheritance, but curiously this was the one right which the earlier jurists did not recognise as part of Scots law.

Jus haereditas in Scots law

Smith presented *jus haereditas* as one of the four real rights recognised in Scots law, (the others being *Dominium*, *Servitus* and *Pignus*), and stated without qualification that these four were "enumerated in the civill law".[51] The civil law that Smith would have drawn on would have been Roman law as received and interpreted throughout the *jus commune* in the seventeenth century. Yet it is not obvious that this reception was uniform. As Feenstra shows, throughout the seventeenth century, European scholars disputed the number and type of real rights: a doctoral thesis by Heinrich Hahn at the University of Helmstadt in 1639 identified five real rights: *dominium*, *pignus*, *servitus*, *possessio* and *hereditas*.[52] Previous scholars had admitted different combinations of real rights, with various groupings of four, five, six or more. The right of *hereditas* was not always included within these groupings, and nor was it free from criticism when an author did choose

---

pp 288–89, footnote omitted. See also the similar text in the third edition (1792) p 203. Millar also discussed the hereditary jurisdiction of barons and lords, and its abolition, but did not include it in his chapter on exclusive privilege, nor did he use the terminology of exclusive privilege: see J Millar, *Lectures on Government, delivered in the University of Glasgow* (MS Gen 180), taken down by William Rae (1789) vol 3, p 661.

50   Kames, *Elucidations Respecting the Common and Statute Law of Scotland* (1777) pp 53–55.
51   Smith, *Lectures* (n 8), at i.16 (at p 10).
52   R Feenstra, "Real rights and their classification in the 17th century: the role of Heinrich Hahn and Gerhard Feltmann" 1982 JR 106, 112.

to include it.[53] Thus, the question of which real rights should properly be included in a finite list of real rights in Scots law (then or now) cannot be answered simply by pointing to the "civill law", since seventeenth century Dutch scholarship illustrates the debate over this point. Moreover, there was consistency up to this point in Scots law that the real rights were ownership, servitude and pledge.[54] Certainly, no legal scholars in Scotland before the 1760s had apparently recognised inheritance – the right of the heir – as a fourth category of real right.

What is critical about the right of *haereditas*, when compared to the other rights Smith enumerated as exclusive privileges, is that the right of the heir to inherit had an established basis as a real right in the civilian tradition – even if there was sometimes doubt surrounding its place in the *numerus clausus*. *Haereditas* thus had a pedigree as a real right, which enabled Smith to extrapolate and encompass *all* the classes of exclusive privilege as real rights. In effect, Smith's reasoning appeared to be:

(i) the right of *haereditas* (or inheritance) is a real right;
(ii) *haereditas* is also a type of exclusive privilege; therefore:
(iii) all exclusive privileges can therefore be classed as real rights.

In Smith's words:

> [i]f therefore we account the right of inheritance to be a real right, as it certainly is, all other exclusive priviledges will for the same reason be accounted real rights.[55]

It is therefore *haereditas* which, through this (arguable) syllogism, opens the door to this new category of real right. Until Smith advanced the real right of inheritance and used it as the basis for exclusive privilege as a unified doctrine, there appears to have been no articulated notion of exclusive privilege as a real right in Scots law. The scholarly writing and the litigation of the time addressed the individual privileges but failed to synthesise them into a broader conceptual classification of exclusive privilege. This appears to be true not only of Scots law but of jurisprudential works more generally. Smith's *Lectures on Jurisprudence* cite Pufendorf and Grotius, which opens the possibility that Smith's development of the doctrine of exclusive privilege could have been inspired by their works.[56] However, a brief review of Pufendorf's *De Jure Naturae et Gentium* (Of the Law of Nature

---

[53] R Feenstra (n 52) pp 114–16, with reference to the scholarship of Baldus, de Mayno, Donellus and Giphanius.

[54] See references to Stair and Bankton, amongst others, cited above.

[55] Smith, *Lectures* (n 8) i.20 (at 11) – a point he repeats at ii.28 (at p 82).

[56] Smith was certainly influenced by some of the leading (and popular) European scholars of the time: the index in Smith, *Lectures* (n 8) contains several references to Pufendorf and Grotius, and Smith certainly referenced both jurists in the text of his lectures.

and Nations) and Grotius's *De Jure Belli ac Pacis* (The Right of War and Peace) does not reveal any notion of "exclusive privilege" – albeit both refer frequently to general privileges of men, sovereigns and nations.[57] It would therefore appear that Smith was entirely original in his development of this doctrine, given the lack of precedent in Scottish and philosophical writings more generally.

From this examination so far, we can see that Smith's work created the doctrine of exclusive privilege in Scots law and in doing so united a wide range of individual rights, ranging from rights to pursue animals and enemy ships to Burgh privileges and literary and patent rights. If Smith did indeed attempt to establish a new legal doctrine, then its longevity would depend on what happened next. It is therefore helpful to examine the work of those who came after Smith.

MID TO LATE EIGHTEENTH CENTURY

Professor John Millar

Relationship with Smith

Returning to the evolution of exclusive privilege as a real right, it is important to consider whether it flourished in academic scholarship subsequent to Smith. The work of Professor John Millar, as Regius Chair of Civil Law in the University of Glasgow from 1761–1801, provides an invaluable yardstick. The close connection between Smith and Millar has been outlined by the late Professor D M Walker, who notes that Millar attended the lectures of Adam Smith on moral philosophy. "His intelligence and ardour soon attracted Dr Smith's notice, and at this time was laid the foundation of that mutual esteem, which, during the few years they were afterwards professors in the same university, produced lasting intimacy and friendship."[58]

If Smith developed the unified theory of exclusive privilege, it is instructive to consider the theory's influence on his pupil, friend and colleague, Millar. Millar's treatment of exclusive privilege is therefore highly relevant, for three reasons. In the first place, Millar was a lawyer, so the

---

[57] The following editions were consulted: S von Pufendorf, *Of the law of nature and nations in eight books* (Oxford, 1703); *Of the law of nature and nations in eight books* (The second edition carefully corrected, and compared with Mr Barbeyrac's French translation) (Oxford, 1710); *The Law of nature and nations* (London, 1749); and H Grotius, *The rights of war and peace, in three books* (To which are added, all the large notes of Mr Barbeyrac, Professor of Law at Groningen) (London, 1738).

[58] D M Walker, *The Scottish Jurists* (1985) p 248, citing the "Account of his Life and Writings" by Millar's nephew John Craig. Walker, at p 253, also suggests that Millar's lectures on public law changed after the publication of Smith's *Wealth of Nations*, and it is suggested that this further illustrates Millar's readiness to take note of Smith's work where he deemed it relevant.

question arises: would a lawyer (albeit one with a strong economic bent) take a different approach to analysing the doctrine than did an economist and philosopher like Smith? Secondly, one of Millar's predecessors in the Regius chair was William Forbes, who, as we have seen, did not recognise exclusive privilege as a real right. Forbes' treatment was consistent with other respected Scottish jurists, such as Kames. Forbes and Kames were legal writers of repute who provided a more traditional model than Smith's. Thirdly, although Millar's lectures were never published, his treatment of exclusive privilege evolved over the course of his tenure. That evolution can be traced by comparing manuscript student lecture notes taken throughout his forty-year tenure in the Regius chair.

Millar's lectures

Millar did indeed advance exclusive privilege as a real right, adopting a similar approach to Smith. In his series of lectures on Scots law,[59] he consistently introduced the notion of real rights by explaining that there are four real rights: "Property, Servitude, Pledge, Exclusive Privilege."[60] This is a clear departure from previous jurists such as Stair, Forbes and Kames, and would appear to make Millar the first lawyer to advance exclusive privilege as a real right. It is inevitable that, in doing so, he was influenced by Smith's work in this area.

Having established exclusive privilege as the fourth of four real rights, Millar then proceeded to examine the concept. Whereas it merited coverage in only part of a lecture in 1776-77,[61] by his later lecture series in the 1790s, Millar devoted an entire lecture to the topic in each year.[62] Although Millar introduced exclusive privilege in the same manner as Smith, there are a number of differences thereafter. Millar did refer to the staples of

---

[59] Unlike the lectures of Adam Smith and Baron Hume, there is no printed record of Millar's lectures as Regius Professor between 1761 and 1801. But a number of copies of lecture notes taken by students, and one volume of his own notes, apparently written up by his son James, survive in the Special Collections of Glasgow University Library. For further details on all of Millar's law manuscripts, see John Cairns, "John Millar's Lectures on Scots Criminal Law" (1988) 8 *OJLS* 364. Of the GUL manuscripts, the most relevant for this paper are: (i) MS Gen 181, *Lectures on the Law of Scotland, by John Millar. Set of lecture notes taken by William Rae* (1790); (ii) MS Gen 347, *Notes taken from a Course of Lectures on the Private Law of Scotland Given annually in the University of Glasgow. Lecture notes of John Robinson* (1776-77); and (iii) MS Gen 1078: *Lectures on Scots Law by John Millar (written up by his son)* (1792).

[60] MS Gen 1078 (John Millar, 1792) (n 59) Lecture 10, 33. See also MS Gen 181 (William Rae, 1790) (n 59) vol 1; and MS Gen 347 (John Robinson, 1776-77) (n 59) Lecture 10, 91.

[61] MS Gen 347 (n 59), where exclusive privilege is covered in the second (albeit largest) part of lecture 26 (from p229), which starts with (a continuation of) a discussion of wadsets.

[62] In both MS Gen 181 (n 59) and MS Gen 1078 (n 59), exclusive privilege is covered in lecture 23. Both sets of notes are almost identical, indicating that Millar stuck closely to his lecture structure in succeeding years.

exclusive privilege, such as the right of the heir or the right to hunt game, but he did so in a distinct manner, setting exclusive privilege in a slightly different light. In all three sets of lecture notes referred to, Millar started by reminding students that the right of property (the primary real right) can be limited in three ways: as to use (by servitude), as to disposal (by pledge) and as to acquisition, by exclusive privilege.[63] He then gave two examples:

> A person may be prevented from acquiring property, by some other having the <u>sole means</u> by which that property is to be acquired. Thus, tho wild animals, in general, belong to the first occupant, the proprietor of a landed estate has a right to prevent any other person from hunting upon it, and consequently has the exclusive right of occupying those subjects while they remain upon their ground. In like manner, a nation, to whom a harbour belongs, may hinder any foreigner from coming into it, and consequently has an exclusive right of acquiring the goods of foreigners in that place.[64]

Millar's discussion of the right to catch wild animals is rather different from the concept of an interrupted chase explored by Smith. Whereas Smith's discussion was concerned with the right to continue once the chase has started, Millar focused on who had the right to hunt in the first place, and the control (the exclusive privilege) that can be exercised by the land owner. This approach led to Millar's quasi-definition of exclusive privilege – apparently given as an aside, as indicated by the square brackets:[65]

> [An exclusive privilege arises from an immediate connection with property, and is therefore a real right, following the thing over which it is exerted.]

Thus, for Millar, a right of exclusive privilege was intimately connected with ownership of a thing, and operated (like servitude and pledge) as a limitation on the primary real right of ownership, by affecting its acquisition or alienation. This can be contrasted with the foregoing discussion of Reid and Smith, wherein the real right of exclusive privilege is the only real right which has no physical object. In fact, Millar's approach makes most sense from a property perspective, providing greater doctrinal coherence with other the real rights which limit the real right of ownership, such as pledge and servitude, which are *jura in re aliena*. The flaw with Millar's approach, however, is that the exclusive privileges typically arise where there is *no* object owned. Thus, the property of the

---

[63] MS Gen 1078 (John Millar, 1792) (n 59) 73; MS Gen 181 (William Rae, 1790) (n 59), 331; and MS Gen 347 (John Robinson, 1776–77) (n 59) 229.

[64] MS Gen 1078 (John Millar, 1792) (n 59), 73, underlining in manuscript See also MS Gen 181 (William Rae, 1790) (n 59), 331; and MS Gen 347 (John Robinson, 1776–77) (n 59), 229–30.

[65] MS Gen 1078 (John Millar, 1792) (n 59) 73. See also MS Gen 181 (William Rae, 1790) (n 59) 331.

deceased, the wild animal being hunted, and the exclusive privileges of burghs and inventors and writers do not operate in relation to objects owned by another. In these instances, the exclusive privilege does not have an immediate connection with any "thing" over which it is exerted. As identified at the outset, exclusive privilege is the only real right, other than ownership itself, which is not a *jus in re aliena*.

Having set out the basis for exclusive privilege, Millar then identified the three chief instances in Scots law: the right of the heir, the right of corporations, and those bestowed upon the inventors of new machines (and also authors).[66] In relation to the right of the heir, Millar stated in his 1776-77 lectures on Scots private law, that:

> The most remarkable instance of Exclusive Priviledge exists in the case of an heir to an Estate. When a man dies, according to the general principle, his property must fall to the first occupant, but this is prevented by the Heir. Still he is not proprietor til he enter; on the contrary he has a time to Deliberate whether he will enter or not. While he does not, he has an Exclusive Privilege, a right of acquiring the property of his ancestor, in preference to every other person.[67]

As regards the other two key privileges, those of corporations and the early intellectual property rights, Millar's treatment was relatively straightforward. In the earlier version of his lectures from 1776-77,[68] Millar dealt with the privileges of the Corporations relatively briefly, although by the 1790s,[69] he had expanded his coverage of them to some extent.

Millar's treatment of exclusive privilege can therefore be viewed as an abbreviated version of Smith's. Its significance derives from two factors: (i) the fact that Millar was the first jurist to advance exclusive privilege as a unified category of real right; and (ii) that he did so throughout his time in the Regius chair, demonstrating that his treatment of exclusive privilege was considered and deliberate – not an impulsive and short-lived experiment. Throughout the forty years of his tenure, during which he was widely regarded as the most famous law teacher in Britain, Millar had the opportunity to influence an entire generation of Scots lawyers.

---

[66] MS Gen 1078 (John Millar, 1792) (n 59) 73. See also MS Gen 181 (William Rae, 1790) (n 59) 333. In MS Gen 347 (John Robinson, 1776-77) (n 59), Millar does not introduce the three chief instances at the outset, but proceeds to deal with them individually throughout the rest of the lecture.

[67] MS Gen 347 (John Robinson, 1776-77) (n 59) 230. See also MS Gen 1078 (John Millar, 1792) (n 59) 73, and MS Gen 181 (William Rae, 1790) (n 59) 333.

[68] MS Gen 347 (John Robinson, 1776-77) (n 59).

[69] See MS Gen 181 (William Rae, 1790) (n 59), and MS Gen 1078 (John Millar, 1792) (n 59).

Baron Hume

Background

David Hume held the Chair of Scots Law in the University of Edinburgh from 1786–1822, before he took up office as a Baron of Exchequer. As a former pupil of Millar's at the University of Glasgow,[70] it is to be expected that Millar's influence would be reflected in Hume's own lectures. Again, Hume's lectures were not published by him. Instead, we are reliant on the publication of original manuscripts now held by the Faculty of Advocates, which were prepared for delivery by Hume in his final year in the Chair of Scots Law, 1821–22.[71] These notes were edited by G Campbell H Paton and published by the Stair Society, in six volumes, between 1939 and 1958. These 1821–22 notes can be read together with manuscript versions of student notes from previous years, from 1788 onwards, a large number of which are in existence.[72]

From these lectures in Scots law, we can see that Hume developed the structure of exclusive privilege which had originated from Smith and been adopted by Millar, but he placed his focus very definitely on the rights of Burghs and the intellectual property rights of copyright and patents. While this approach remained constant throughout his tenure, there is a significant difference between the initial introduction to the subject in Hume's earlier lectures (1788 and 1790) and his later ones (at least 1810 onwards, as well as the 1822 version).

Hume's earlier treatment: 1788–90

From the academic session 1788–89, we have access to two out of four volumes of notes taken in Hume's class by one George Joseph Bell,[73] who, in 1822, succeeded Hume in the Chair of Scots Law. Lecture 22 given by Hume introduced the division between personal rights and real rights: "We shall divide what we have to say upon Real Rights into 4 branches – 1. Property – 2. Servitude. 3. Pledge – and 4thly Exclusive Privilege."[74] The

---

[70] At Hume's own request, according to Prof D M Walker: *The Scottish Jurists* (1985) p 316. Walker records that Hume studied under Millar in 1775 and boarded with him in the year 1776–77.

[71] G C H Paton (ed), *Baron David Hume's Lectures 1786–1822 Vol IV* (Stair Society vol 17, 1955) p v.

[72] In researching this work, I consulted a number of manuscript versions of notes from Hume's lectures held in Edinburgh University's Centre for Research Collections ("CRC"), dating from 1788–89 to 1820–21. Where relevant, these will be referred to below to supplement the Stair Society's published edition of Hume's lectures.

[73] Only volumes II and III of Bell's notes are available in the CRC (n 72) referenced Dc.5.37 and Dc.5.38 (1788–89) respectively: fortunately, vol II contains Hume's treatment of real rights.

[74] Hume's *Lectures*, vol II, CRC (n 72).

coverage of real rights occupied the whole of the second volume of Bell's manuscript notes, and the final two lectures in the volume (Lectures 39 and 40) are dedicated to exclusive privilege.

Hume commenced his treatment of exclusive privilege with the statement that:

> This is not treated as a real right by any of the writer [sic] on our law – It seems however entitled to a place among these rights – this will appear from the law of all nations with regard to a person duly possessed of property.[75]

Thus, Hume appears to found exclusive privilege as a real right based on the "law of all nations" – and reminiscent of Smith's broad reference to the "civill law". Hume set out the rationale for this in detail, and the basis is clearly tied to the right of the heir, as it was with Smith and Millar:

> When a man dies possessed of any property we should naturally imagine that that property would return to the Common Stock in consequence of the dissolution of the connection which had been formed betwixt the property and its possessor – but by the law of (it would seem) all Countries the heir of the deceased proprietor has an interest in his predecessor's property. This is not a right of property but it is the next step to it – it is a right by which the heir may exclude all others from the possession of the subject by which he is entitled to take up the possession & he alone. In the person of the heir then this interest in his predecessor's property is a real right, it is formed not in consequence of any personal connection betwixt John and James; but in consequence of a connection betwixt the heir and the subject itself. The Romans accordingly enumerated this right of succession among real rights – another instance of the Right of Exclusive Privilege is the property that the owner of the ground has over the wild beasts taken on it.[76]

The rest of Hume's first lecture covered the exclusive privileges of the Royal Burghs, while the second lecture addressed patents and copyright.

Hume's sources

Comparing Hume's approach with the notes from Smith and Millar, the similarities between Millar's approach and Hume's are undeniable, not least when considering their coverage of the exclusive privilege of the owner of land in relation to wild beasts, which differs from Smith's account of the interrupted chase. The similarity of approach by Hume and Millar is not coincidental: Hume explicitly acknowledges his debt to Millar in his very next sentence: [77] "We are indebted for this view of

---

[75] Hume's *Lectures*, vol II, CRC (n 72) 142 (page numbers in this volume are not, however, consistent).

[76] Hume's *Lectures*, vol II, CRC (n 72) 142 onwards.

[77] Hume's *Lectures*, vol II, CRC (n 72) 142 onwards. This acknowledgment is also contained in the 1790 lectures notes, indicating that it was more than a one-off or throwaway comment: CRC (n 72) Dc.6.123.

Exclusive Privilege & the invention of the name to Mr Millar, the Glasgow Professor".

The new Professor of Scots Law at Edinburgh is therefore quite explicit that he has adopted the concept of exclusive privilege as the fourth category of real right from the Glasgow Professor. This appears to contradict his opening sentence that no other writer in Scots law treats exclusive privilege as a real right.[78] Nevertheless, it provides explicit evidence that Hume was directly influenced by Millar in his analysis of exclusive privilege.

Hume's later treatment: 1822

By 1822, however, Hume's starting point was no longer the right of the heir, but the right of thirlage. This is the miller's exclusive right to grind all the corn grown in the vicinity of the mill, and which imposes a corresponding obligation on all farmers in that area to take their corn to that mill. Given the dual aspect of thirlage – both imposing an obligation and granting a monopoly – it is not surprising to find it classed alternatively as a right of servitude and as a right of exclusive privilege. Writers before and since have been split as to its correct classification:[79] Hume attempted to run with the hares and hunt with the hounds:[80]

> [Thirlage] is treated, and arranged, in all our Books of Law, as a Servitude (And of course it is better not to deviate from that arrangement). But still, Thirlage is, in truth, not properly speaking a servitude, farther than as, in a loose way, any burden on a property may be called a servitude. It is just an instance of the real right of exclusive privilege, – an exclusive title in the owner of the mill to perform a certain operation ...

With thirlage as his starting point for introducing the right of exclusive privilege (while not wishing to appear controversial in doing so), Hume then moved on to *haereditas*. Here his account does not differ significantly from that given above, in his earlier lectures. In particular, he comments that the right of inheritance:[81]

---

[78] Hume's comment that Millar invented the name also indicates that he was unaware that Millar was following Smith in this approach.

[79] Stair treated thirlage as a servitude: *Inst* II.7.15–27; *contra* Smith, *Lectures* (n 8), ii.37–38 (at 85). Even scholars who did not recognise exclusive privilege as a real right still challenged the classification of thirlage as a servitude: for example, Bell subsequently dealt with thirlage in his treatment of servitudes, but argued that it was in fact a sort of taxation and was in any event in a state of gradual extinction: Bell's *Principles of the Law of Scotland* 4th edn (1839, republished 2010) § 1017. Those in favour of classifying thirlage as a servitude appear to have won the day, although the position is academic since the abolition of thirlage on 28 November 2004, by the Abolition of Feudal Tenure etc (Scotland) Act 2000, s 55.

[80] Hume, *Lectures* (n 71) 38, footnote omitted. Bell, *Principles* (n 79) § 1016 agrees.

[81] Hume, *Lectures* (n 71) 38, emphasis added.

is something short of property; yet it is the next step to it. It is a preferable and an exclusive
title on his part ... [and any attempt to interfere with this is an] usurpation ...
an infringement of the exclusive privilege of their heir. He may vindicate – may
recover – the succession ... and his right is thus marked with all the characters of
a proper legitimate and real right.

Significantly, all acknowledgment of the debt owed to Professor Millar has
gone by the time of these lectures. This acknowledgement is also missing
from the 1810–11 manuscript notes,[82] suggesting that, while Hume was
conscious of Millar's influence at the outset of his lecturing career, this
diminished over time, especially after Millar's death.[83]

Hume on burgh and intellectual property rights

Throughout Hume's tenure, however, he was consistent in devoting the vast
majority of his coverage of exclusive privilege to the burgh rights and the
intellectual property rights of copyright and patents. The weighting given
to these is perhaps unsurprising, in view of the significance of the burgh,
and its privileges at this time.[84] The importance of these monopolies can be
seen in the Treaty of Union 1706, which dedicated a specific article solely to
maintaining these rights.[85] With the intellectual property rights, especially
copyright, Hume (and Smith and Millar before him) may have had a much
more personal interest in their significance, given their own publications:
all three would have been conscious of the value of literary property and,
presumably, the need to protect it.

A further indicator of the legal importance of the exclusive privileges
of the burghs, and the rights they delegated to the guilds and trades, can
be deduced from the volume of litigation these rights generated, as the
freemen of the burgh attempted to enforce their privileges, particularly with
regard to imports of foreign commodities. *Morison's Dictionary* provided
Hume with ample material for his review, together with the statutes of the
Parliament of Scotland and, latterly, the British Parliament, granting and
regulating these privileges. In addition to outlining the different privileges
enjoyed by the merchants (to trade) and the incorporated crafts (in relation
to manufactures), Hume provided fascinating detail as to the scope and
limits of these exclusive privileges.[86]

---

[82] CRC (n 72) ref Gen 1394 vol IV, 1 ff.

[83] A more prosaic explanation may be that the students in question failed to note down Hume's
acknowledgment. But Hume's own 1822 notes contain no such acknowledgment.

[84] For an excellent historical account of Scottish burghs, see T C Smout, *A History of the Scottish
People 1560–1830* (1969; repr 1998), chapter 7.

[85] Article 21 of the Treaty of Union 1706, as ratified by the Union with England Act 1707
(APS, xi, 406, c 7; RPS 1706/10/257): "That the rights and privileges of the royal burghs in
Scotland, as they now are, do remain entire after the union, and notwithstanding thereof."

[86] Hume, *Lectures* (n 71) 39–59.

THE NINETEENTH CENTURY

Exclusive privilege, as developed by Smith and adopted by Millar and Hume, was presented as a unified category of real right, in an apparent departure from what had gone before. It is therefore instructive to see how subsequent scholars engaged with the doctrine. From this point onwards, however, the right appears to vanish as a distinct real right, albeit the individual privileges remained important aspects of Scots law.

Bell

Hume's successor in the Chair of Scots Law at Edinburgh University was Professor George Joseph Bell. In his *Principles of the Law of Scotland*, Bell did not use the terminology of "real rights" – there is no entry for such in the index – although his Introduction did distinguish between real and personal rights. The former are "available against the thing itself, in whose hands soever it may be found".[87] Such "rights real" are discussed as "property, heritable and moveable", in Part II of the *Principles*. Within Part II, Bell followed the institutional scheme of rights, discussing ownership and limitations on absolute ownership, including nuisance, servitudes, thirlage and liferent, but there is, however, no mention here of exclusive privilege.[88]

Instead, Bell treated the different privileges simply as individual rights – the Burgh privileges, for example, were discussed within his section on Royal Burghs[89] and also under the heading "Fairs and Markets".[90] Patents and copyrights are covered in a separate section on "Incorporeal Moveable Subjects".[91] In relation to literary property (copyright), Bell employed the phrase "exclusive privilege" interchangeably with monopoly. "There is no exclusive privilege in any subject of inquiry", Bell writes. "No one by writing on any subject can pre-occupy it to the exclusion of another."[92] Bell followed a similar pattern in his *Commentaries*, although here (unlike his *Principles*), there was an index entry for exclusive privilege, which made specific reference only to copyright and patents. Again, real rights were dealt with through property rights and ownership, and exclusive privilege was not addressed here.[93] Despite the use of the term, "exclusive privilege", there was no attempt to engage with the unifying theory advanced by Smith, Millar or Hume. For Bell, this cannot be attributed to a lack of awareness, since

---

[87] Bell, *Principles* (n 79) § 3.
[88] Bell, *Principles* (n 79) § 359 ff
[89] Bell, *Principles* (n 79) § 2174 ff, especially §§ 2183–89.
[90] Bell, *Principles* (n 79) §§ 664–66.
[91] Bell, *Principles* (n 79) § 1355 ff.
[92] Bell, *Principles* (n 79) § 1358.
[93] G J Bell, *Commentaries on the Law of Scotland and on the principles of mercantile jurisprudence*, 5th edn (1826) (the last edition prepared by Bell); 7th edn by J McLaren (1870).

we have clear evidence, from his own lecture notes, taken in Hume's classes of 1788–89, that he heard the doctrine being expounded as a unified real right. Bell's divergence from Hume and his coverage of different exclusive privileges in different places must either have been a deliberate decision to reject the approach or, possibly, an imperfect recollection of what he studied thirty years earlier.

More

John Schank More succeeded Bell in the Chair of Scots Law at Edinburgh in 1843, a post he held until 1861. His *Lectures on the Law of Scotland* were published shortly after his death, edited by John McLaren. The first volume contained a section on "Invasion of Exclusive Privileges", arranged within the chapter on "Obligations Arising from Delict, or Quasi Delict". The coverage extended to trading privileges (a very short section, which noted "they are now a matter of history, and no longer of the least practical importance");[94] patents; and copyright. The sole reference to exclusive privilege in the second volume was to the rather curious privilege of magistrates or friendly societies in letting out mortcloths.[95] It is clear from More's treatment that he viewed exclusive privilege simply as a collective term for a limited number of monopolies, being the Burgh rights, patents and copyright,[96] rather than a broader category of real right.

Later editions of Erskine

Erskine's first works were published in the eighteenth century, and have been examined above. His final works (from 1769 and 1773) contain no reference to exclusive privilege as a real right.[97] However, Erskine's *Principles* and *Institute* are also of interest in the period after Hume, as edited editions were published throughout the nineteenth century and, in the case of his *Principles*, up to 1911. A review of successive editions of these reveals very little of note in relation to exclusive privilege: on occasion the *Principles* contain a footnote reference to an exclusive privilege of a town clerk,[98] while

---

[94] J S More, *Lectures on the Law of Scotland*, edited by John McLaren (1864) I, 349. The section on "Invasion of Exclusive Privileges" covers pp 319–57.

[95] More, *Lectures* (n 94) I, 83, noted in the context of a wider discussion of prescription and the acquisition of exclusive rights and privileges by this method.

[96] This is particularly clear in the Index to the *Lectures*, at the end of vol II, which reads "Exclusive Privilege: See Burgh – Patent – Copyright".

[97] Erskine, *The Principles of the Law of Scotland* 4th edn (1769); Erskine, *An Institute of the Law of Scotland* (1773).

[98] J Erskine, *Principles of the Law of Scotland* 14th edn (1870); 15th edn (1874); 16th edn (1881); and 17th edn (1886) each contain passing references in footnotes to the exclusive privilege of town clerks as notaries, in Bk II, Tit III, "On the Constitution of Heritable Rights". The many other editions of the *Principles* apparently contain no reference to "exclusive privilege" at all.

the *Institute* does contain references to exclusive privilege, but only as far as copyright, patents and Burgh rights: again, there is no consideration of the doctrine as a category of real right.[99]

The editor of the final four editions of Erskine's *Principles* was Sir John Rankine KC, Professor of Scots Law at Edinburgh from 1888. Student lectures notes from Rankine's lectures on Scots law delivered in 1890–91 are available and also reveal no analysis of exclusive privilege, or indeed any detailed account of real and personal rights. His treatment of copyright and patents was very brief, and without reference to exclusive privilege.[100]

Bell's *Dictionary and Digest*

Robert Bell's *Dictionary and Digest of the Law of Scotland* was published throughout the nineteenth century, with seven editions spanning 1807 to 1890. It started with no entry for "exclusive privilege"[101] and, when it acquired one in its 3rd edition in 1826, the focus was firmly placed on the privileges of Burghs and of literary property of copyright.[102] By the time of the final edition in 1890, the entry simply recorded that "This term is used in a limited acceptation, to signify the rights and franchises of the nature of monopolies, [formerly] enjoyed by the incorporated trades of a royal burgh".[103] The entry finished with a cross reference to the entry on copyright, noting "As to the exclusive privilege granted to authors, see *Copyright*". There is thus no wider treatment of exclusive privilege in the *Dictionary*, beyond identification of these two monopolies.

Later works

Similar approaches can be found in other nineteenth and early twentieth century texts. Green's *Encyclopedia on the Law of Scotland*, first published in 1897 and followed by a second edition in 1911, contained a short

---

[99] See, for example, the index entry and references therein, in J Erskine, *An Institute of the Law of Scotland* 8th edn by J B Nicolson (1871).

[100] T Wilson, "Notes on Professor Rankine's Lectures – Scots Law – 1890–1891", manuscript notes (Edinburgh University Library ref *KK Wil), Lectures 47 and 58 contain a brief discussion of land ownership and ownership of moveables, including copyright and patents.

[101] Robert Bell, *Dictionary and Digest of the Law of Scotland* (1807), 2nd edn (1815). Only the first two (of seven) editions were compiled by Robert Bell.

[102] Robert Bell, *Dictionary and Digest of the Law of Scotland* 3rd edn by William Bell (1826). This inclusion of exclusive privilege for the first time focused on the monopolies of incorporations and burghs, with a final reference to literary property. The definition remained the same in the 4th edn by William Bell (1838) and in the 5th edn by George Ross (1861).

[103] *Bell's Dictionary and Digest of the Law of Scotland* 7th edn by George Watson (1890; reprinted 2012) 429. The rights of the Burghs had been abolished by the time of the 7th edition and this is noted in the entry for Exclusive Privilege. The definition was modified between the 5th edition (1861) and the 6th edition (1881), which was the first edited by George Watson. The wording remained unchanged in the 7th and final edition cited here.

definition of "exclusive privilege", stretching to little more than fifty words, and referring to two very specific examples of the right. But there was no wider conceptual consideration.[104] In 1927, the first edition of Gloag and Henderson's formative *Introduction to the Law of Scotland* contained no reference to "exclusive privilege" at all.[105]

Discussion

The picture emerging from the nineteenth and early twentieth centuries is clear. Although the terminology of exclusive privilege was still in limited use, and individual categories were still recognised, there was apparently no understanding of exclusive privilege as a unified category or real right in the period between Hume's final lecture in 1822 and Reid's title on *Property* in the *Stair Memorial Encyclopedia* in 1993. Despite the pre-eminence and well-established reputations of each member of the Smith-Millar-Hume triumvirate, no other scholars who published work then or after adopted exclusive privilege as a category of real right. The doctrine remained marginal and neglected until rediscovered by Reid.

It is a matter of speculation why the conceptual category of exclusive privilege was overlooked. One possibility is lack of access to the works of Smith, Millar and Hume – a possibility strengthened by the fact that Millar's lectures remain unpublished today, while Smith's and Hume's were only published in the second half of the twentieth century. This theory is, however, significantly weakened by the fact that there were a large number of manuscript versions of notes of Hume's *Lectures* in circulation, while manuscript notes for Millar and Smith certainly existed, as evidenced above. Millar and Hume each lectured for over thirty years, and the evidence is that they both covered exclusive privilege throughout that time.[106] Their students were therefore exposed to the concept of exclusive privilege, with every opportunity to apply it in practice thereafter. Moreover, we have clear evidence, discussed above, that Bell was introduced to the concept of exclusive privilege through his attendance at Hume's lectures in 1788–89, yet did not include it, for whatever reason, in his own work. Thus, the lack of formal publication can only be at best partially responsible for the lack of wider awareness of the doctrine.

---

[104] J Chisholm (ed), *Green's Encyclopaedia of the Law of Scotland* (1897), 2nd edn (1911), vol V "Election Petition to Fire-Raising". The entry for "Exclusive Privilege" remains unchanged between the two editions. The two rights referred to in it are the rights of burgesses in Royal Burghs, and the intellectual property rights granted to authors, artists and inventors.

[105] W M Gloag and R C Henderson, *Introduction to the Law of Scotland* (1927). The index contains no entry for "privilege" or "exclusive privilege". The only monopolies covered are the intellectual property rights, in the chapter on "Moveable Property".

[106] See MS Notes of Millar's lectures, 1766–1801 (n 59), and the notes of Hume's *Lectures*, 1788–1822 (n 72) and (n 73) above.

A second explanation reflects the changing society of the nineteenth century. Whether one had a right to chase down deer or pursue enemy shipping was of significantly less importance than in previous centuries; and the burgh privileges were abolished during the course of the nineteenth century. The rights which retained considerable economic importance, then as now, were the rights of copyright and patent, and these were increasingly regulated by statute and harmonised with English law. In time, they came to be treated as *sui generis* statutory rights or even as full property rights. The transition from the era of Smith–Millar–Hume to that of the nineteenth century jurists accompanied the industrial revolution, and the older exclusive privileges gave way to free competition.

A third possible reason for the lack of uptake amongst subsequent scholars is a much more fundamental one: that the doctrine lacks internal coherence and intellectual rigour. It is to that assessment we now turn.

EXCLUSIVE PRIVILEGE: A DOCTRINAL ASSESSMENT

Introduction

Reid defines exclusive privilege as "an exclusive, and valuable, right to do something and, hence, to stop others from doing the same thing".[107] All the examples of exclusive privilege given by Smith and examined above are capable of meeting this definition. However, a right which can encompass heirs, hunters, Burghers, tradesmen, writers and inventors must be framed so widely as to undermine its very utility as a conceptual category. The above definition could in fact be applied to almost any real right – and thus exclusive privilege risks losing any internal coherence.

It is possible, however, to identify four shared features of these privileges, which may be enough to give exclusive privilege the necessary internal coherence as a unified category, and thereby unite the different privileges encompassed within it. Critically, such an exercise, if successful, would also give us the necessary legal certainty to allow other privileges to be included, or not, on a principled basis in the future. It would therefore enable exclusive privilege to operate as a useful right in the twenty-first century.

Four features

Good against the world

The first and most fundamental feature of exclusive privilege is that it is good against the world. The classes of exclusive privilege covered by Smith, Millar and Hume were all enforceable against anyone who attempted to

---

[107]   Reid, *Property* (n 3), para 5.

challenge or interfere with the right. In particular, when talking about the right of the heir, Smith, Millar and Hume all emphasised the *erga omnes* nature of his right to the inheritance in the interim period between the death of the ancestor and taking entry. For Smith, this was the right to prevent others "meddling" with it, and to obtain reparation for any damage suffered;[108] for Millar, the heir had the right "in preference to every other person";[109] while for Hume, the heir "may vindicate – may recover – the succession".[110] This essential shared feature helps explain the treatment of exclusive privilege as a real right, and also points to the second shared feature, since there is at least one critical difference between the classes of exclusive privilege and the other real rights.

No physical object

The second unifying feature of exclusive privilege is therefore that, in each instance, there is no thing which is the object of the right. Unlike the other real rights, there is no requirement for there to be a thing at the heart of the right.[111] Even in the case of the exclusive privilege in chasing deer or ships, where it might appear that the right subsists in a physical object, this is not so. The exclusive privilege does not arise in the deer or ship itself – although once caught, a real right of ownership will, all other things being equal, arise in that object. The exclusive privilege is a right to prevent others from stepping in.[112] In the case of inventions and books, where it could be argued that there is a "thing" – the invention or book – it is in fact the right to make (in the case of patents) or copy (in the case of copyright) which is the valuable right. Moreover, unlike the other traditional real rights, no exclusive privilege is a *jus in re aliena*: they place no burden on anything owned by another. Exclusive privilege is therefore good against the world,

---

[108] Smith, *Lectures* (n 8), at i.19 (at p 11), emphasis added.

[109] MS Gen 347 (John Robinson, 1776–77) (n 59) 230; MS Gen 1078 (John Millar, 1792) (n 59) 73; and MS Gen 181 (William Rae, 1790) (n 59) 333.

[110] Hume, *Lectures* (n 71) p 38 (emphasis added).

[111] For a review and analysis, see S van Erp and B Akkermans (eds), *Cases, Materials and Text on Property Law* (2012), pp 51–53, and chapter 4, discussing whether property rights can be held in respect of incorporeal objects; also G L Gretton, "Ownership and its objects" (2007) 71 RabelsZ 802.

[112] If the chase were interrupted and another party made off with the deer, it is not clear from the reports of the time whether the injured party would have a right to possess the deer, or to receive compensation for infringement of the right (the exclusive privilege) to finish the chase. It is submitted that the latter is the correct response in theory, to reflect the "loss of a chance" that was infringed by intercepting the chase, although Stair, while not dealing specifically with exclusive privilege, asserts that an intercepted chase would be grounds for restoring the resulting property to the original pursuer: Stair, *Inst* II.1.33, discussed above. Accordingly, it may be that either remedy should be available. For the current law in this area, see D L Carey-Miller with D Irvine, *Corporeal Moveables in Scots Law* 2nd edn (2005) paras 2–04 and 2–05.

but not tied to or dependent on any prior ownership right. Instead, it is in all these cases a right to be the only person entitled to *do* a specific act – a monopoly right.

Inalienable

A third shared feature is that these rights are, from the available evidence, inalienable. The clear exception is the intellectual property rights (and even then, the moral rights of authors are inalienable, in the case of copyright). Here, however, the ability to license, assign, or pass on through testamentary disposition derives from extensive statutory developments in the nineteenth and twentieth centuries.[113] Whether copyright could be passed by will was litigated in the eighteenth century and, in a dispute between two publishers, the court upheld the right of the original publisher to publish letters received by the deceased son from his father, the Earl of Chesterfield, which had been assigned to the publisher by the son's widow. This would seem to indicate that the original publisher had a protected right in the copyright of the letters, which had passed from the original writer and recipient on death, via the widow. The Court of Session rejected the defence that the copyright was personal and incapable of testamentary disposition, thereby allowing for the transmission of copyright on death.[114]

In all other cases, however, the right appears to be personal to the privilege holder. Smith, Millar and Hume do not specifically address this point yet there is no evidence that the exclusive privileges they discussed were freely transferable. Indeed, in the case of the pursuit of deer or enemy shipping, it would seem a practical impossibility to effect a transfer in the time available. The privileges of craftsmen, merchants and freemen of Burghs also appear to be personal to the person who has served the apprenticeship or paid the dues. In the case of discharged soldiers, or "King's freemen", statutory provision entitled them to exercise the privilege of a craft or guild "as if regularly entered" therein.[115] This right could be continued after the soldier's death, by his widow and children. At first sight, therefore, this looked like an exclusive privilege

---

[113] For the right to license and assign patents, see the Patents Act 1977, s 30 (re England) and s 31 (re Scotland). In the case of copyright, see the Copyright, Designs and Patents Act 1988, s 90.

[114] See *Dodsley v M'Farquhar* (1775) Mor 8308.

[115] Hume, *Lectures* (n 71) p 58. Unsurprisingly, this generated some litigation between the freemen who had paid their dues and served their time, and the King's freemen and their relatives seeking to take advantage of their statutory right: so much so that *Morison's Dictionary* contains a section dedicated to such litigation: Mor 2014, "Burgh Royal: Section VIII 'Privilege to Soldiers Exercising Trades within Burgh'". See also *Corporation of Wrights and Masons in Portsburgh v Chalmers* (1804) Mor 11821.

which was alienable and transmissible. However, the right of the widow and children was in fact granted by a separate statute, the Privileges of Exercising Trades Act 1762,[116] and therefore this right to continue the soldier's trade after his death was not a right passed by the solider to his surviving family, but apparently a new statutory grant of a privilege specifically addressed to those relatives. Thus, the rights encompassed by exclusive privilege are inalienable, other than by specific statutory provision.

Limitation of time or space

The fourth commonality is that the privilege is always limited in one of two ways: in time or in space. Unlike ownership, the right of exclusive privilege will either extend over a limited geographical area, or will be effective in the whole of the jurisdiction but of limited duration. Thus, the privilege of the craftsman or the merchant in the Burgh only covered the territory of the Burgh and, even then, was limited in other ways. For example, those who were not burghers could manufacture crafts for personal use and consumption, or an inn keeper could brew beer and bake bread for sale to his customers without infringing the privileges of the brewers and bakers, since these activities were ancillary to his primary business as inn keeper.[117] The exclusive privileges of copyright and patents were not limited by territory, and thus applied throughout the kingdom, but they were limited as to time. Litigation to attempt to found an unlimited copyright arising at common law was unsuccessful, with the Court of Session holding that there was no copyright other than the (time-limited) right granted by statute.[118] The original time limits may have been extended over the centuries, at least in the case of copyright, but it remains the case that copyright and patents are still time-limited statutory monopolies.[119]

Limitations as to time and space are arguably least clear as regards those privileges said by Smith to arise from natural reason, that is to say, the right of the heir, the right to hunt down deer, and the right to chase down enemy ships.[120] While no specific time limit is attached to the right to chase down

[116] 3 Geo III c 8.

[117] Hume, *Lectures* (n 71) p 45 (personal use and consumption) and p 46 (innkeepers).

[118] *Hinton v Donaldson* (1773) Mor 8307. For the same case and outcome in English law the following year, see the decision of the House of Lords in *Donaldson v Beckett* (1774) 2 Bro PC 129.

[119] Patents Act 1977, s 25; Copyright, Designs and Patents Act 1988, s 12.

[120] Although whether the right to chase down enemy shipping can be said to arise solely from "natural reason" is open to debate, since it was a right typically granted and regulated by the state on a war-by-war basis and enemy captures would in some instances be commandeered by the state: see Bell, *Principles* (n 79) § 1295; Bankton, *Inst* II, 523, 11.

deer or shipping, the very nature of the activity means that it will have a finite, and relatively short, duration. The chase will end with either the capture or escape of the quarry, at which point the exclusive privilege will come to an end.

Discussion

These four factors do appear to unite the various classes of exclusive privilege, over and above the basic aspect of their monopolistic nature. The fact remains, however, that exclusive privilege did not flourish in the nineteenth century. While the reason for its demise at this time may never be known, a number of possible reasons can be reviewed.

THE DEMISE OF EXCLUSIVE PRIVILEGE

Despite the shared features of exclusive privilege, identified above, which give internal coherence to the doctrine as a category of real right – most notably, as the only real right other than ownership which is not a *jus in re aliena* – there are a number of inconsistencies.

No uniformity

In the first place, there is no uniformity in the origins of the different classes of exclusive privilege. As a general rule the older rights, such as hunting deer and the inheritance of the heir, were based on "natural reason" (although, as noted above, the right to pursue enemy shipping arose from a grant from the Crown), while the newer and more commercial classes, concerning Burghs, literary property and patents, were statutory in origin, or originated in an express or implied grant from the Crown. As "natural reason" faded from the scene, so too did the older rights.

Division of purpose

Moreover, the rights which owed their origin to natural reason were also typically interim rights which existed only to protect a limited interest until a full right of ownership could be established – or the object of ownership was lost altogether. This was clearly the case regarding the right of the heir and of the hunter. In both cases, the exclusive privilege protected the prospective holder in the vulnerable stage before his full ownership was established. In contrast, the statutory grants of exclusive privilege may have been time limited (as in the case of the intellectual property rights) but they were never interim: they were never intended to lead to full ownership in due course. There is therefore a theoretical divide between the purpose of the different exclusive privileges.

Overlap with public law rights

A further distinction can be seen when the burgh rights are contrasted with the rights of the heir, the hunter and creators and inventors. Whereas the latter privileges were all primarily concerned with private law interests, the burgh rights were very much an area of public law, wherein the state regulated the nature and extent of the rights granted to the holders. One writer who did identify this aspect was Forbes, the first holder of the Regius Chair in law at Glasgow. Although he did not identify exclusive privilege as a coherent doctrine, he dealt with the privileges of trades, handicrafts, fairs and markets as public law matters, in his volume dedicated to "Publick law".[121] While the public law/private law distinction is not insurmountable, it does indicate a sharp divide between the functions of the different classes of exclusive privilege.

These distinctions may not have been enough, in and of themselves, to cause writers who followed Hume to depart from the attempted classification of exclusive privilege as a real right. However, they may have had a cumulative effect, especially when combined with two further, very practical, factors: desuetude, and professional practice.

Desuetude

Smith, Millar and to some extent Hume were writing in a different era from Bell and his successors. The impact of commerce and industrialisation was changing the world and consequently the law. By the start of the nineteenth century, the rights brought together by Smith under the banner of exclusive privilege were losing their significance. As these individual rights fell into desuetude, there was correspondingly little need for a coherent doctrine to unite or explain them. The rights which actually increased in importance as a result of these industrial and commercial changes were the intellectual property rights, which were developed on a UK-wide basis through legislation – again potentially minimising the perceived need for a coherent common law "home" for them.

Professional practice

In professional practice, meanwhile, there was (and still is) little incentive for solicitors or advocates to spend their time or their clients' money exploring theoretical concepts. Litigation, which drives the development of the common law, typically focuses on the most direct route to a practical

---

[121] Forbes *Great Body* (n 39) vol 3, Publick Law, Pt 1, Book 2, Chapters 2 and 3.

outcome for the litigants.[122] It is therefore not entirely surprising that
Millar's and Hume's students, after learning about exclusive privilege in
their lectures on Scots law, did not seek to entrench this through their
professional practice. A review of the cases reported in Morison's Dictionary
supports this. Although there are innumerable references to the various
individual exclusive privileges, there is no entry for "exclusive privilege" as a
unified category, suggesting that litigation at least did not seek to locate the
individual rights within a broader class of real right.

EXCLUSIVE PRIVILEGE TODAY

In light of the lack of detailed academic consideration of exclusive privilege
since Hume, together with the lack of modern relevance for most of the
rights it encompassed, it is not easy to see how exclusive privilege could be
rehabilitated in the twenty-first century. Two suggestions can be made.

The first is that the one category of exclusive privilege identified by
Smith which continues to play a key role today is intellectual property.
There is considerable controversy surrounding the legal nature of the
various intellectual property rights: are they property capable of ownership,
incorporeal moveables, or a *sui generis* right? The current statutory bases
of the various intellectual property rights assert their status as "property":
the Copyright, Designs and Patents Act 1988 opens with the statement
that "Copyright is a property right";[123] under the Trade Marks Act 1994 a
"registered trade mark is a property right",[124] and the Patents Act 1977 states
that, in Scotland, any "patent or application for a patent, and any right
in or under any patent or any such application, is incorporeal moveable
property".[125] Nonetheless, the debate continues as to whether intellectual
property and other incorporeals can correctly be classed as real rights since
there is no tangible "thing" at the heart of the right.[126]

In fact, a return to Smith's original classification of intellectual property
rights as exclusive privileges addresses this debate, and provides a coherent
intellectual home for these rights. As an exclusive privilege, there is no need

---

[122] This can be seen in the development of unjustified enrichment through litigation in the
1990s and 2000s in Scots law, which was at times irregular. But the development of the law
in this area does illustrate that greater doctrinal coherence can arise through the activity of
the courts.

[123] Copyright, Designs and Patents Act 1988, s1(1).

[124] Trade Marks Act 1994, s 2(1).

[125] Patents Act 1977, s1(2) – and can be licensed, assigned or be made the subject of a standard
security: ss 31(3) and 31(4).

[126] H Beverley-Smith, *The Commercial Appropriation of Personality* (2000) p 278, for example,
comments that "in the case of intellectual property, the term 'property' is used in a purely
metaphorical way"; and, more generally, at pp 277–83. See also see Gretton (n 111).

for intellectual property rights to subsist in relation to a corporeal "thing", nor must they place a burden on the property of another, since exclusive privileges are not *jura in re aliena*. Recognition of intellectual property rights as exclusive privileges in the twenty-first century would therefore provide an underlying doctrinal certainty for these rights, over and above the statutory basis upon which they rely.

The statutory origin of exclusive privileges also supports the second proposition regarding modern exclusive privileges: any new addition to the category would have to be statutory in origin, as there seems to be no common law basis for recognising a new privilege, not least since "natural reason" is no longer deemed sufficient as the basis for a right in law.

As I have suggested elsewhere, exclusive privilege could provide a coherent and useful home for a new right in Scotland to protect publicity rights, or image rights.[127] These are rights to respect the economic and dignitarian interests that an individual has in his "persona", which comprises his name, image, reputation, and other indicia of identity. Moreover, a right of publicity for the individual must be balanced with competing interests, such as the right of third parties to use his name and image to convey meaning, under freedom of expression. Since exclusive privilege is not a full right of ownership, however, it does not bring with it the full range of rights of the owner. Instead, the right can be shaped, through statute, to reflect the competing interests of all parties concerned.[128] Although not currently protected in a comprehensive fashion in Scots law, a statutory right of publicity could grant a *limited* monopoly to the individual – and would therefore be very much in keeping with the concept of an exclusive privilege, as expounded by Smith, Millar and Hume.

CONCLUSION

This analysis has shown for the first time how Smith, followed by Millar and Hume, attempted to draw together a range of discrete monopolies under one conceptual category, closely allied with other real rights. Smith's originality has been demonstrated by comparing his work to that of other jurists both before and after. The right of exclusive privilege is an attractive proposition, and the broad definition could potentially lend itself to extensive application in modern society. Nevertheless, the right did not flourish after its initial emergence. While the reasons for this are hard to

---

[127] See my previous attempt to classify a Scottish right of publicity as a modern example of exclusive privilege, reflecting its "IPish" nature: Gillian Black, "Publicity and image rights in Scots law" (2010) 14 Edin LR 364; and *Publicity Rights and Image: Exploitation and Legal Control* (Hart, 2011).

[128] Gillian Black, *Publicity Rights and Image*, chapters 9 and 10.

establish with any certainty, it is possible that the main reason for its demise was largely pragmatic: the classes of exclusive privilege identified and brought together were decreasing in importance in the course of the eighteenth century, such that there was limited need to try to find a meaningful home for them in Scots law in the nineteenth century or thereafter. Conversely, those elements of exclusive privilege which grew in importance – principally the rights of copyright and patents – were increasingly governed by UK-wide statutes, and therefore were accommodated without the need for a specific home in Scots law.

By refining the doctrine to acknowledge the (practical) redundancy of the historical elements, I have sought to show how exclusive privilege could provide a much-needed conceptual home in the twenty-first century for the statutory intellectual property rights. In doing so, it could also offer a principled classification for new legal developments, such as a right of publicity, where there is no object of the right which is susceptible to ownership, but which nevertheless bears the hallmarks of a real right and is good against the world. The legacy of Smith and Millar in relation to exclusive privilege could thus live on in Scots law, nearly three hundred years after their work first identified it.

"A Rule of Great Value and Importance": Aspects of Confidentiality and Privilege in Civil Litigation in Scotland

K J Campbell

Confidentiality attaches to a number of aspects of the dealings between lawyers and their clients, some of which inhere in the relationship, while others arise from the character of the service being provided. The aim of this essay is to consider some more recent developments in the application of the doctrine of confidentiality in Scots law so far as relating to lawyers or to legal process. In relation to lawyer–client confidentiality, an effort is made to consider those developments in light of the origins of the principle, while the broader context of developments in other areas will also be addressed.

LAWYER–CLIENT PRIVILEGE

Lawyer–client privilege, also commonly referred to as legal professional privilege, is well understood and well established in Scots law, with substantive discussion usually found in treatises on the law of evidence,[1] though there are many judicial dicta across the common law world emphasising that its importance goes far beyond the rules of evidence. In proceedings arising from an attempt to make a client's communications with his lawyer available at a murder trial, Lord Taylor of Gosforth explained the position thus:[2]

> The principle which runs through all these cases … is that a man must be able to consult his lawyer in confidence, since otherwise he might hold back half the truth. The client must be sure that what he tells the lawyer will never be revealed without his consent. Legal professional privilege is thus much more than an ordinary rule of evidence limited in its application to the facts of a particular case. It is a fundamental condition on which the administration of justice as a whole rests.

Further, the importance of this principle is such that it transcends any debate about whether it is a procedural right or a substantive law right.[3]

---

[1] See eg *Narden Services Ltd v Inverness Retail and Business Park Ltd* 2008 SC 335, and also F P Davidson, *Evidence* (2007) paras 13.18–13.46; M L Ross and J Chalmers, *Walker and Walker The Law of Evidence in Scotland* (3rd edn, 2009) ch 10, particularly para 10.2.

[2] *R v Derby Magistrates, ex p B* [1996] AC 487 at 507D. His Lordship had surveyed a series of cases spanning 400 years of English law.

In that regard, it is important to note that the discussion in more recent cases – and some statutes – has been under reference to "legal professional privilege", but it is suggested that the principle is perhaps more accurately characterised as "lawyer–client privilege" or "lawyer–client confidentiality".[4] Use of the latter formulations avoids the misleading impression that the privilege is that of the lawyer, and instead focuses on the essential point that the source of the confidentiality is the relationship of lawyer and client.[5] Lord Rodger captured this with typical pithiness: "In relation to legal advice privilege what matters today remains the same as what mattered in the past: whether lawyers are being asked qua lawyers to provide legal advice."[6] As will become apparent later, it is the character of that relationship rather than the nature of the information communicated which is critical to the existence of the protection of confidentiality in documents and other material.[7] Nonetheless, the terminology "legal professional privilege" has been adopted by the Inner House in a relatively recent discussion of the issue, so that it may now be an accepted term of art in Scotland.[8]

It is important also to note at the outset that, in Scotland, the law in this area has developed from separate roots from the origins of the law of confidentiality in England.[9] However, the direction of travel has been similar, and while "[t]here are a number of differences in the case law in relation to particular aspects of the law … the general principle, its fundamental importance, and the considerations of public policy which underlie it, are common to both systems".[10]

---

[3] *Three Rivers District Council v Bank of England (No 6)* [2005] 1 AC 610 at para 26 per Lord Scott of Foscote.

[4] For a critique of the use of the phrase "legal professional privilege" in health and safety legislation applicable in Scotland see V Ogston and A Seager, "Legal professional privilege: an examination of its meaning and application in Scots law" 1987 JR 38.

[5] Cf *Ventouris v Mountain* [1991] 1 WLR 607 at 611 per Bingham LJ.

[6] Cf *Three Rivers* (n 3) at para 58 per Lord Rodger.

[7] The principle is also found in Civilian systems, but with a rather different conceptual underpinning. For an accessible, if now slightly dated, account of the Civilian tradition see D A O Edward, "Confidentiality in the EEC: lawyer–client relationships" (1978) 19 JLSS 19. See too *R (Prudential plc) v Special Comr of Income Tax* [2013] UKSC 1, [2013] 2 AC 185 at para 115 per Lord Sumption.

[8] *Narden Services Ltd v Inverness Retail and Business Park Ltd* 2008 SC 335 at para 7 per Lord Johnston. Interestingly, in *Prudential* Lord Reed approved the Inner House's use of the term "legal professional privilege" on the basis that it was employed "in preference to the older term 'confidentiality', which could lead to confusion between the privilege and the different sense in which 'confidentiality' is employed in other contexts". See *Prudential* (n 7) at para 108.

[9] The history of the recognition of lawyer–client privilege in English law is set out by Lord Taylor of Gosforth in *R v Derby Magistrates, ex p B* (n 2) at 504A–D. For a provocative account of the development of the law in England, see J Auburn, *Legal Professional Privilege: Law and Theory* (2000).

[10] *Prudential* (n 7) at para 103 per Lord Reed. This important decision is discussed further below.

These are, of course, not new ideas in Scotland or England. Thus, the final section of Sir George Mackenzie of Rosehaugh's tract *Observations made upon the 28 (sc 18) Act, 23 Parl. K. James VI. against dispositions made in fraud of creditors etc.* addresses lawyer–client confidentiality.[11] While Mackenzie deals at length with a range of topics arising from the 1621 Act, it is the last section of his text in which the nature of the relationship between lawyer (specifically the advocate) and client is explored and the source of confidentiality, as Mackenzie saw it, explained. Mackenzie expounded his analysis essentially as part of the law of evidence, though the underlying basis of the principle of confidentiality was as much about the status of the office of advocate as the public interest in confidentiality. This is not the place to explore the richness of the sources to which Mackenzie refers in his tract,[12] but what does emerge is a two-stranded rationalisation for upholding confidentiality of lawyer–client communings. The first is consistent with Mackenzie's Ciceronian ideal of the advocate as a learned orator and lineal successor to those of Classical antiquity.[13] Mackenzie's second strand is rather more consistent with our contemporary understanding of a public interest in unfettered frankness in communications between client and lawyer. Thus he notes that:[14]

> [H]is client has deposited in [the lawyer's] breast his greatest secrets, and it is in the interest of the Commonwealth to have that freedom allowed and secured without which men cannot manage their affairs and private business; and who would use that freedom if they might be ensnared by it? This were to beget a diffidence between such, who should of all others, have the greatest mutual confidence in one another.

As will be immediately apparent, this is exactly the rationale at the heart of Lord Taylor's dictum set out above.

Stair by contrast deals with the matter quite briefly, noting that "advocates, agents and factors" are "not obliged to depone as to any secret committed to them".[15] Though that idea is not further elaborated, nor does Stair refer to any particular source; his formulation is consistent with

---

[11] *Observations made upon the 28 (sc 18) Act, 23 Parl. K. James VI. against dispositions made in fraud of creditors etc.* (Edinburgh 1675) [Adv Lib C.24.3]. At least two later editions, 1698–99 and 1712, also survive, and the text also appears in *Sir George Mackenzie's Works* (Edinburgh 1755) vol 2, p 1. The discussion of confidentiality is at pp 189–202 in the 1675 edition.

[12] See K Campbell, "The advocate as *civis Romanus* in Mackenzie's *Observations made upon the 28 Act, 23 Parl. K. James VI*" (forthcoming article).

[13] On Mackenzie's views about the nature of the advocate as a neo-Ciceronian, see his *Oratio Inauguralis* given on the occasion of the inauguration of the Advocates Library in 1689, and see also J Cairns, "Sir George Mackenzie, the Faculty of Advocates and the Advocates Library" in J Cairns and A Cain (eds), *Oratio Inauguralis* (1989) p 18.

[14] Mackenzie, *Observations* (n 11) pp 190–91.

[15] Stair, *Inst* IV.43.8.

a Civilian view of professional secrecy (the more so as Stair includes a reference to trustees in the list of persons covered).[16] Writing a generation later, Bankton approached the matter slightly more broadly, describing the privilege as covering both "the secrets of the cause" and "such matters which they [ie the lawyers] know only from their client's information".[17] Indeed, Bankton went further, explicitly asserting that the privilege also precluded any person present when advice was tendered from being produced as a witness.[18] It is worthy of note that both Stair and Bankton dealt with the topic as part of their treatment of witnesses, and in particular those classes of person who could not be compelled to give evidence and in what circumstances. There is no trace in either writer of the part of the justification based on the nature of the office of advocate given by Mackenzie in his tract, nor does either advance any other argument based on status of the lawyer; and indeed Mackenzie's own *Institutions* treat evidence and procedure in much less detail than the other two writers.[19]

By the end of the eighteenth century, the Court of Session had been recorded as determining[20] that lawyer–client confidentiality did indeed extend "to every thing he [ie the lawyer] was informed of as agent",[21] while by the middle of the nineteenth, it was recognised that "the rule by which communications between clients and their legal advisers are protected from discovery, is one of great value and importance".[22] Further, by the same period "[i]t [was] quite a settled point that the plea of confidentiality is not limited to documents passing subsequently to the date of raising an action".[23] The latter observation was made by the court putting to rest an argument that confidentiality was confined to litigious cases, and that only after proceedings had been commenced. That aspect of confidentiality does, of course, have application to other types of communication between persons other than clients and their lawyers, in the form of *post litem*

---

[16] Cf Edward (n 7).

[17] Bankton, *Inst* IV, xxx, 12.

[18] Bankton, *Inst* IV, xxx, 12.

[19] Book IV of Mackenzie's *Institutions of the Law of Scotland* contains but four titles or topics, one of which is the criminal law and it amounts to considerably less than a quarter of the text.

[20] This is not the place to consider the problems of eighteenth-century law reporting in Scotland. The position is sketched out in J Cairns, "Historical introduction", in K G C Reid and R Zimmermann (eds), *A History of Private Law in Scotland*, vol 1 (2000) p 14 at 172–75. See too A Stewart and D Parratt (eds), *The Minute Book of the Faculty of Advocates 1783–1798* (Stair Society vol 53, 2008) pp xxix–xxxiv and K Campbell, "'Takin' doon ma very words': the trials of early Scots law reporters" (paper presented at the British Legal History Conference July 2013, and forthcoming article).

[21] *Count Leslie v Grant* 8 January 1760, Brown's Supplement vol V, p 874.

[22] *McCowan v Wright* (1852) 15 D 229 at 237 per Lord Wood.

[23] *Hay Thomson & Blair v The Edinburgh & Glasgow Bank* (1858) 20 D 701 at 703 per Lord Justice-Clerk Hope.

motam privilege: in the words of Lord Justice-Clerk Thomson, "Once the parties are at arm's length, or are obviously going to be at arm's length, the details of their preparation of weapons and ammunition are protected as confidential."[24] Such protection is about fairness in the conduct of litigation, allowing a party to prepare his position without the concern that other parties might have access to the fruits other than at proof, and thus addressing a rather different public interest from the confidentiality of relations between clients and their lawyers.

Concern for such lawyer–client dealings has been the consistent position in the court's decision-making since the nineteenth century. In the most recent general discussion of the subject, *Narden Services Ltd v Inverness Retail and Business Park Ltd*, the Inner House was able to take as its starting point that:[25]

> The notion of LPP [ie legal professional privilege] is enshrined in the common law of Scotland. There is (in broad terms) a right of absolute privilege in respect of communications emanating between a solicitor and a client relating to advice and also in respect of any documents, including those coming from accountants, which were prepared in contemplation of litigation.

Note that Scots law has not, thus far, developed doctrinally separate notions of litigation privilege and advice privilege.[26] Instead, these are treated as instances of privileged communications. In *Narden Services Ltd*, the court also satisfied itself that the existing Scots common law afforded sufficient protection to meet the requirements of articles 6 and 8 ECHR.[27]

In addition to the evidential rules so far discussed, it should also be noted that professional obligations of confidentiality remain part of the codes of conduct of both advocates and solicitors in Scotland today.[28] Thus while advocates and solicitors are competent and compellable witnesses in both civil and criminal causes, they may not give evidence of matters relating to their clients' affairs, nor may they produce documents in answer to commission and diligence, without the sanction of the client.[29] Those

---

[24] *Young v National Coal Board* 1957 SC 99 at 105. See also M L Ross and J Chalmers, *Walker and Walker: The Law of Evidence in Scotland*, para 10.4 and F P Davidson, *Evidence*, paras 13.40–13.46.

[25] 2008 SC 335 at para 11(1) per Lord Johnston.

[26] The distinction and its scope in England are discussed in *Three Rivers* (n 3) at para 10 per Lord Scott of Foscote and paras 51–54 per Lord Rodger. Cf para 105 per Lord Carswell, who held legal professional privilege to be a "single integral privilege, whose sub-heads are legal advice privilege and litigation privilege". See too the appellant's argument noted at p 617D–G.

[27] At para 11(4) per Lord Johnston.

[28] See *Guide to the Professional Conduct of Advocates* (5th edn, 2008) section 1, paragraph 2.3 and section 9; Law Society of Scotland Practice Rules 2011 rule B1 para 1.6. The advocates' guide is available online at *http://www.advocates.org.uk/downloads/guidetoconduct_5thedition.pdf*.

[29] M L Ross and J Chalmers, *Walker and Walker: The Law of Evidence in Scotland*, para 10.2.

are aspects of professional discipline as well as rules of evidence, for the confidentiality has long been definitively established to be that of the client, which the client may waive.[30] So far as advocates are concerned, the *Guide to Conduct* contains an explicit statement that the rationale for the obligation is that discussed already in relation to the law of evidence, namely the client must be able to consult counsel freely and without concern that what has passed may subsequently be disclosed to a third party – particularly a potential or actual opponent.[31] Nor is the practitioner's obligation time limited.[32]

WAIVER

Confidentiality being that of the client rather than of the lawyer, the privilege may be waived by the client. Express waiver is conceptually straightforward, though there is a potentially troubling issue which may well arise in some cases about whether the waiver has been properly informed. In other areas of practice, consideration has been given to the extent to which waiver of fundamental rights must be on an informed basis in order to be recognised as effective. This issue arose most starkly in the somewhat analogous context of waiver of the right to legal representation by persons detained by the police. The UK Supreme Court held that for waiver of such fundamental rights to be effective, the right holder must be told of his right; he must understand what the right is; he must understand that he is waiving it and that the waiver is made freely.[33] Given that the majority of cases involving waiver will arise either in court or in the margins of some sort of contested process, there is likely to be judicial oversight or legal advice available (or both). For any cases occurring outwith those settings, it is suggested that the same formulation would be an appropriate test for a court to apply in judging the efficacy of waiver, since it represents the minimum effective guarantee of the lay client's right to confidentiality.

In the absence of express waiver, there may be cases where there is argument about whether waiver can be inferred from actings or from circumstances. There may also be a question about the extent of the waiver. Both issues have lately been the subject of consideration by the Inner House in *Scottish Lion Insurance Co Ltd v Goodrich Corporation & ors*.[34] Those confidentiality issues arose as part of a larger litigation about a petition for approval of a scheme of arrangement under section 899 of the Companies

---

[30] Cf F P Davidson, *Evidence*, para 13.31 and authorities mentioned there.
[31] *Guide to the Professional Conduct of Advocates* (n 28) para 2.3.1.
[32] Paragraph 2.3.3.
[33] *McGowan v B* [2011] UKSC 54, 2012 SC (UKSC) 182 at paras 46–54 (esp para 46) per Lord Hope.
[34] [2011] CSIH 18, 2011 SC 534.

Act 2006. However, their importance may be gauged from the fact that the hearing on the confidentiality points before an Extra Division lasted three days.[35]

In *Scottish Lion*, the scheme of arrangement was for settlement of claims present and future by creditors of a solvent insurance company. Meetings of creditors were held in accordance with the Companies Act[36] and creditors voted on proposals in the scheme. Weighting of the votes was one of the issues in controversy in the proceedings, and creditors were invited to submit documents supporting their respective valuations. In the unusual circumstances of the case, the Lord Ordinary ordered the hearing for sanction of the scheme of arrangement to proceed as a proof,[37] and in that connection ordered the production of documentation submitted in support of the creditors' valuations of their claims.[38] A question then arose of whether creditors were entitled to object on the basis of legal professional privilege to production of certain documents and to their inspection by the court or a reporter appointed by the court.[39] The Lord Ordinary held that privilege could not be claimed because, if there had been privilege attached to particular documents, it had been waived when they were submitted to the petitioner in connection with the valuation.[40] Certain creditors reclaimed, and the reclaiming motion afforded the Inner House an opportunity to affirm a number of core principles and also to address the issue of waiver. Applying the Privy Council decision *B & ors v Auckland District Law Society & anor*,[41] the court began by observing that since the purpose of lawyer–client privilege[42] is to maintain confidentiality, the privilege was lost if there was no longer any confidentiality to maintain.[43] Waiver was to be distinguished from loss of privilege, and arose:[44]

> in circumstances where it can be inferred that the person entitled to the privilege has given up his right to resist the disclosure of the information in question, either generally or in the particular context. Such circumstances will exist where

---

[35] See the procedural history summarised in 2011 SC 534 at 536.

[36] The court had made orders in terms of s 896 for the creditors' meetings.

[37] Ie a hearing at which evidence would be led; usually the final hearing on a petition for sanction of a scheme of arrangement would be confined to legal submissions about the scheme and the report of the court appointed reporter.

[38] The procedural history is summarised at 2011 SC 534 at 535, and explained in more detail by Lord Reed, giving the opinion of the court at paras 32–42.

[39] In accordance with the court's usual procedure in Companies Act petitions, a reporter (an experienced company law solicitor) had been appointed to enquire into and report on the proceedings at the creditors' meetings and other steps taken in connection with the scheme.

[40] *Scottish Lion Insurance Co Ltd, petitioner* [2010] CSOH 87.

[41] [2003] 2 AC 736.

[42] The Extra Division used the term "legal professional privilege".

[43] *Scottish Lion* (n 34) at para 46.

[44] *Scottish Lion* (n 34) at para 46.

> the person's conduct has been inconsistent with his retention of that right:
> inconsistent that is to say, with the maintenance of the confidentiality which the
> privilege is intended to protect.

Further, applying the general law of waiver,[45] the court held that waiver of lawyer-client privilege is not dependent on the subjective intention of the client, but is judged "on an objective analysis of the conduct of the person asserting the privilege".[46] Given the breadth of the classes of right which may validly be waived,[47] it is suggested that the application of the general law of waiver in this context is unexceptionable. On the question of whether there has been a waiver, an objective test seems entirely appropriate, given the importance of the public interest consistently reaffirmed in the case law, and the role of the court in balancing the interests of all parties involved.

In *Scottish Lion*, it was evident that the documents had been submitted by the creditors specifically for the purpose of voting on the proposed scheme of arrangement, and in the knowledge that an application was being made to the court for approval of the scheme. The complaining creditors sought to rely on confidentiality agreements entered into with the petitioner, which included provisions asserting that disclosure of the information covered by the agreements did not constitute waiver. These agreements themselves were disclosed to the court in part only[48] but, on construction, the court concluded that the agreements did not bear on the present dispute because in one case they related to an earlier, abortive, scheme of arrangement, and in the other to settlement of liabilities in the insurance market.

The Extra Division also held that it was possible for lawyer-client privilege to be waived for a particular purpose, without being waived generally: "in other words, the right to resist disclosure may be given up in relation to a particular context".[49] That plainly requires a close examination of the circumstances of a given case, and the Extra Division correctly observed that earlier cases in which this issue has arisen have been very different in their context, for example attempts by clients engaged in litigation with their former lawyers to prevent reference to material relevant to the lawyers' defence of the action, or where there is an apprehension that disclosure has been selective.[50] However, expressly adopting the reasoning of the Privy

---

[45] See *Armia Ltd v Daejan Developments Ltd* 1979 SC (HL) 56; cf E C Reid and J W G Blackie, *Personal Bar* (2006) paras 3.10–3.14.

[46] *Scottish Lion* at para 47, under reference to *Great Atlantic Insurance Co v Home Insurance Co & ors* [1981] 1 WLR 529.

[47] Cf Reid and Blackie, *Personal Bar* para 3.08.

[48] *Scottish Lion* at para 53.

[49] Paragraph 47.

[50] Paragraph 48.

Council in *B v Auckland District Law Society*,[51] the court held that disclosure of a document covered by privilege for a plainly limited purpose did not mean that the privilege was lost in any subsequent context.[52] The careful analysis of the circumstances by the court indicates that this question is determined objectively.

ATTEMPTS TO EXTEND THE SCOPE OF PRIVILEGE

From the discussion thus far it may appear that the boundaries of lawyer–client privilege are well settled, and that the scope for significant further development is limited. However, in *R (on the application of Prudential plc & anor) v Special Commissioner of Income Tax*,[53] the UK Supreme Court was called upon to determine whether lawyer–client privilege – in the form of the English law classification "legal advice privilege" – should be extended to persons other than lawyers providing legal advice. Although the appeal was determined in accordance with English law, Lord Reed also expressly considered the position under Scots law, and laid down what might be considered a checklist of issues for argument were the question to arise in a Scots case.[54] For that reason alone, quite apart from the striking reasoning from first principles by several justices, the case merits consideration.

Although the *Prudential* case presented in the form of a question about whether the appellant company was entitled, on the basis of legal professional privilege, to refuse to produce documents called for by a tax inspector in connection with a tax investigation (which documents contained legal advice produced by an accountant rather than a member of the legal profession), it was accepted at all hands that a much more general question arose about the proper extent of legal professional privilege.[55] The issue arose in this way because the advice in question had been provided by an accountant in connection with a tax avoidance scheme, subsequently the subject of a Revenue investigation. There was no dispute that had the advice been provided by a member of the legal profession, privilege would have applied and the material would not have been recoverable. The case for the appellant company, supported by the Institute of Chartered Accountants in England and Wales, was that the privilege (designated as legal advice privilege) should attach to the communications in question.

---

[51] [2003] 2 AC 736 at paras 66–69 per Lord Millett.
[52] *Scottish Lion* at para 63.
[53] [2013] UKSC 1, [2013] 2 AC 185.
[54] Cf para 113 per Lord Reed.
[55] Thus in addition to the parties, before the UK Supreme Court there were five interveners, being several legal professional bodies and regulators, the Institute of Chartered Accountants in England and Wales, and the International Association for the Protection of Intellectual Property.

That was on the basis that the privilege was a common law right created by the judges, which should be applied, and if necessary extended, so as to accord with the principles said to underlie and justify the right. Thus the privilege was argued to be justified by the rule of law, and to exist for the benefit of the client who seeks and receives legal advice – for instance on tax matters – so that there could be no principled basis upon which the privilege could be restricted to cases where the adviser was a member of the legal professions, as opposed to a qualified accountant. It was argued that was *a fortiori* in modern conditions where the great majority of legal advice on tax matters was given by accountants rather than lawyers.[56] For the Revenue, supported by the legal professional bodies and the International Association for the Protection of Intellectual Property, the starting point was the universal understanding that legal advice privilege was restricted to advice given by lawyers. That position should, it was argued, be maintained because any extension would involve a potentially nuanced policy decision, with unpredictable and potentially wide-ranging public and forensic consequences. Further, Parliament had legislated on a number of occasions on the assumption that legal advice privilege was restricted to advice given by lawyers, and had in fact considered and rejected a proposal to extend privilege to non-lawyer tax advisers.[57]

A court of seven justices held by a majority of five to two that legal professional privilege should not be extended to the provision of legal advice by persons other than members of the legal profession, even where that advice addressed a topic on which that person was qualified to advise. Thus the existing law was reaffirmed by the court; however, the justices approached the question from a number of directions to reach that result. The dissenting judgments also repay study, both for Lord Sumption's argument from first principles and Lord Clarke's explicit invitation to early parliamentary consideration of the issue.[58]

In the leading judgment, Lord Neuberger stressed the generally understood scope of "legal advice privilege", and its long-standing foundation in consistent case law of the highest authority. His Lordship also noted that several attempts had been made in the last thirty years to extend the scope of the privilege to other professional groups, which the courts had on each occasion rebuffed.[59] In the cases of trademark agents and patent attorneys, those rebuffs had subsequently been reversed by limited statutory extensions of the privilege; however, the very character of the statutory extensions "plainly implies that [Parliament] assumes that [legal advice

---

[56] See *Prudential* at paras 25–26 per Lord Neuberger PSC.
[57] See paras 27–28 per Lord Neuberger PSC.
[58] Paragraph 139.
[59] Paragraph 31.

privilege] is limited to advice given by lawyers".[60] Even more significant was the fact that in the very area in which the appeal arose, namely tax advice, there had been parliamentary consideration in 2008 of a proposal to extend legal advice privilege to tax advice provided by accountants. Though the matter had been the subject of debate in committee, the proposal had been taken no further and the relevant legislation maintained a distinction between a "professional legal adviser" (with whom communications were privileged in the context of a Revenue investigation) and a "tax adviser" (with whom they were not).[61] Against that background, Lord Neuberger correctly, it is respectfully suggested, recognised that allowing Prudential's appeal would result in a significant extension of the boundaries of legal professional privilege "beyond what are currently, and have for a long time been understood to be, its limits".[62] In that conclusion, his Lordship was rejecting the functional approach central to the analysis offered by Lord Sumption in the leading dissent, considered below, while accepting that analysis was powerful and principled. Nonetheless, Lord Neuberger expressly recognised that there were strong policy arguments which could be advanced in support of the positions on each side of the appeal;[63] in other words, this was a case which truly involved a determination of judicial policy, rather than being confined to clarifying the applicable law.

Three reasons of policy led Lord Neuberger to the decision not to extend legal professional privilege. In the first place, although it might be possible to reformulate the ambit of the privilege to cover "members of a profession which ordinarily gives legal advice", that was a significant change from the current formulation, which was well understood by all who had to address the issue. That class extended beyond lawyers and their clients to the courts, the executive and ultimately to the public more generally.[64] It was very likely that there would be difficult questions at the margins which were simply avoided by the present formulation. In his Lordship's view, it was conceivable that a court dealing with a claim for confidentiality under a reformulated version of the principle might well be compelled to enquire into matters of professional organisation, as well as having to determine whether a profession was one which "ordinarily includes the giving of legal advice".[65] With respect, the first of those rationalisations is considerably less convincing than the second. Structural, regulatory and disciplinary considerations relating to an advice-giver seem unlikely to be determinative

---

[60] Paragraph 35.
[61] Paragraph 36.
[62] Paragraph 37.
[63] Paragraphs 39–46.
[64] Paragraphs 53–54.
[65] Paragraph 57.

in a case arising under Lord Sumption's formulation. However, the question of scope posed by the proposed test of whether the advice-giver was a member of a profession "ordinarily giving legal advice" would indeed be much more challenging, particularly in modern conditions where many activities, private as well as commercial, are the subject of detailed regulation about which advice is often provided by non-lawyer professional people who have a deep knowledge of a narrow area of law. Precisely because of such difficulties of boundary setting, Lord Neuberger concluded that the matter was one for Parliament.[66] Separately, and secondly, the matter was one for Parliament because it might be that on consideration of the issue more broadly, the privilege might be extended on different, and perhaps more restricted terms, to non-lawyer professional groups. That was a matter for Parliament and not the courts.[67] The final consideration which led his Lordship not to support extension of confidentiality was the fact, already noted, that there had been recent parliamentary consideration and rejection of extending the privilege in the very area out of which the appeal arose, while there had been specific and confined statutory extension in other cases.[68]

Lord Sumption's dissent took as its starting point the character and function of the advice sought and obtained by the client, rather than the circumstances of its being tendered. At the outset of his judgment, his Lordship set out his opinion that:[69]

> The law is that legal professional privilege attaches to any communication between a client and his legal adviser which is made (i) for the purpose of enabling the adviser to give or the client to receive legal advice, (ii) in the course of a professional relationship, and (iii) in the exercise by the adviser of a profession which has as an ordinary part of its function the giving of skilled legal advice on the subject in question.

In his Lordship's view, the test is functional,[70] and the case law discussion, since the late eighteenth century at least, affirming that client confidentiality applied to advice from lawyers alone was explained on the footing that until modern times, "lawyers were the only source of skilled legal advice".[71] In an echo of the Ciceronian strand of Sir George Mackenzie's analysis, Lord Sumption referred to the earlier history of the compellability of professional advisers as witnesses in English practice. It appears that

---

[66] Paragraph 62.
[67] Paragraphs 62–67, particularly para 65.
[68] Paragraphs 68–69.
[69] Paragraph 114.
[70] Paragraph 122.
[71] Paragraph 121.

"[b]y the early eighteenth century most writers were agreed that [protection of confidences] was based on the protection of the honour of the adviser, who would be discredited by being required to disclose them. It followed that the adviser was permitted but not compellable to give evidence of them".[72] That doctrine had been brought to an end by Lord Mansfield in *The Duchess of Kingston's case*, and had thereafter been reformulated by the judges in favour of clients by reference specifically to their communings with their legal advisers.[73] Accepting the summary of the history of English law in the eighteenth century, it is respectfully suggested that basing the right of confidentiality in functional test rather than on the professional nature of the advice-giver is an *ex post facto* rationalisation which underplays the consistent direction of judicial characterisation of the right over two centuries.

As already indicated, Lord Reed was the only member of the court to consider the position in Scotland, and his Lordship observed that in Scotland, as in England and Wales, all the cases in which the privilege has been upheld appear to have concerned lawyers acting in a professional capacity, clerks or assistants acting on their behalf, or other intermediaries to whom a communication had been made for transmission to or from such a person. Indeed it had been held (albeit in an old case) that the privilege did not attach to communications made to an accountant, though the case was not one involving the giving of legal advice, since it came from an era when that would simply not have occurred.[74] It was not apparent to his Lordship whether the Scots courts had "hitherto been required to make a judgment as to whether the privilege ought to be confined to legal advice given by lawyers acting as such, as opposed to legal advice given by members of other professions".[75] That meant, in Lord Reed's view, that "the authorities do not foreclose the possible application of the privilege to advice given by accountants".[76]

However, as in England and Wales, the general understanding was that the privilege applied only to members of the legal professions. Interestingly, in that context Lord Reed referred to the use by the Inner House of the expression "legal professional privilege" in *Narden Services Ltd v Inverness Retail and Business Park Ltd*, which was discussed above, as potentially indicating "that documents prepared by accountants may come within the scope of litigation privilege (in the older terminology, *post litem motam* confidentiality) if they were prepared in contemplation of litigation, but

---

[72] Paragraph 115.
[73] Paragraph 115.
[74] *Wright v Arthur* (1831) 10 S 139.
[75] *Prudential* at para 107.
[76] Paragraph 108.

that legal advice privilege is confined, in broad terms, to communications between a solicitor and his client". That, with respect, involves a degree of speculation and inference, for as his Lordship himself observed, "[t]he court [in *Narden*] was not however addressing the question whether the scope of the privilege might be extended where legal advice was given by accountants".[77] That general understanding was evident from both the standard legal texts and also the work of bodies concerned with law reform. In that connection, Lord Reed mentioned the Scottish Law Commission's Memorandum No 46, *Law of Evidence*, where the Commission expressed the view that "solicitor/client privilege is reasonably well-defined and works satisfactorily in practice",[78] and noted that "[t]he Commission did not suggest that the privilege applied, or ought to apply, in situations where legal advice was sought from members of other professions; nor was that issue touched upon in the reports which followed upon the consultative memorandum".[79] As with England and Wales, there was also legislation applicable which assumed that legal advice privilege was confined to advice given by lawyers. Some of those were UK-wide statutes such as the Taxes Acts and Copyright, Designs and Patents Act 1988 and section 87 of the Trade Marks Act 1994, while other enactments related to the regulation of the provision of legal services in Scotland.[80] The gravamen of the latter was that, for the purposes of the regulatory regime, legal professional privilege attached only to licensed providers of legal services.

USE OF DISCLOSED MATERIAL IN OTHER PROCEEDINGS

Several different aspects of confidentiality arise in relation to the use (or proposed use) of privileged or potentially privileged material which has been disclosed in one set of proceedings in subsequent proceedings.

Material – real evidence as well as documents – may be recovered in the course of an action by commission and diligence at common law, or prior to commencement of proceedings or thereafter by means of an order under section 1 of the Administration of Justice (Scotland) Act 1972, and the party recovering the material will in most cases use the material for the purposes of the action in the course of which the material is recovered, or, in the case of recovery using section 1 of the 1972 Act, the proceedings which were contemplated at the time the order for recovery was made. However, there will also be circumstances in which the party recovering the material may at the time of recovery, or thereafter, desire to make

---

[77] Paragraph 108
[78] Scottish Law Commission, *Law of Evidence* (Scot Law Com Mem No 46, 1980) para 21.
[79] *Prudential* at para 110.
[80] Paragraphs 111–12.

use of that material in a second set of court proceedings in Scotland or in another jurisdiction. Perhaps surprisingly, the competency of and terms under which such subsequent use might be made were not authoritatively determined until 1998. In *Iomega Corporation v Myricia (UK) Ltd*,[81] the First Division held that:[82]

> A party who, as a result of commission and diligence, obtains possession of documents or other items [is] subject to an implied obligation or undertaking to the court not to use them nor to allow them to be used for any purpose other than the conduct of the actual or prospective proceedings in respect of which they have been recovered.

This significant restriction is not cast in terms of confidentiality; however, it is suggested that the limits placed on disclosure by the court clearly partake of some of the same characteristics: the limitations on the use of disclosed material, and the active oversight by the court. However, adopting an approach not unlike that taken to confidentiality restrictions, the First Division went on to hold that the court had power to permit items recovered for the purposes of particular proceedings before it to be used in separate parallel proceedings before it or another court "where that would be in the interests of justice".[83] These results can be rationalised in terms of the public interest in the need for material to be available to the court for the resolution of a given dispute, being balanced by limiting the interference in the rights of litigation party haver or the third party haver, so that disclosure is not a once-and-for-all act.

In *Iomega*, both the initial disclosure and the subsequent proceedings involved court actions. Until 2012, the Court of Session had not had an opportunity to consider the extent of privacy and confidentiality in relation to material initially produced in an arbitration which was sought to be recovered in subsequent court proceedings. However in *Gray Construction Ltd v Harley Haddow LLP*,[84] the question arose for consideration directly. In that case, one of the issues in the court proceedings related to the terms of settlement of a previous arbitration involving one of the parties to the court proceedings and another party not involved in the litigation, but concerning the same construction project which was the subject of the court action. A motion was made by the litigation party which had not been involved in the arbitration for recovery of documents which would disclose *inter alia* the precise issues which had been referred to arbitration, the basis on which the arbitration had been compromised, and the legal advice tendered about

---

[81] 1998 SC 636.
[82] At 641A per Lord President Rodger.
[83] At p 641F per Lord President Rodger.
[84] 2012 SLT 1034.

the basis of settlement. In support of that motion it was argued that, in order for the court to consider whether settlement of the arbitration had been reasonable, details of the settlement and the rationale for it would require to be put in evidence, and that the affidavit offered by the litigation party which had been involved in the arbitration was insufficient as a source of evidence.[85] It is also worth noting that the non-litigation party to the arbitration participated in the hearing about disclosure, which took the form of a debate about whether a confidential bundle should be unsealed by the court.

Arbitration is, of course, a contractual and private dispute resolution process, and it was common ground between the parties that confidentiality extended to all documents produced or created by (or on behalf of) the parties in connection with arbitration proceedings. In the absence of Scots authority, parties were prepared to agree that proposition by analogy with English authority.[86] The Lord Ordinary was content that, in the absence of express contractual provision, such an implied obligation of confidentiality did indeed arise in Scots law.[87] Because, with limited exceptions, the documents in issue were not inherently confidential – unlike, for example, trade secrets – but were fixed with confidentiality because of the background circumstances, the court did not consider it necessary to delineate the boundaries of the obligation of confidentiality nor define exhaustively the nature of the documents covered.[88] Nonetheless, the Lord Ordinary pointed out that there might be cases in which documents were produced in an arbitration which were not otherwise publicly available, or documents which had been produced under compulsion, which might have attached an implied term restricting their use in proceedings other than the original arbitration. Equally, where a party requires to use such documents to enforce the award, confidentiality might not apply, and likewise where disclosure was otherwise in the public interest.[89]

That the court is empowered to order disclosure of documents otherwise subject to private law obligations of confidentiality is well established in Scots law.[90] The power requires consideration of the circumstances of each individual case, rather than a formulaic test. So far as arbitration was concerned, in *Gray Construction* the Lord Ordinary considered that it was "at least arguable that in an arbitration the private obligation of confidentiality may be supported by the public interest in enabling people

---

[85] At para 3.
[86] At para 4, under reference to *Dolling-Baker v Merrett* [1990] 1 WLR 1205.
[87] At para 5.
[88] Paragraph 6.
[89] Paragraph 6.
[90] *Santa Fe International Corporation v Napier Shipping SA* 1985 SLT 481.

to resolve their disputes privately if they so wish".[91] However, that was not an end of the matter, and the court had an overriding power to dispense with confidentiality if that was in the interests of justice.[92] In balancing these important rights:[93]

> Where it is necessary to recover documents which a party holds subject to an obligation of confidentiality in order to achieve the fair disposal of an action, the court will as a norm order the production of those documents. The test is not one of absolute necessity; the court, in deciding how to achieve a fair disposal of the action, may take into account how a party can reasonably prepare to present his case. If the documents are not essential to the action, or if the information can be recovered elsewhere without breaching a confidence, the court may exercise its discretion to refuse recovery.

CONCLUSIONS

That confidentiality attaches to various aspects of communings between clients and their lawyers is well established in Scots law. Shifting terminology from confidentiality to legal professional privilege, which assimilates the nomenclature used in England, may seem to obscure the essential principle that the confidentiality arises from the nature of the relationship and belongs to the client. *Pace* powerful dissenting voices in the UK Supreme Court, the right – or, better, the group of associated rights – is not best characterised in functional terms. Rather, confidentiality rights should be understood as arising from the relationship between clients and their lawyers, and legal process. Though not confined to judicial process, the confidentiality rights are plainly most important in the context of judicial process, and the recent case law demonstrates that the Court of Session and the UK Supreme Court remain alive to the necessity for judicial protection of these rights.

---

[91] *Gray Construction* at para 8.
[92] Paragraph 8
[93] At para 9.

Resorting to Crime

James Chalmers*

Good evening, and thank you for coming. We are very fortunate in the Law School to have fantastic administrative staff. One of them, Jenny Crawford, has put a huge amount of work, for which I am very grateful, into organising tonight. I have been bothering her repeatedly over the last few weeks to ask how many people have registered for the lecture, terrified of speaking to an empty room. I may have been worrying a little too much.[1] I am delighted to see so many people here. I should say in particular that I am very grateful that the Principal and Professor Anderson, the Head of the College of Social Sciences, have given up their time to be here tonight: I know that both of you have a huge number of commitments and I very much appreciate you giving up your time to listen to a lecture outside your own areas of academic interest. I can promise one mention of a Professor of Political Economy over the course of the next hour but less, I'm afraid, on human-computer interaction.

THE NATURE OF AN INAUGURAL

I can think of no better venue in which to deliver an inaugural lecture, but this is not my inaugural in the strict sense. My first lecture in this institution took place on 18 September last year, in the less auspicious

---

* This is the text of my inaugural lecture, delivered in the Bute Hall of the University of Glasgow at 6 pm on Thursday 17 January 2013. For the purposes of publication, and in the interests of providing an accurate historical record, I have sought to keep the text as close as possible to that which was delivered that day, save for some minor emendations and alterations where the text as delivered would be unclear in the absence of images which were displayed during the lecture. I am grateful to Lindsay Farmer, Gerald Gordon, Fiona Leverick, Rosemary O'Neill and Ondine Tennant for comments and assistance relating to the text, and to Nigel Dewar Gibb, Nigel Dewar Gibb (Andrew Dewar Gibb's son and grandson, both of the same name) and Sally Harrower for assistance relating to Andrew Dewar Gibb's papers, held by the National Library of Scotland. I am also grateful to Bill McBryde for taking a photograph of the lecture (specifically, of the audience's reaction to one particular point) which has been deposited in the University Archives along with other photographs taken by him as a record of the tercentenary year.

[1] The exact attendance at the lecture was not recorded, but appears to have been between 200 and 250.

surroundings of the Boyd Orr Building.[2] On that occasion, I gave the third lecture to the incoming class of LLB students on the subject of criminal courts. Encouragingly, the lecture was followed by a queue of students with questions. The first of these looked at me nervously, before offering my first ever question from a Glasgow student. She said: "Could you tell me how I would go about quitting law?"[3] I hope not to elicit the same reaction from you tonight.

Various friends and colleagues have made suggestions as to what I should cover in this lecture. These have included "the history of the Regius chair", "something interesting" (I cannot remember whether that was a rejoinder to the first suggestion), "the Act of 1701", a "manifesto", and a joke about a magic tractor. (I understand that it turned into a field.) And for Shona Wilson, who is I think one of only two people – along with Colin Campbell – to have attended both my *real* inaugural lecture at Aberdeen in 2000 and this one, and is now pursuing a PhD on law reform at Cambridge, I will even say something about the Law Commission, which I hope persuades your College that you are entitled to reimbursement of your travel expenses.

It was not until Tuesday that anyone here tonight asked me what my title actually means – collectively, you are taking an awful lot on trust! In this tercentenary year, it is of course appropriate that I should say something about the Regius chair and my predecessors in this role. There is more I want to say, of course, although as this is an inaugural lecture I take it that I have thirty years to answer any questions which I raise. A copy of this lecture has been placed on the tercentenary pages of the School of Law's website and will become available overnight: should you disagree with anything I say, I assure you that the necessary qualifications or explanations will be found in the copious footnotes.[4]

THE REGIUS CHAIRS IN LAW

There are five Regius chairs in law in the British Isles: in addition to this one, there are the Regius Chairs of Civil Law at Oxford and Cambridge, the Regius Chair of Public Law and the Law of Nature and Nations at Edinburgh,[5] and the Regius Chair of Laws at Dublin. At one time, there

---

[2] Coincidentally, this was the date of Kenneth Reid's inaugural (in the modern sense) lecture in the Chair of Scots Law at Edinburgh University, which took place in the Old College at that institution that evening.
[3] She did not quit law.
[4] This is not true.
[5] On which, see J Cairns, "The origins of the Edinburgh Law School: the Union of 1707 and the Regius Chair" (2007) 11 Edin LR 300.

were in fact six, Dublin having two,[6] but one of those was discontinued in 1934.[7]

There is, so far as I know, no official list of Regius professorships. An online encyclopaedia lists around fifty in all disciplines in the United Kingdom and Ireland.[8] Not all of these chairs are currently occupied: at least one of those listed has been abolished.[9] Another is effectively defunct because it exists in a subject which the university concerned no longer teaches.[10] The existence of these professorships is more contingent and arbitrary than the grand titles might suggest. All are of considerable antiquity,[11] and were not necessarily known as "Regius chairs" at their outset. Such chairs were often simply founded as a chair, with the support of the reigning monarch,[12] and in most cases were the only chair in their discipline at the institution when created. Today I am one of well over a dozen professors in the Glasgow Law School, together with over twenty lecturers and a considerable number of part-time teaching staff. But it is not so long since the Regius professor was the only teacher of law in the entire university, and even in comparatively recent times the holder might have been expected personally to deliver the entire course of lectures in Scots law.

Shortly after my appointment, one of my new colleagues expressed some confusion as to how the school would operate with me in post. There had, he pointed out, never been both a head of school and a Regius professor simultaneously during his time at Glasgow. That query seemed to me to be odd: I am simply one professor among many and I do as my Head of School tells me – mostly.

---

6   See Royal Commission on Trinity College, Dublin, and the University of Dublin, Appendix to the Final Report; Minutes of Evidence and Documents (Cd 3312: 1907) p 459. At this time, Trinity College Dublin had six Regius professorships, including both the Regius Professorship of Law, founded in 1668 and held concurrently with the Chair of Civil Law and General Jurisprudence, and the Regius Professorship of English and Feudal Law, founded in 1761. Election to both posts was by nomination of the Council of the College, subject to the approval of the Provost and Senior Fellows; the latter chair required its holder to be a barrister of two years' standing. At this time, the chairs were held respectively by H Brougham Leech and J V Hart. The other Regius professorships were in Divinity (carrying a salary of more than the other five Regius professors combined), Physic and Surgery.

7   V T H Delany, "Legal studies in Trinity College, Dublin, since the foundation" (1957) 89 Hermathena 3 at 11.

8   http://en.wikipedia.org/wiki/Regius_Professor, but see n 11 below.

9   The Regius Professorship of Humanity at the University of Aberdeen. See P G Walsh, "Souter, Alexander (1873–1849)", Oxford Dictionary of National Biography (2004).

10 The Regius Professorship of Greek at the University of Aberdeen.

11 Shortly after this lecture was delivered, twelve Regius chairs were created in celebration of the Queen's Diamond Jubilee: https://www.gov.uk/government/news/the-queen-awards-prestigious-regius-professorships-to-twelve-universities-2.

12 Note, however, that the Professorship of Divinity at Dublin was founded in 1607 and became a Regius professorship in 1761: see Royal Commission on Trinity College, Dublin (n 6) p 459.

But if the question seems odd in an era where all professorships are rightly regarded as equal in standing,[13] it is not so strange when the history of the chair is considered. When it was advertised in 1957, for example, leading to David Walker's appointment the following year, the particulars for the post made it explicit that the holder would bear responsibility for the work of the Department of Scots Law.[14] That was inevitable; there was no other occupied chair in the Department at the time.[15] This leadership role, however, related to the Department of Scots Law and not to the Faculty of Law as a whole, in which there were two other professors.[16] T B Smith, who played the role of kingmaker in the appointment[17] – more on this later – emphasised to the Scottish Office that the holder of the chair had to be *primus inter pares* in relation to the other two chair-holders.[18] But although that view seems to have been accepted, it was not formally any part of the role.

I mention all this only to indicate that although the Regius chair is central to the history of the Glasgow Law School, it is not a static institution. The meaning of being the Regius Professor of Law has changed over time, due to context, contingency and the characteristics of the individual holders. The meaning of my tenure in the chair will fall to be judged at some future date by persons other than me. All I can say is that it is a considerable honour to have been appointed, that I am deeply touched by the confidence placed in me by the university, and that I intend to do my best to repay that trust.

SOME NUMBERS

This lecture, in the style of a popular children's programme, is brought to you by the letters ER and three numbers. The significance of the second of these will be obvious: 1713 marks the foundation of the Regius Chair of Law, the tercentenary of which we celebrate this year. In fact, although the

---

[13] The University of Glasgow formally removed distinctions between holders of established and personal chairs in 1995, at which point personal professors became *ex officio* members of the University Senate.

[14] NAS, HH91/824.

[15] There was a Chair of Mercantile Law, but the particulars noted that the university had decided not to fill it and instead to appoint a lecturer in that subject.

[16] The Chair of Jurisprudence (held by Walker immediately before his appointment to the Regius chair) and the Douglas Chair of Civil Law (then held by J A C Thomas).

[17] It seems unlikely that Walker was aware of this. Even if he was, it did not temper his criticism of Smith's own work subsequently: see K G C Reid, "While one hundred remain: T B Smith and the progress of Scots law", in E Reid and D L Carey-Miller, *A Mixed Legal System in Transition: T B Smith and the Progress of Scots Law* (2005) p 1 at 14–15.

[18] NAS, HH91/824, note of meeting between Sir David Milne and T B Smith, 5 May 1958. See also Smith to Milne, 6 May 1958.

chair was founded in December 1713,[19] the first appointment was not made until January 1714, meaning that we shall be able to celebrate a second tercentenary next year if this one goes well.

The third number, 3,023, I intend to say nothing about at this stage. I doubt that more than three people in the hall will recognise it. But it is thought to be important, and many leading criminal lawyers and criminologists – for example, Andrew Ashworth,[20] Adam Crawford,[21] Nicola Lacey,[22] Robert Reiner[23] and Lucia Zedner[24] – have cited it in recent years, as have lesser authors such as myself.[25] All these writers have drawn a variety of conclusions from the number, which is thought to tell us something about the state of criminal law in the United Kingdom today. Unfortunately for all of us the number is nowhere near being correct. In an attempt to build suspense, I will say no more about this until later.

1451: A PREHISTORY

The first number is here as a reminder that although the foundation of the Regius chair represents the origin of the Glasgow Law School in its modern form, legal teaching and scholarship in this institution has a rather longer history. We know, in fact, that legal teaching can be traced back to the foundation of the University in 1451, although we know relatively little about it and it appears to have ceased in the sixteenth century.

Glasgow's place in Scottish legal history prior to the Regius chair's foundation owes less to this early teaching and more to the contribution of James Dalrymple of Stair, who graduated Master of Arts in 1637 and subsequently taught – probably philosophy – in the University. He went on, of course, to become Lord President, Viscount Stair and the author of *The Institutions of the Law of Scotland*, the foundation of modern Scots law.

---

[19] With an assignation of £90 *per annum* from Queen Anne. See J W Cairns, "The origins of the Glasgow law school: the professors of civil law, 1714–61" in P Birks (ed), *The Life of the Law: Proceedings of the Tenth British Legal History Conference, Oxford 1991* (1993) p 151 at 154.

[20] A Ashworth and L Zedner, "Defending the criminal law: reflections on the changing character of crime, procedure and sanctions" (2008) 2 Criminal Law and Philosophy 21 at 22 and 32.

[21] A Crawford, "Governing through anti-social behaviour: regulatory challenges to criminal justice" (2009) 49 Brit J Crim 810 at 826.

[22] N Lacey, "Historicising criminalisation: conceptual and empirical issues" (2009) 72 MLR 936 at 938 and 951 (avoiding, however, direct reference to the number).

[23] R Reiner, "Citizenship, crime, criminalization: marshalling a social democratic perspective" (2010) 13 New Criminal Law Review 241 at 259.

[24] Ashworth and Zedner (n 20).

[25] In a piece with Fiona Leverick, whom I would not wish to describe as a lesser author. See J Chalmers and F Leverick, "Fair labelling in criminal law" (2008) 71 MLR 217.

Andrew Dewar Gibb, one of my predecessors as Regius Professor of Law, was concerned for some time that Stair's links with Glasgow were not properly recognised. In the early 1950s, he engaged in discussions with Lord Cooper, then Lord President, about the possibility of a memorial. In 1951, Cooper wrote to Dewar Gibb in somewhat negative terms. He had discussed the matter with the Edinburgh legal community, who felt that a memorial to Stair should wait until 1971, when the anniversary of his appointment as Lord President would come around. Moreover, it should not be in Glasgow. Edinburgh was the preferred location, although "[n]o one [was] keen on a statue to be placed anywhere, Edinburgh being choked with statues". Glasgow University, it was suggested, could erect a "simpler memorial, such as a tablet".

Dewar Gibb's response to this was to arrange for perhaps the least simple tablet imaginable to be erected, in the most prominent of locations, and well before 1971. This tablet sits at the foot of the stairs in the university's main building. Although now some distance from the Law School's location in the Stair Building, it was at the time "as near as possible to the Law Class-Room", something which Dewar Gibb considered important for the encouragement of current students.[26] Whether this accords with what Cooper had envisaged I do not know, but he did agree to unveil it.[27]

SELECTING A REGIUS CHAIR

Although the appointment of a Regius chair is formally a matter for the monarch, the selection process is in the hands of the university, subject to confirmation by Royal Warrant thereafter.[28] The selection process has varied over time – William Forbes, the first holder, was appointed after the Professor of Greek was appointed to go to Edinburgh and find a suitable candidate.[29]

In modern practice, the recruitment process is the same as for any other chair, save for the process of submitting the name of the preferred candidate to the Scottish Ministers for confirmation. This can take some time – I

---

[26] "Twenty Five Years in the Faculty of Law", delivered to the Juridical Society on 7 January 1958: NLS Dep 217, Box 11, folder 4.

[27] Some of his remarks on the occasion are excerpted in D M Walker, *The Scottish Jurists* (1985) p 119.

[28] The appointment of Regius chairs in Scotland has not in modern times been as politically sensitive as in England: see S Targett, "A Regius rumble", Times Higher Education Supplement, 1 March 1996. The position in England has now changed, and appointments are in the first instance a matter for the universities concerned.

[29] Specifically, to "inform himself who is esteemed the fittest to undertake the ... profession of Law". He reported that Forbes was "Esteem'd a man very well skill'd in the Civil Law and Capable to teach the same": see Cairns (n 19) at p 155.

was not permitted to identify myself as the Regius chair until almost two months after I arrived at Glasgow. The holder receives a Royal Warrant, now signed by the Queen and the First Minister, and the appointment is announced in the Edinburgh Gazette.

Other steps have changed over time. Andrew Dewar Gibb, when offered the chair, was sent a form letter requesting that he pay ten shillings stamp duty in order that the Royal Warrant be issued.[30] I received no such letter, thanks to the little-known current suspension of stamp duty for first-time Regius chair holders. Surprisingly, this innovation has failed to lift the British economy out of economic stagnation, and so the Cabinet Office has announced a programme of quantitative easing, whereby the supply of Regius chairs in the economy will be significantly increased.[31]

All applicants for any post at Glasgow, no matter its nature, must fill out the same online form. This requires the applicant to declare all their qualifications from Standard Grade onwards. Being an obedient sort of individual – and hopeful that my A in Higher Economics might impress the Principal – I dug out my certificates and completed the form in full.

In the process, I came across a document, which is of interest for a number of reasons. A report from the staff partner in a firm of solicitors, it represents my first real encounter with the discipline of law, when as a school pupil I spent a week in each of two successive years on work experience with an Aberdeen firm of solicitors, AC Morrison and Richards.

Very flatteringly, many friends and colleagues have reacted to my appointment by commenting that I must be the youngest person to hold the chair. (In academia, the adjective "young" is used in a more flexible manner than in other walks of life.) However, John Millar was twenty-five when appointed in 1761.[32] It should also be noted that David Walker, although thirty-eight when appointed in 1958, had interrupted his studies to serve in the Second World War, and was appointed to the Regius chair within a decade of graduating with the degree of LLB. Even more remarkably, this was his second chair.

So I cannot claim any sort of record in that regard. I can, I believe, claim to be the first holder of the chair to have attended a comprehensive school. As, however, Inverurie Academy has now had an alumnus holding a chair

---

[30] NLS Dep 217, Box 3, folder 4.

[31] Cabinet Office, "Queen to bestow new Regius Professorships on outstanding universities", 12 October 2012, available at *http://www.cabinetoffice.gov.uk/news/regius-professorships-universities*. See n 11 above.

[32] He was born on 22 June 1735, with the royal warrant appointing him to the chair being issued on 15 June 1761 and the university admitting him to it on 15 July that year: see K Haakonssen and J W Cairns, "Millar, John (1735–1801)", *Oxford Dictionary of National Biography* (2004).

within the Glasgow Law School continuously since 1969[33] (and, indeed, a current visiting professor in the Edinburgh Law School),[34] my kid from the wrong side of the tracks argument is unlikely to convince anyone.

Of more interest, perhaps, are the comments of Morrison and Richards' staff partner on this form, which read as follows:

> He is a nice young man but if he wants to become a lawyer, he will have to be more outward-looking. Clients expect to have confidence in their lawyer which does require a more extrovert (without being too extrovert) type of person.
>
> P.S. He was very good at figures. Maybe he should consider accountancy!

I can tell you why I did not consider accountancy. Inverurie Academy had a careers fair one evening where pupils were encouraged to meet local employers. The local accountant told me quite firmly that if I wanted to enter his profession, I would have to play golf. I have played golf. My best round was, I think, a little under 90 strokes. That is a reasonable score for a dilettante playing an 18-hole course. It was not an 18-hole course.

So, I chose law. My experience at Morrison and Richards was important for other reasons. Like all law firms faced with occupying a school pupil for a week, they packed me off to the sheriff court, where I sat listening to the debate on a no case to answer submission in a sexual offences trial. I sat through a lengthy discussion of what sounded like the "More-of principle" – a name which made sense, because it referred to whether the claims made by two separate child victims of sexual abuse could support each other's accounts – and returned later that day to Morrison and Richards' law library to try and work out what it was I had been listening to.

The answer was that I had been listening to a discussion of the *Moorov* doctrine. I learned this from a book entitled *The Law of Evidence in Scotland*, better known as "Walker and Walker". I suspect I am the only legal academic to be now a co-author of the first legal textbook they ever read,[35] in doing so citing the appeal from the first trial they ever saw.[36] I am very grateful to

---

[33] Bill Gordon, who attended Inverurie Academy and thereafter Robert Gordon's College in Aberdeen, was appointed to the Douglas Chair of Civil Law in 1969. He became an Emeritus Professor on his retiral in 1999 until his death on 1 September 2012: see P Davison, "Obituary: Professor Bill Gordon", *The Herald* 20 September 2012.

[34] Harvey McGregor QC, who attended Inverurie Academy and thereafter Scarborough Boys' High School: see CV available at *http://www.hailshamchambers.com/barristers/harvey-mcgregor-cbe-qc.asp*.

[35] It may not have been the first legal text of any sort which I read. Either around the same time or earlier, I read S R Moody and J Tombs, *Prosecution in the Public Interest* (1982), a copy of which was held by the Carnegie Public Library in Inverurie.

[36] *Smith v HM Advocate* 1995 SLT 583. See now M L Ross and J Chalmers, *Walker and Walker: The Law of Evidence in Scotland* (3rd edn, 2009) para 5.2.1.

Margaret Ross for giving me the opportunity to be involved in revising and updating this classic text.[37]

My use of the library is, even today, recorded in Morrison and Richards' records (according to which I seem to have been capable of borrowing a book and returning it the previous day). This includes the consultation of my predecessor David Walker's classic text on *The Scottish Legal System*, although I have no special recollection of it.

I do recall, however, that one wall of the library contained a set of the now defunct *Statutes in Force*. *Statutes in Force* was a collection of over 100 brown loose-leaf binders, designed to hold the complete and up-to-date text of all United Kingdom Acts of Parliament. By the time I found myself in Morrison and Richards' library, it was already a dismal failure, increasingly out of date.[38] But I knew nothing of its deficiencies, and I distinctly remember being surprised that "all the law" took up such a relatively small amount of shelf space. It struck me that a diligent student could conceivably memorise the entire contents of such a set of volumes, and thus know the complete law of the land. You will deduce from this absurd thought that I had yet to attempt reading a statute at this point. There is, however, something of importance in this naïve observation which I shall return to later. But first, given that this is the tercentenary year, I should say something about my predecessors.

THE EIGHTEENTH CENTURY: AUSPICIOUS BEGINNINGS

I do not want to say too much about the Regius chair in the eighteenth century. This is in part because of pressure of time, but also because so much work has been done on the early history of the School of Law by John Cairns, to whom Glasgow owes an enormous debt. Anything I could say on the subject would be a pale and inadequate summary of John's detailed and scholarly accounts, which I commend to you.

There were four holders of the Regius chair in the eighteenth century. Of the middle two – William Crosse and Hercules Lindseay – there is little to be said. Crosse treated the chair as a sinecure and was after a few years replaced by Lindseay.[39] Lindseay published nothing, but all the evidence points to him having been an able teacher, well respected by his colleagues.[40]

---

[37] The gap between the first and second editions of *Walkers on Evidence*, at thirty-six years, may be some sort of record.

[38] P Clinch, "Statutes probably not in force" (1994) 15 Stat LR 64.

[39] See J W Cairns, "William Crosse, Regius Professor of Civil Law in the University of Glasgow, 1746-1749: a failure of enlightened patronage" (1993) 12 History of Universities 159.

[40] See Cairns (n 19) at p 185.

The contribution of the first and last holders of the chair in the eighteenth century, however, is far more significant. William Forbes, the first holder, is best known for his somewhat neglected *Institutes of the Law of Scotland*, published in two volumes.[41] The first dealt with private law, the second with criminal. Many modern academics publish too much (or, as Kenneth Reid has put it, write too much and read too little).[42] Not so Forbes. He wrote a *Great Body of the Law of Scotland*, a "gigantic seven-volume manuscript"[43] held in the Glasgow University Library which he never published. The value of Forbes's work is not in doubt, and there is good reason to hope that greater use will be made of it in the future. Thanks to the efforts of Ross Anderson and Ronan Deazley, and the support of the University's Chancellor's Fund, the *Great Body* is now available online.[44] In addition, the *Institutes* have very recently been reprinted by the Edinburgh Legal Education Trust. If I may be permitted a sales pitch, I would draw your attention to the limited number of discounted copies available for sale at tonight's wine reception: get yours while stocks last!

To Millar, it is impossible to do justice in the time here and I will not attempt it. He published widely, but rather than being concerned with doctrinal law, his work is perhaps best characterised as social theory and history, and so his name is not as recognisable to Scots lawyers as it should be. As a teacher, he radically overhauled and expanded the curriculum, making Glasgow Britain's leading law school, to which students resorted from all quarters of the country.[45] His success in the chair is unparalleled. Unfortunately, the momentum he developed was entirely lost after his death in 1801.

THE NINETEENTH CENTURY: DECLINE

The story of the Regius chair in the nineteenth century is not a happy one. David Walker, Regius Professor from 1958 until 1990, has offered blunt assessments of the nineteenth-century professors in his *History of the School of Law*, and a sufficient picture can be obtained by quoting from his commentary.

---

[41] In 1722 and 1730.

[42] "Smoothing the rugged parts of the passage: Scots law and its Edinburgh chair", 18 September 2012, *http://www.youtube.com/watch?v=YTFW7XXqBxY*.

[43] "[W]hich must provide the fullest account available of Scots law in the early eighteenth century": H L MacQueen, "Introduction" in W Forbes, *The Institutes of the Law of Scotland* (Edinburgh Legal Education Trust reprint, 2012) p v at vi.

[44] *http://www.forbes.gla.ac.uk/contents/*.

[45] See the quotes offered by J W Cairns, "'Famous as a School for Law, as Edinburgh ... for medicine': legal education in Glasgow, 1761–1801", in A Hook and R B Sher (eds), *The Glasgow Enlightenment* (1995) p 133 at 134.

Robert Davidson, appointed in 1801, "probably owed his appointment to being the son of the Principal: He seems to have been competent ... in 1802 and 1803 he had no students at all".[46]

Allan Maconochie, appointed in 1842, "left no published work [but] seems to have made a genuine effort to teach his subject".[47] George Skene, appointed in 1855 "merely read lectures to the class ... 'though earnest and conscientious, [he] had no illumination'".[48] He was succeeded in 1867 by Robert Berry, who "did not write and left no particular reputation".[49] Finally, Alexander Moody Stuart held the chair from 1887 to 1905. "He too made no particular mark in the law."[50]

"In truth", Walker concludes, "the Regius Professors of the nineteenth century were a mediocre bunch".[51] In his work on *The Scottish Jurists*, he ignores them, mentioning only that after John Millar the chair "was held by several undistinguished persons".[52] Certainly, they left no scholarly mark: Davidson seems to have been the only one to have published anything on law.[53] Walker describes his contribution as a "small book on Scottish poor law".[54] This is unusually charitable: the "book" is all of twelve pages long.[55] Twelve pages of scholarship in a century – one page every eight and a half years – is a poor record. Why was this so?

We might note, first, that the problem was not unique to Glasgow. The position elsewhere is instructive. The Regius chair at Edinburgh, while held with great distinction by James Lorimer from 1862 onwards, was vacant for

---

[46] D M Walker, *A History of the School of Law, The University of Glasgow* (1990) p 39. That was particularly distressing given Millar's great success in the chair. It has been suggested that student numbers had declined towards the end of Millar's tenure: see J D Mackie, *The University of Glasgow 1451–1951: A Short History* (1954) p 166, n 3. Mackie argues that Millar, "[l]ike other Professors ... may have gone on too long" (p 234, see also p 187). However, the only evidence Mackie offers for this is Davidson's own low student numbers. As John Cairns has demonstrated, they do not support this conclusion, and the available evidence is to the contrary: J W Cairns, "From 'speculative' to 'practical' legal education: the decline of the Glasgow Law School, 1801–1830" (1994) 62 Tijdschrift voor Rechtsgeschiedenis 331 at 334–35.

[47] Walker, *History* (n 46) p 40.

[48] Walker, *History* (n 46) p 55, quoting D Murray, *Memories of the Old College of Glasgow: Some Chapters in the History of the University* (1927) p 232. Murray goes on to say (at p 234) that "though George Skene was not a distinguished professor, he was an excellent man. What he lacked was animation; he did not do himself justice ... he was a Scottish gentleman of the finest type".

[49] Walker, *History* (n 46) p 55. Berry has, however, been credited with reviving the teaching of civil law in 1873–74: J Coutts, *A History of the University of Glasgow* (1909) p 452.

[50] Walker, *History* (n 46) p 56.

[51] Walker, *History* (n 46) p 56.

[52] Walker, *Scottish Jurists* (n 27) p 410. He mentions Davidson, but only in a list of many students of David Hume's "who later attained distinction": p 319.

[53] Skene, however, had previously published *The Chronology of the Old Testament, and its Connection with Profane History* (1836).

[54] Walker, *History* (n 46) p 39.

[55] R Davidson, *A Short Exhibition of the Poor Laws of Scotland* (3rd edn, 1816).

a lengthy period in the middle of the nineteenth century.[56] Around that time, a Select Committee of the House of Commons was appointed in 1846 to enquire into the state of legal education in England and Ireland. In the course of their researches, they looked into the activities of the Regius professors there. The picture was not attractive.

Joseph Phillimore, Regius Professor of Civil Law at Oxford from 1809 until 1855, reluctantly admitted to the Committee that his subject had not been taught at Oxford for over a century.[57] His duties, the Committee concluded, had "dwindled down to a mere sinecure".[58] Matters were somewhat better at Cambridge, where the Regius Professor had "generally a good attendance on his lectures, but not such as to be called a very large one",[59] although the other professor – the Downing Professor of English Laws – did not teach at all.[60] The Regius Professor at Dublin gave evidence as follows:[61]

> How often in a year are you required to give lectures? – The charter says twice a week during the College term.
> At what hour in the day? – Nine o'clock in the morning.
> Are the lectures generally well attended? – No, I should say not.

His attendance "did not exceed seven", consisting of barristers rather than students, to whom no fees were charged: "if there were any fees there would be no attendance at all".[62] Allan Maconochie's average attendance of thirty students[63] was stellar by comparison.

---

[56] In addition, John Cairns and Hector MacQueen have referred to the "largely undistinguished men" who held the Edinburgh Chair of Scots Law in the second half of the nineteenth century: J W Cairns and H L MacQueen, *Learning and the Law: A Short History of the Edinburgh Law School* (2013) p 18.

[57] B Nicholas, "Jurisprudence", in M G Brock and M C Curthoys (eds), *The History of the University of Oxford. Volume VII: Nineteenth-Century Oxford, Part 2* (2000) p 385 at 385. Phillimore appears to have published some law reports but little else: see N Doe, "Phillimore, Joseph (1775–1855)", *Oxford Dictionary of National Biography* (2004).

[58] *Report from the Select Committee on Legal Education, Together with the Minutes of Evidence* (PP 686, 1846) p lv. The Committee found that the "department of Common Law is somewhat more efficiently managed", with a course of twenty-four lectures being delivered (ibid).

[59] *Report from the Select Committee on Legal Education* (n 58) p v. Geldart, the Regius Professor, did not give evidence. Starkie, the Downing Professor, was asked whether Geldart's lectures were better attended than his ones had been and replied "Yes, I think more; but I do not think it is a very large attendance" (Q 30).

[60] *Report from the Select Committee on Legal Education* (n 58) p v, recording rather curiously that there were "no lectures given, and no attendance whatever".

[61] *Report from the Select Committee on Legal Education* (n 58) QQ 2830–32.

[62] *Report from the Select Committee on Legal Education* (n 58) p vii.

[63] *Report from the Select Committee on Legal Education* (n 58) Q 3886. It is not clear how many students attended the Vinerian Professor's lectures at Oxford: his (J R Kenyon's) evidence was that "there has been very little disposition to attend; but there is an increasing disposition now" (Q 1455). The Downing Professor at Cambridge had "somewhere about 10 or 12" students in his first year; "the next year not so many"; he had not lectured since (Q 26).

But that is a comparison, not an explanation, and the different model of legal training in Scotland at the time undermines its value. A more direct explanation is that the chair was not, at the time, a financially attractive proposition to a first-rate lawyer. It had been suggested to George Jardine, the Glasgow Professor of Logic, that his son might seek the chair on Millar's death. Jardine's response is instructive: "None who like the Bar and have any prospect of rising there could be tempted by it."[64] The chair seems also to have been relatively poorly paid, at least in the latter half of the century, compared to other professorships in the University.[65]

John Cairns has charted how the Glasgow Law School declined over this period as it moved from the "speculative" education of Millar to Davidson's self-described "practical" approach. That did not change with Davidson's departure. Indeed, it was given emphasis by the fact that Maconochie's 1842 appointment was, unlike his predecessors, to teach "Scots law" and not Civil (that is, Roman) law. This, it seems, was because the Glasgow legal profession had made representations to the Lord Advocate that the function of the chair should change in this way.[66] Maconochie was still required to teach Civil law if sufficient students requested it, and appeared keen to do so, but they did not.[67] He saw this as evidence of a change in the kind of education which students wanted. When Millar had lectured, he said, "men's minds were particularly turned to the discussions then going on in Europe regarding the principles of government". A course of lectures such as Millar's, he thought, "would draw no attendance now in Glasgow". He ascribed this to:[68]

> ... the utilitarian notions of the present day; that where a young man does not see the immediate advantage which he is to reap by undergoing any particular course of instruction, he will neglect it, and adopt only that which is to be immediately conducive to his patrimonial advantage ... I always find that when my lectures are to be upon the history or principles of our jurisprudence, the attendance of students is comparatively small; but when I lecture upon the mercantile parts of our system of law, and more especially when last winter I delivered lectures upon the statutes relative to joint-stock companies, my class-room was crowded.

[64]   Cairns (n 46) at p 339 (citing Jardine to Hunter, 16 July 1801, GUL, MS Gen 507/118).

[65]   See eg Scottish Universities Commissioners, Ordinance (No 25), Glasgow No 3 (1893) pp 8–9. This does not appear to have changed with Gloag's appointment: see *Annual Statistical Report by the University Court of the University of Glasgow to the Secretary of State for Scotland, under the provisions of section 30 of the Universities (Scotland) Act, 1889, for the year 1905–06* (1907).

[66]   *Report from the Select Committee on Legal Education* (n 58) Q 3885. Subsequently, Skene's appointment referred to the "sole profession of law". Walker says that this "was the basis of the claim sometimes asserted by successors that they would, if they chose, teach Roman law or Hindu law and could not be stopped from doing so": Walker, *History* (n 46) p 41.

[67]   *Report from the Select Committee on Legal Education* (n 58) Q 3885.

[68]   *Report from the Select Committee on Legal Education* (n 58) QQ 3935–36.

Seduced by a badly-remembered golden past, academics are prone to characterise their students as instrumental and strategic, not interested in learning for learning's sake like their predecessors. Perhaps, nearly two centuries after Maconochie, we might at least have the wit to avoid parroting complaints of such antiquity.

THE TWENTIETH CENTURY: REVIVAL

The fortunes of the Regius chair changed dramatically when, upon Moody Stuart's retirement in 1905, Willliam Gloag was appointed. Even before then, Gloag had already made a greater contribution to scholarship than all the Regius professors since Millar combined, having co-authored a significant volume on *Rights in Security and Cautionary Obligations*.[69] But it is his classic work on *The Law of Contract*[70] and his co-authorship of Gloag and Henderson's *Introduction to the Law of Scotland*,[71] today in its thirteenth edition,[72] which have ensured his leading place in Scottish legal history. He is also the only Regius professor ever to have published a book of poetry.[73] And, unlike me, he could play golf, scoring a hole in one in the 1907 Senate Match between the Universities of Aberdeen and Glasgow.[74]

Considered a distinctive personality[75] and an inspired teacher,[76] Gloag was described by Andrew Dewar Gibb as "beyond all question the most remarkable legal scholar who has ever held this Chair".[77] David Walker, by contrast, thought that Gloag's *Contract* contained "many flaws" and that *Gloag and Henderson* "cannot be said to be a satisfactory book at all".[78] On

---

[69] W M Gloag and J M Irvine, *Law of Rights in Security, Heritable and Moveable, Including Cautionary Obligations* (1897). See A J M Steven, "One hundred years of Gloag and Irvine" 1997 JR 314. Irvine was to become Professor of Scots Law at the University of Aberdeen two years later, serving until 1919. See M C Meston, "The civilists of Aberdeen: 1495–1995" 1995 JR 153 at 164.

[70] W M Gloag, *The Law of Contract* (1914), 2nd edn (1929). See H L MacQueen, "Glory with Gloag or the stake with Stair? T B Smith and the Scots law of contract" in Reid and Carey-Miller (eds), *A Mixed Legal System in Transition* (n 17) p 138 at 140–41.

[71] W M Gloag and R C Henderson, *Introduction to the Law of Scotland* (1927).

[72] H L MacQueen and Lord Eassie, *Gloag and Henderson: Introduction to the Law of Scotland* (13th edn, 2012).

[73] W M Gloag, *Carmina Legis, or Verses Illustrative of the Law of Scotland* (1920). See also J Blackie, "A serious poem by Gloag" (2005) 9 Edin LR 331.

[74] H L MacQueen, "Gloag's golf: a past Master" *Scots Law News* 10 April 2012.

[75] Walker, *Scottish Jurists*, p 411.

[76] A F Rodger, "Gloag, William Murray (1865–1934)", rev *Oxford Dictionary of National Biography* (2004).

[77] A Dewar Gibb, "Law", in J B Neilson (ed), *Fortuna Domus: A Series of Lectures Delivered in the University of Glasgow in Commemoration of the Fifth Century of its Foundation* (1952) p 157 at 167.

[78] Walker, *Scottish Jurists* pp 412–13.

the basis of this evaluation, he concluded that Gloag was "the outstanding jurist of the century".[79]

On Gloag's death in 1934,[80] he was succeeded by Andrew Dewar Gibb. Dewar Gibb had studied under Gloag and was then leading a peripatetic and contradictory existence as simultaneously lecturer in English law at Edinburgh and lecturer in Scots law at Cambridge. That made him, perhaps, uniquely qualified to lecture on the relationship between the two systems.[81] Dewar Gibb was a significant figure both academically and politically: he had been a Unionist candidate twice in the 1920s and a founder of the Scottish National Party in 1934, serving as its chairman from 1936 to 1940.[82] He published on Scots law, English law, and politics,[83] leaving a considerable body of work, the diversity of which has proved difficult for subsequent commentators to analyse.[84]

Dewar Gibb's contributions to legal academia beyond publication appear to have been important, yet little recognised. He was critical of the Juridical Review, at the time the only legal journal in Scotland of an academic nature. Its content, he said, was "extremely diffuse", and "one gains the idea that the editor is casting around desperately for something to publish".[85] Dewar Gibb led efforts to remedy the situation, with an initial proposal to create a new periodical resulting in the reconstitution of the Juridical Review as a universities' journal on a model which continues to the present day.[86] We know similarly that he was instrumental in the development of Scottish Current Law, a crucial service in the days before electronic databases,[87] and active in the reform of the law degree,[88] but his contributions both to legal publishing and legal

---

[79] Walker, *Scottish Jurists* p 413.

[80] It is indicative of Gloag's modest personality that his short will stated that he "should desire to be cremated, with as little ceremony as possible": typescript extract of holograph will of William Murray Gloag, NAS/IRS20/137.

[81] On 27 May 1936, he delivered a "Special University Lecture on Laws" at King's College London, with the title "The inter-relation of the legal systems of Scotland and England".

[82] E A Cameron, "Gibb, Andrew Dewar (1888–1974)", *Oxford Dictionary of National Biography* (2009).

[83] *Scotland in Eclipse* (1930), *Scottish Empire* (1937) and *Scotland Resurgent* (1950).

[84] See, however, L Farmer, "Under the shadow over Parliament House: the strange case of legal nationalism", in L Farmer and S Veitch (eds), *The State of Scots Law: Law and Government After the Devolution Settlement* (2001) p 151.

[85] "Proposed Universities Law Legal Journal", dated 1/12/53: NLS Dep 217, Box 3, folder 1.

[86] "Twenty Five Years in the Faculty of Law", delivered to the Juridical Society on 7 January 1958: NLS Dep 217, Box 11, folder 4. See also "Note on the Juridical Review", 17 February 1956, NLS Dep 217, Box 3, folder 1.

[87] T B Smith, in an appreciation delivered at Dewar Gibb's memorial service (1974 SLT (News) 38), suggested that Dewar Gibb had not received enough credit for this.

[88] A Dewar Gibb, "Reform in the Scottish Law School: A lecture not yet delivered" 1943 JR 152.

education have yet to be properly detailed or assessed. Like Gloag before him, he lived in one of the houses in Professors' Square. This proximity to the teaching rooms had enabled Gloag to offer alcoholic breakfasts to select students: it is said that it enabled Dewar Gibb to turn up to 8.30 am lectures wearing pyjama bottoms, combined with a suit jacket, tie and academic gown.

David Walker, his successor, claimed that towards the end of his tenure Dewar Gibb was "a rather depressed, disappointed man, feeling that he had not achieved what he had wanted or hoped to do".[89] Perhaps it was not always clear what Dewar Gibb had wanted or hoped to do: he told the publishers W Green in 1946 that he was "writing or editing no more law books for a long time ever".[90] Over the next decade, he supplied Greens with two more editions of Gloag and Henderson,[91] a new edition of his own Preface to Scots Law,[92] and four brand new books.[93]

Following Dewar Gibb's retiral, David Walker was appointed to the Regius chair in 1958, shortly after his thirty-eighth birthday. Just as Dewar Gibb had studied under Gloag, Walker had studied under Dewar Gibb. The process was a prolonged one: the Scottish Office had invited applications by 8 February that year, but Walker was not notified that he was to be offered the chair until late May. In his History of the School of Law, he suggested that this was because the Scottish Office had thought him too young to hold the post.[94]

In fact, Walker's age never entered into the question. The Scottish Office, which handled the recruitment process directly, was concerned that it had received only two applications.[95] Walker was the only applicant from

---

[89] Walker, History (n 46) p 58.

[90] Dewar Gibb to G R Thomson, 14 July 1946, NLS Dep 217, Box 3, folder 1.

[91] He co-edited three editions of Gloag and Henderson: A Dewar Gibb and N M L Walker (eds), Introduction to the Law of Scotland, 4th edn (1946), 5th edn (1952) and 6th edn (1956). The timing of his comments to Thomson may indicate that producing the fourth edition had not been a pleasant experience, but that is speculation.

[92] A Dewar Gibb, A Preface to Scots Law (2nd edn, 1950). The first edition had been published in 1944. A third (1961) and fourth (1964) followed after his retiral from the chair.

[93] Law from Over the Border: A Short Account of a Strange Jurisdiction (1950); Perjury Unlimited: A Monograph on Nuremberg (1954); Fragmenta Legis (1955); Judicial Corruption in the United Kingdom (1957).

[94] Walker, History (n 46) p 65.

[95] See NAS, HH91/824. This was seen internally as surprising given that a "large" number of enquiries (nine) had been received from individuals who did not submit applications. This mismatch is, however, readily explicable. With at most two exceptions, those who requested copies of the terms and conditions but who submitted no application were unqualified for the chair, as having no knowledge of Scots law. The necessity of this was not explicit in the advertisement, but the requirement to take responsibility for the Department of Scots Law, as set out in the particulars, should have made this clear. One enquirer, L A Sheridan (later founding Dean of the Faculty of Law in the University of Malaya, now the National University

within Scotland; the other candidate was Scottish and had studied law at Aberdeen, but had pursued his academic career in Canada.[96] Both were regarded from the outset as strong candidates, eminently appointable, with Walker the stronger of the two. The civil servants, however, seemed worried purely about the numbers: something had surely gone wrong in the process if the field was so limited.

The Scottish Office was concerned, therefore, that steps should be taken to expand the field. The process followed seems, in retrospect, somewhat farcical. Names were sought and received from various quarters. Discussions ensued between the University Principal, the Scottish Office, the Lord Advocate and the Court of Session judge Lord Cameron. Eventually, it was accepted that there was no point in approaching any of the individuals whose names had been mentioned to ask whether they wished to be considered. There was no way in which any of them could be considered a better candidate than Walker. The futile escapade was brought to an end, and the Principal told Walker that he had the post.

In all of this, a crucial role was played by T B Smith, then Professor of Scots Law at Aberdeen and shortly to take up the Chair of Civil Law at Edinburgh, and often portrayed as a combative rival to Walker. Smith was regarded both by the Principal and the Scottish Office as the obvious adviser on the issue. His advice was pivotal. He dismissed suggestions by the Lord Advocate that the post might not have been properly advertised to members of the Bar. Anyone potentially interested and qualified would have been aware that Dewar Gibb was due to retire.[97] "Academics", he said, "like Regular Army, are as a rule keen students of necrology."[98] Walker was the "outstanding man available";[99] the lack of other applicants could be explained by the assumption that his appointment was "virtually a foregone conclusion".[100] It was Smith's counsel which secured Walker's appointment to the chair.

Walker's contribution to Scots law has never been properly evaluated. Given its scale, it perhaps never can be. Both Smith and Walker were deeply concerned about the lack of literature on Scots law, but they attacked the problem in very different ways. Alongside his own substantial scholarly

        of Singapore) did press the point. The Secretary to the University Court (Hutcheson) was
        consulted, confirmed that a knowledge of Scots law was essential, and this was duly relayed
        to Sheridan by the Scottish Office.
 96   Ian F G Baxter, then Professor at the Osgoode Hall Law School.
 97   And again, salary was an issue: "these legal chairs had little, if any, financial attraction to
        outstanding members of the legal professions, as the salaries attached compared unfavourably
        with those of Sheriff-Substitutes": note of meeting between Smith and Milne, 5 May 1958.
 98   Smith to Milne, 6 May 1958.
 99   Smith to Maclay, 20 January 1958.
100   Smith to Milne, 6 May 1958.

contributions, Smith was instrumental in establishing the Scottish Universities' Law Institute and the *Stair Memorial Encyclopaedia*, thereby encouraging academics and practitioners to write widely across the entire sphere of Scots law.[101] Walker had a different approach: he would do all the writing himself.

That is a caricature of the differences between the two men, but Walker's published output defies belief. He has been described as "perhaps the most prolific legal writer in the British Isles".[102] This is surely true, and perhaps best illustrated by a photograph of his works (displayed in the lecture) rather than an attempt to list them all.[103] It is emphasised further by his single-handed *Oxford Companion to Law*, published in 1980, recording his opinions on everything from A and B lists to the Belgian jurist Franciscus Zypaeus. It is not without its flaws, as another distinguished Glasgow graduate was to point out. Perhaps if only David Walker could produce a book such as the *Commentary* single-handed, only Alan Rodger could write an essay-length review of the results.[104] But it is an astonishing accomplishment by any standard. There is now a *New Oxford Companion to Law*, published in 2008. While Walker wrote his alone, the *New Companion* required 710 authors.

In a 1993 article, shortly after his tenure in the chair came to an end, he explained that he had written so much for two reasons: first, because when he began to write, "there was a desperate need in Scotland for new, modern textbooks on all the central subjects of private law",[105] but also because of:[106]

> ... an incurable disease with which I became afflicted in student days and for which no one has been able to offer any palliative. It is called *daimonia scribendi* – the existence within me of a tyrannical daimon that relentlessly pursues me with whips and scorpions if I do not do something every day, evening, weekend, holiday and any other time not absolutely spent on eating and sleeping (and formerly teaching, examining, and administering). I get a little relief daily from a medicine called *canis ambulatio* (walking the dog), and during our summer

---

[101] Reid (n 17) at pp 25–27. See also K G C Reid, "The third branch of the profession: the rise of the academic lawyer in Scotland", in H L MacQueen (ed), *Scots Law into the 21st Century: Essays in Honour of Bill Wilson* (1996) p 39.

[102] B A Garner, *Garner on Language and Writing: Selected Essays and Speeches* (2009) p 358.

[103] He is not one of the Walkers of *Walkers on Evidence*. As it happens, he had intended to be initially – the book was to have been by Walker, Walker and Walker – but as the preface to the first edition records, he had to withdraw due to pressure of work.

[104] A Rodger, "Good companion" (1981) 1 OJLS 257.

[105] D M Walker, "How I write" (1993) 4 Scribes Journal of Legal Writing 65 at 68. This was one contribution amongst a number which the journal's editors had solicited from "some of their favorite legal writers", inspired by Bertrand Russell's essay of the same name.

[106] Walker (n 105) at p 69.

vacation I take treatment called *montium peregrinatio* (walking the hills) and frequent doses of *librorum lectio* (reading books). Writing has been my consuming interest and hobby to the exclusion of sports and relaxations, and I have enjoyed it.

Walker was succeeded in the chair in 1991 by Joe Thomson. As Joe is present tonight, and still very active as an academic, it would be wrong of me to embarrass him by listing his many accomplishments. His contribution to Scots law, both in this chair and in his role as a member of the Scottish Law Commission, is widely recognised by both academics and practitioners and deservedly so. It is an honour to succeed him.

THE END OF GENERALISM

These, then, are the men whom I follow in the chair today. (And they are all men: it is a matter of some regret that save for Frances Moran's appointment to the Dublin Regius Chair of Laws in 1934, there have as yet been no female occupants of any of the Regius chairs in law.[107])

All of the twentieth-century appointees to the Glasgow Chair produced generalist texts on the subject of law. Gloag co-authored *Introduction to the Law of Scotland*; Dewar Gibb wrote his *Preface to Scots Law*; Walker his *Principles of Scottish Private Law* and Thomson his *Scots Private Law*. But generalism of the sort embodied in the chair has been under increasing pressure for some time as the body of the law has grown.

As early as 1821, the American Supreme Court Justice Joseph Story had identified the problem in the most memorable of terms. The "mass of the law" and the "ponderous volumes, which the next half century will add to the groaning shelves of our jurists", threatened "the fearful calamity ... of being buried alive, not in the catacombs, but in the labyrinths of the law".[108] The solution, he thought, was regular codification and recodification, reducing the past "to order and certainty".[109] None of this has happened in this jurisdiction – indeed, Story's proposal of regular recodification has perhaps not taken root anywhere. But lawyers have not yet been buried by their books. With the aid initially of all manner of indexing and digesting schemes and more recently the technology of electronic databases, we have devised ever more elaborate means for

---

[107] Moran was one of the first women to be admitted to the Irish Bar and also, in 1941, the first woman to become senior counsel in Ireland: see I Bacik, C Costello and E Drew, *Gender InJustice: Feminising the Legal Professions?* (2003) pp 58–61.

[108] J Story, "An address delivered before the Members of the Suffolk Bar, at their anniversary, on the fourth of September, 1821, at Boston" (1829) 1 American Jurist 1 at 31.

[109] At 32.

keeping abreast of a literature which grows exponentially. A resort to specialism has necessarily been part of this process.

Generalism is sustainable (and necessary) for a longer period in a small jurisdiction. Probably no holder of the two great chairs of English law – the Downing Professorship at Cambridge and the Vinerian Professorship at Oxford – has produced a generalist text since William Geldart's *Elements of English Law* in 1907,[110] a book which Dewar Gibb saw as a model for his own *Preface to Scots Law*.[111] In an unpublished talk, probably delivered in the late 1940s, Dewar Gibb drew attention to this problem:[112]

> The 230 odd years which have passed since 1713 have been marked by an amazing growth in the complexity of our civilization. The law too has in that period grown infinitely more complex since law inevitably reflects the nature and quality of a civilisation. Thus it has been found necessary as time went on to add to the students' knowledge of the Civil Law a rather sketchy outline of the principles of the law of Scotland, a more detailed knowledge of the complicated land laws, the law of the constitution, international law, jurisprudence and mercantile law.

He was less than impressed by the University of Glasgow's response, commenting that:

> Few chairs have been created and it has to be recorded that an ancient University which boasts a professorship of Heat Engines, still lacks a Chair of Jurisprudence. There is, mercifully, contemporary evidence of a more enlightened policy in the future.

A Chair of Jurisprudence was created by the University in 1952, and first held by David Walker.

I mention this not because I want to say anything in particular about generalism. If it is dying, that death is probably both regrettable and unavoidable. To borrow an old joke, we live in times when everyone is becoming more and more knowledgeable about less and less, and we will soon have professors who are unsurpassed in their knowledge of nothing at all. But I want to express some self-doubt at this point. Although I have written on private law and the Scottish legal system more generally, I am primarily a criminal lawyer. What precisely, am I doing in a chair of Scots law?

---

[110] The Vinerian Chair, which fell vacant with Andrew Ashworth's retirement in 2013, was advertised in 2012 on the basis that the successful candidate "will be a leader in scholarship and teaching in one or more of the areas within the field [of English law]": University of Oxford, "Job description and selection criteria: the Vinerian Professorship of English Law" (2012) p 1.

[111] See correspondence with W Green in NLS Dep 217, Box 3, item 6.

[112] "The Faculty of Law in the University of Glasgow" (nd): NLS Dep 217, Box 11, folder 6.

CRIMINAL LAW'S PLACE

To answer this question, I want to make a detour to Dublin, to consider the views of another Regius professor. The wonderfully named Mountifort Longfield was a generalist *par excellence*, having been not only the Regius Professor of English and Feudal Law in that institution but also the Professor of Political Economy.[113] He explained his approach to teaching law as follows:[114]

> I try to take a two years' course; in the course of two years to go through the body of law, except that I have never lectured on criminal law, not considering it worth calling the attention of students to. There are no fixed principles in it, except that men must not commit certain crimes, and if they do, there are certain punishments.

In the 1910–11 academic year, when Dewar Gibb was Gloag's student in Glasgow, Gloag delivered ninety-two lectures, of which it seems that only the last two contained any discussion of criminal law.[115] I say "it seems" because Dewar Gibb slept in on the day of lecture 90 and missed it, and was honest enough to record this for posterity in his notes. The content of lecture 91 seems, however, obviously to have been the start of Gloag's treatment of the subject, and so we can safely say that two lectures it was.[116] This compares with, for example, twenty-four lectures on the law of obligations.[117]

Was that adequate? David Walker thought the treatment "had to be" very brief, because Gloag's task of "covering the main topics of the whole private law in less than 100 lectures" was "impossible".[118] The latter claim may be true, but there is an interesting assertion of priority here. Criminal law is recognised as essential to a complete course in Scots law, even if it had sometimes been omitted. But on Gloag and Walker's account, the most cursory of nods would suffice. Criminal law was to be resorted to for completeness, nothing more.

Gloag did (along with Henderson) include a chapter on criminal law in his *Introduction to the Law of Scotland*, but it does not suggest that either

---

[113] A A Tait, "Mountifort Longfield 1802–1884: economist and lawyer" (1982) 133 Hermathena 15. Longford was appointed to the Chair of Political Economy in 1832 and to the Regius Chair of English and Feudal Law in 1834. He resigned the former – which had a maximum tenure of five years – in 1836.

[114] *Report from the Select Committee on Legal Education* (n 58) Q 2835.

[115] Dewar Gibb's notes of Gloag's lectures (and others) are held by the National Library of Scotland (NLS Dep 217, Box 12, item d). These meticulous notes of one Regius professor's lectures by his eventual successor are a tragically under-utilised resource.

[116] Walker (*Scottish Jurists* (n 27) p 411) says "two or three", perhaps on account of Dewar Gibb's notes.

[117] Fourteen on contract, six and a half on delict, and three and a half on prescription and remedies.

[118] Walker, *Scottish Jurists* (n 27) p 411.

author was much interested in the subject: it bears a striking similarity to the corresponding chapter in Erskine's *Principles*, the textbook it was intended to replace. It does not survive: the editors of the tenth edition announced that they had felt the time was right to excise the chapter (but without explanation).[119] Dewar Gibb certainly was interested in criminal law, and lectured rather more extensively on it. Walker may not have been, but he once wrote a book chapter on the topic perhaps just to show that he could.[120]

The place of criminal law in the Scots law curriculum has varied over time. We know that the two great eighteenth-century Regius professors, Forbes and Millar, were both deeply interested in the subject and devoted significant attention to it.[121] That level of attention seems to have diminished greatly when Millar was succeeded by Davidson.[122] David Hume, Professor of Scots Law at Edinburgh from 1786 to 1822, described criminal law as "certainly the noblest and most interesting part of [the lawyer's] profession"[123] and devoted a separate summer course to it.[124] These lectures formed the basis for his *Commentaries*, the outstanding work on Scots criminal law for some time and by some distance. By contrast, his successor in the chair, Bell, ignored the subject altogether. In turn, he was sharply criticised by his own successor for so doing.[125]

But I do not want to be too critical. The fact is, Longfield had a point and was honest enough to admit it. Criminal law *was* devoid of fixed principles. The attempts by earlier scholars and lecturers to categorise and order offences created the illusion of principles where they did not exist. One nineteenth-century Scottish text gave up on these attempts and simply listed crimes alphabetically in the form of a dictionary,[126] and a modern text takes a similar approach.[127] Criminal law's lack of principle made it impossible to give a short overview of the topic, and Gloag's two lectures lack any coherence. The only way to give a proper account of the criminal

---

[119] W A Wilson and A D M Forte (eds), *Introduction to the Law of Scotland* (10th edn, 1995) p ix.

[120] D M Walker, "The interaction of obligations and crime", in R F Hunter (ed), *Justice and Crime: Essays in Honour of the Right Honourable the Lord Emslie* (1993) p 15.

[121] This is self-evident from the treatment of criminal law in Forbes's *Institutes*. On Millar, see J W Cairns, "John Millar's lectures on Scottish criminal law" (1988) 8 OJLS 364.

[122] See Cairns (n 46) at pp 352–55, comparing the headings of lectures in Millar, Hume and Davidson's lectures. Davidson's lectures have a single heading "Of crimes", while Millar has five relevant headings along with two more relating (one only in part) to criminal procedure. But the headings are not equivalent to individual lectures and so, not having consulted the original materials, I make this claim tentatively.

[123] D Hume, *Commentaries on the Law of Scotland, Respecting Crimes* (4th edn, 1844) pp i, 2.

[124] Cairns (n 121) at p 396.

[125] J S More, *Lectures on the Law of Scotland* (J McLaren ed, 1864) vol I, p 15.

[126] J W Angus, *A Dictionary of Crimes and Offences According to the Law of Scotland* (1895). A second edition was published in 1915 and a third in 1936.

[127] P Hamilton, *A Fingertip Guide to Criminal Law* (6th edn, 2013).

law was to aim at comprehensiveness.[128] That explains why in the eighteenth and nineteenth centuries, some teachers developed the subject into a separate summer course.[129] That would not, however, have been attractive to professors with limited interest in the subject.[130]

Hume's masterful *Commentaries* are sometimes described as "principled",[131] but in fact he was quite explicit that he had "no intention of bringing forward a Philosophical Treatise of Criminal Jurisprudence" or to attempt to ascertain "on abstract and universal principles, the nature of the several offences".[132] His *Commentaries* are not unprincipled in any pejorative sense, but they are an attempt comprehensively to document, systematise and understand the great body of the criminal law, not to reduce it to the fixed principles which Longfield found lacking. There are many magisterial works from which key points, capable of exposition in a lecture or two, can be distilled. Hume's *Commentaries* is unquestionably magisterial, but it is not and was never meant to be a work capable of such reduction.

But just as legal generalism becomes less and less feasible as the body of the law grows, so does an attempt to treat the criminal law in a comprehensive fashion as the legislature resorts ever more frequently to that device. When Macdonald, later Lord Justice-Clerk, published his *Practical Treatise on the Criminal Law of Scotland* in 1867, he sidestepped this problem, stating at the outset that he would deal only with those offences punishable by death or immediate imprisonment.[133] Dealing with other offences would take up too much space, and they could not in any case "truly be described as crimes".[134] There is something to be said

---

[128] Note also Erskine's statement that "the Doctrine of Crimes, if properly explained, would take up a whole Course of Lectures by itself": Cairns (n 121) at p 395, quoting from Signet Library, MS 7 (law), vol 2, 313.

[129] Such as Hume, and also Bayne (the first Professor of Scots Law at Edinburgh). Millar's lectures on criminal law at Glasgow were more detailed but did not, as has sometimes wrongly been suggested, form a separate summer course. See generally Cairns, "Millar's lectures".

[130] It also raises the question of how attractive such courses were to students in comparison to the general Scots law course.

[131] See eg G H Gordon, *The Criminal Law of Scotland* (1968) pp 3–4 (referring to Hume's discussion of the "principles of Scots criminal law"). Of course, much depends on what a "principle" is taken to be in this context. See L Farmer, "The Idea of Principle in Scots Criminal Law", in J Chalmers, F Leverick and L Farmer (eds), *Essays in Criminal Law in Honour of Sir Gerald Gordon* (2010) p 86.

[132] Hume, *Commentaries* vol 1, p 14.

[133] J H A Macdonald, A *Practical Treatise on the Criminal Law of Scotland* (1867) p 1 ("those offences only, for the suppression of which the law has entrusted the judge or magistrate with the power of pronouncing a sentence of death or immediate deprivation of liberty, without the offender being entitled the option of paying a pecuniary penalty").

[134] At p 1. Macdonald's work went through five editions, the last being published in 1948, and was the standard work on Scottish criminal law prior to G H Gordon, *The Criminal Law of Scotland* (1968).

for this limiting device – although as Macdonald himself admitted, it was far from perfect.

It was not until 1959, when perhaps the most important PhD thesis to be completed in this law school was submitted, that matters changed. That was Gerald Gordon's *Criminal Responsibility in Scots Law*,[135] and I am greatly honoured by Sir Gerald's presence here tonight.

Gordon's work – later published, in expanded form, as *The Criminal Law of Scotland* in 1968 – was genuinely principled in a way that previous treatments of Scottish criminal law had not been. In a similar vein to the groundbreaking English work of Glanville Williams a few years earlier,[136] it sought to impose "some sort of theoretical order"[137] on the law, focused on individual responsibility and reflecting the author's dual philosophical and legal training. In its published form, it differed significantly from Williams's work, in that it addressed both the "general part" and the "special part" – that is, particular crimes. The latter part, save for homicide, had not formed part of Gordon's thesis, but the Scottish Universities' Law Institute felt it necessary to make the book a more attractive commercial proposition.[138] Principles, set alone, do not sell well.

There has been much disappointment expressed about the fact that Williams never wrote a "special part" for English law. But that is perhaps not surprising: Williams had at length defended the view that a crime was simply anything which could be prosecuted in the criminal courts, and that further definition was neither possible nor helpful.[139] If that view is taken to its logical conclusion, the special part is unwriteable. There is too much criminal law, and has been for a very long time, for anyone to attempt that enterprise without becoming demented.

But somehow, we still teach and write on criminal law, and most of us stay relatively sane. How?

VARJE ABSTRAKT BILD AV VÄRLDEN ÄR LIKA OMÖJLIG SOM RITNINGEN TILL EN STORM

Or, in English, every abstract picture of the world is as impossible as the blueprint of a storm. I use this quote, from the Nobel Prize winning

---

[135] This thesis is now available electronically via the Glasgow Theses Service, at *http://theses. gla.ac.uk/2753/*. This archive primarily contains theses submitted relatively recently, but a number of other older PhD theses have been made available. In addition to Gerald Gordon's, these include William McBryde's *Void, Voidable, Illegal and Unenforceable Contracts in Scots Law* (1976), at *http://theses.gla.ac.uk/2488/*.

[136] G L Williams, *Criminal Law: The General Part* (1953).

[137] Farmer (n 131) at p 98.

[138] Farmer (n 131) at p 98, n 56.

[139] G Williams, "The definition of crime" (1955) 8 CLP 107.

poet Tomas Tranströmer, for two purposes. First, to illustrate the curious coincidence that both Andrew Dewar Gibb and I spent time learning Swedish for reasons which seem equally obscure.

Tranströmer does not deny the existence of abstract pictures in this line – that might be an odd thing for a poet to do. The problem is both their impossibility and their necessity. In teaching or writing on criminal law, we offer an abstract picture of it, selecting from its chambers in a way which we hope makes some sense of the topic, but which can never be a true blueprint of our subject. The topics we cover in our courses and books are arbitrary and contingent. Almost all criminal law courses and books spend a considerable amount of time on the law of homicide. Why? We rarely think about this. If pressed, we might say it is an important offence which we use to illustrate general principles. But in fact, the entire structure of homicide is a mess which is replicated nowhere else in the criminal law. Perhaps it is because it is so serious – but few courses discuss the offence of genocide. Perhaps that is because it is serious and actually prosecuted in the Scottish courts – but few courses do more than touch on offences such as causing death by dangerous or careless driving.

Practice is by no means uniform, but most (not all) university criminal law teachers say little or nothing about road traffic offences, misuse of drugs or offensive weapons, crimes far more commonly prosecuted than some of those which we lecture on. And, like many law teachers, we say relatively little about statutes for no reason other than an instinctive aversion to them, preferring to concentrate on the humanity of case law.

I do not mean to condemn the enterprise of teaching criminal law, and I am as guilty as anyone else of any charges I might lay here. Much of what we do, we do for a reason, and it can be justified – although we have rarely bothered to articulate those justifications and I am not sure that we have much sense of what they are. But we should pause to consider whether the abstract picture we are offering is really "the criminal law". We operate on the understanding that criminal law is a device by which the community calls serious offenders to account for their wrongs. And criminal law is an important part of that – but only in part.

RESORTING TO CRIME

Earlier on in the lecture, I mentioned the number 3,023, and it is to that number that I now turn. This number came to prominence in August 2006, when it was reported in the press that this was the number of offences which New Labour had created since coming to office in May 1997: almost one for every day in office.[140] This represented everything that was wrong about New Labour. They had been "seduced by the politics of penal populism",[141] seeing the criminal law as "a multi-purpose solution to contemporary social ills".[142] The idea that New Labour had resorted too readily to the criminal law gained considerable traction, and the Coalition government committed itself to "introduc[ing] a new mechanism to prevent the proliferation of unnecessary new criminal offences".[143] When the press release announcing this was issued, the next paragraph committed the Coalition to criminalising the possession of illegal timber:[144] a sensible editor moved the two commitments rather further apart in the final document.

The figure of 3,023 was important, because it evidenced the fact that we have practically no systematic understanding of what the criminal law actually is. Let me demonstrate by inviting you to play a short game. Take the following supposed offences (under English rather than Scots law):

- Wearing armour in the Houses of Parliament
- Handling salmon in suspicious circumstances
- Dying in Parliament
- Allowing a boy under the age of ten to see a naked mannequin

Do you think these are crimes? Give it some thought while I explain the background. I mention these because they have all been listed in the media as examples of crazy laws at one time or another. Last year, the Law Commission for England and Wales decided to perform a public service by researching a whole number of supposed "crazy laws" and publishing the true position. The Law Commission, and its counterpart the Scottish Law Commission, are statutory bodies tasked with keeping the law under review and recommending reform. Law Commissioners are some of the most learned lawyers in the country.

So you can rely on what the Law Commission says – or you should be able to, but with an embarrassing lack of confidence in its own abilities, it headed up the list with a disclaimer that "readers should not rely on it without conducting their own research".[145] Never mind. What are the answers?

---

[140] N Morris, "Blair's 'frenzied law making': a new offence for every day spent in office", *The Independent* 16 August 2006. For more detail on the origins of this figure, see J Chalmers and F Leverick, "Quantifying criminalisation", in R A Duff and others (eds), *Criminalization: The Aims and Limits of the Criminal Law*, forthcoming.

[141] D Wilson, "Seduced by the politics of penal populism", *The Independent* 16 August 2006.

[142] Crawford (n 21) at p 826.

[143] HM Government, *The Coalition: Our Programme for Government* (2010) p 11.

[144] And its import: see sections 10 and 11 of the text at http://www.guardian.co.uk/politics/2010/may/12/lib-dem-tory-deal-coalition.

[145] Law Commission, *Legal Curiosities: Fact or Fable?* (2012), available at http://lawcommission.justice.gov.uk/docs/Legal_Oddities.pdf.

The first two are in fact offences, under the 1313 Statute Forbidding Bearing of Armour and the Salmon Act 1986[146] – so now you know. The third is not. (You might think that in any event it would be difficult to prosecute someone for an offence of "dying", but we used to prosecute dead people for treason in Scotland, even digging up their corpses to present before the court, so it is not impossible.[147]) And the fourth, which was publicly listed as an offence by a Swansea firm of solicitors in 2006?[148] Here is the Law Commission's response:

"No evidence."

Let me emphasise that: "no evidence". The Law Commission does not know what the law is. How is anyone else supposed to?

THE CHAOS OF THE CRIMINAL LAW

How could the Law Commission not know whether something was a criminal offence or not? The answer is that our criminal law is far more chaotic than we generally admit. Offences might be found anywhere in the vast range of statutes enacted and statutory instruments made each year.

Nevertheless, that is a closed list of material, well documented in commercially available databases. Surely the Commission could confirm that it contained no mannequin-related offences? But it is not just Parliaments and governments who make criminal law. In another recent project, the Law Commission estimated that criminal law could also be made by 486 local authorities, an unspecified number of trading standards authorities and "over 60" national regulators.[149] Note that "over 60". Not only do we not know how many criminal laws exist, we are not even sure how many *legislators* there are. Nor is there any systematic publication of the offences which they create.

Were you shocked when I said that New Labour had created 3,023 criminal offences in ten years? Perhaps you remembered that I had said earlier on that the figure was badly wrong, and chalked it up to media hyperbole. There was never much reason to think it reliable. It had been compiled by the efforts of the Liberal Democrats, who had struggled for years to extract information from different government departments about how many offences they were creating. But it is difficult to see how

---

[146] Section 32.

[147] See W K Dickson, "The Scots law of treason" (1898) 10 JR 243.

[148] "Where mince pies break the law ...", *BBC News Online* 23 December 2006. Mince pies do not break the law.

[149] *Criminal Liability in Regulatory Contexts* (Law Com CP No 195, 2010) para 1.21.

they had arrived at their final figure, because they had been stonewalled so often. Not because the relevant departments did not want to tell them, but because they did not know themselves.

The only way to find out how many offences are being created is systematically to review the legislation produced each year (although even that will give an incomplete picture, because of the other legislators I mentioned just now). It is a tedious job, and while various academics have expressed the view that someone ought to do it, none of them has cast themselves in the role of someone.

If you have remembered my thoughts about the statutes in Morrison and Richards' library, or the comments of their staff partner on my work experience report, you may have sensed where this is going. Fiona Leverick and I, along with a research assistant, Peter Lewin, have attempted to make a start on just this task. I have said nothing about Fiona Leverick so far, so it is at this point that I should embarrass her by emphasising just how lucky I have been to have worked with her, first at Aberdeen, then at a distance for some years when she moved to Glasgow and I to Edinburgh, and now in the same institution again. All my most valuable work has been done in conjunction with her (you may safely assume that the better parts of those works are hers and not mine) and I would undoubtedly not have been appointed to this chair were it not for the opportunity I have had to work with her over the years. Both of us were also extremely fortunate to have been taught criminal law by Michael Christie and Chris Gane.

Our work identified 1,395 offences created by the New Labour government. You may be relieved to learn that matters are not as bad as the media suggested. But 1,395 offences is still a lot. Also, I am taking advantage of the fact that you are now tired and thinking about the wine reception to play a little trick on you. We did identify 1,395 offences. But we were only looking at a single year. 1,395 is the number of offences created by New Labour in the twelve months after the 1997 general election. This suggests that New Labour might have created something in the region of *fourteen thousand criminal offences* in its first decade. Of course, we cannot know whether the rate of creation remained constant over that time, although we have as yet no reason to think that the first year was atypical. And crucially, at this stage in our research, it is not possible to identify the rate at which criminal offences are repealed. Many of these offences will have been the result of legislative churn as legislation was consolidated or replaced.

But, you might think, most of this is not "real crime" – whatever that means. In the absence of any better definition, we might take Macdonald's dividing line of imprisonment: an offence is only a "real crime" if you can be sent to jail for committing it. On that basis, New Labour created 906 real crimes in its first year, hardly a more encouraging figure.

I said earlier that the Coalition had sought to do something about this. Its solution is a purely administrative one. A civil servant who wants to create a criminal offence must send an email to offencesgateway@justice.gsi.gov.uk asking for permission, and the Secretary of State decides whether permission is to be granted. There is no identified test to be applied, although there is a list of factors to be taken into account.[150]

Has this worked? Possibly. The Ministry of Justice published figures of the number of criminal offences created in the year before and after the Coalition took power, purporting to show a drop of just over 60 per cent in the number of offences created.[151] But our research suggests that the Ministry has somewhat undercounted the number of offences it created in that year – they think it was 174; it was actually 608[152] – and as we have not examined the previous year ourselves, we cannot judge their claim.

But a reason to think that it might have made a difference is offered by this table.

Total number of offences created in England and Scotland, 1997–98 and 2010–11 (including both Westminster and Holyrood legislation)		
Geographical applicability	1997–98	2010–11
England	1,235	634
Scotland	1,238	1,223

In brief, twice as many criminal offences were created applying to Scotland in the first year of the Coalition government than were created applying to England. At first sight, these figures seem to imply that the Scottish Government has been much more willing to resort to the criminal law than

---

[150] Ministry of Justice, *Criminal Offences Gateway Guidance* (2011).

[151] Ministry of Justice, *New Criminal Offences: England and Wales 1st June 2009–31st May 2011* (2011).

[152] Actually, the time periods we have assessed are slightly different, and our figure of 608 corresponds to only 157 identified by the Ministry over the same time period. The difference exists in part because the Ministry appears to have missed some offences entirely, but also because of differences in approach to the question of how "a" criminal offence has been committed. These are discussed further in J Chalmers and F Leverick, "Tracking the creation of criminal offences" [2013] Crim LR 543, and space precludes a full explanation here, save to note that the Ministry's approach makes any count overly dependent on the vagaries of drafting technique, so that it cannot be assumed to have resulted in an accurate comparison between the two years.

its Westminster counterpart. However, much more work has to be done to understand the difference.

THE CONCEPT OF CRIMINALISATION

Criminalisation is a tricky concept, and means many different things. Nicola Lacey has observed that we should distinguish between "formal" criminalisation – the law on the books – and "substantive" criminalisation – the law in action.[153] We actually know a great deal about substantive criminalisation, through official statistics and empirical research, although as with most subjects we will never know as much as we might like to. The surprising thing is that we have next to no systematic knowledge about formal criminalisation. It is tempting to respond "so what": surely only substantive criminalisation matters? But aside from the fact that substantive criminalisation requires formal criminalisation as a prerequisite, the data we have on substantive criminalisation will never show us the full picture. Any data available always invites us to consider a different stage: when we look at prosecution figures, we should think of alternatives to prosecution; when we look at alternatives to prosecution we should think of informal interactions by police and regulators; when we look at informal actions we should think of the steps people take to comply with the criminal law without official intervention. Understanding formal criminalisation is no magic bullet: it is simply one element of a complex reality. And the "headline figures" I gave you earlier, while striking, are in many ways a trivial matter – since no-one knows how many criminal offences there ought to be, simply knowing how many there are would not actually tell us very much. It is the more detailed analysis – which could occupy many lectures – that is more enlightening and useful.

In a draft paper which Fiona Leverick and I circulated to colleagues in late 2012, we described this lack of knowledge as "embarrassing", which provoked an interesting response: a number of our commentators took issue with this. *They* were not embarrassed, although I think they thought someone ought to be. But it is embarrassing: those of us working in the field teach criminal law without really knowing what criminal law is. There is a temptation to focus on what we see as "fundamentals", treating all these new offences as noise to be disregarded. But that is to ignore the fact the fundamentals were only ever deductive principles discerned from the great body of the criminal law. The idea that we can disregard that ever greater body and cling to what we know best as the wreckage accumulates around us has little to commend it.

---

[153] See Lacey (n 22).

THE FUTURE

I said earlier that I had thirty years to answer any questions posed tonight, and I hope you will forgive me for taking advantage of at least some of that time. It has been fashionable in recent years to make claims of over-criminalisation. The restatements and reformulations of general principle which have flowed from those debates are hugely valuable, but demonstrate a huge gulf between theoretical accounts of the criminal law and the practical reality. Until we understand what the criminal law actually is, how governments resort to it, why they do so, and what alternative strategies might be advocated, our efforts to temper criminalisation are likely to be of limited success.

I do not offer that quite as a manifesto. In any case, we know what happens to manifesto commitments. And I hope that my contribution in this chair will not be confined to the issues I have discussed tonight. Nevertheless, I hope I have given you some hope that my tenure in the Chair might be of some value. And if not, wine has been provided for you to drown your sorrows.

Thank you for listening.

Learning from W D Lamont:
Towards a Science of Situated Judgement

Maksymilian Del Mar[*]

INTRODUCTION

There are some striking parallels between the late Ronald Dworkin and the now largely forgotten Glaswegian moral philosopher, W D Lamont (1901–82). Apart from numerous articles and a few short books on Scottish local history, Lamont published three important books: *The Principles of Moral Judgement* (1946); *The Value Judgement* (1955); and *Law and the Moral Order* (1981). In the first and the third of these, Lamont engages with the law. (He examines economics in the second.) In the first, Lamont argues that legal reasoning (in so far as it is understood to be a matter of applying rules) needs to be supplemented by moral principles[1] – obviously enough, this prefigures the early Dworkin. In the later book, Lamont characterises the law as part of the moral order, thereby again prefiguring Dworkin's picture (articulated in *Justice for Hedgehogs*, 2011) of law as a branch of the tree of morality.[2] There is no evidence that either read the other, but of course, Lamont's work appeared considerably before Dworkin's.[3]

This little introductory observation might help persuade that Lamont deserves more attention than he has hitherto been granted. References to his work appear here and there: John Rawls acknowledges him,[4] and Alexander Broadie lists him in the same breath as other "major representative[s] of Scottish philosophy up to the end of the 1950s", including Charles A

---

[*] I would like to thank the most helpful and hospitable staff at the University of Glasgow Archives.

[1] See *The Principles* (1946) pp 49–55, eg "It can be shown that the interpretation and application of existing law assumes that existing rules and principles are complementary, in the sense that the interpretation of rules always or generally requires looking beyond the rules to the principles which they are supposed to express" (p 54); and *The Value Judgement* (1955): "[L]aw in action demands something more than a system of rules to be applied in making a judicial decision. There must be a system of rules plus some principle or principles in the light of which the rules are 'appropriately' applied" (p 299).

[2] For an exposition of this shift in Dworkin, see J Waldron, "Jurisprudence for hedgehogs" (2013), available at *http://papers.ssrn.com/sol3/papers.cfm?abstract_id=2290309*.

[3] Of course, in other respects, Lamont's work is quite different from Dworkin's – if only at the methodological level, with Lamont proposing a scientific approach to morality.

[4] See J Rawls, "Justice as fairness" (1958) 67 The Philosophical Review 164 at 166, n 3.

Campbell, John Macmurray, and Donald MacKinnon.[5] As precious as they are, these are rare appearances for someone with Lamont's prodigious output.

For present purposes, a particularly noteworthy and indeed moving source is Neil MacCormick's obituary of Lamont.[6] MacCormick was taught by Lamont at the University of Glasgow, and listed him as one of his most important early influences.[7] MacCormick's obituary emphasises Lamont's last book, which he reminds us was published when Lamont was eighty-one years old. MacCormick elaborates as follows: "For those of us who were his students at Glasgow, it was and is a tangible reminder of his extraordinary vividness and lucidity as a teacher, and of the imaginative sympathy which he brought to his restatement of Kantian philosophy."[8] MacCormick was undoubtedly influenced by Lamont: both Kantianism, and attempts at softening it (eg via Adam Smith's sentimentalism), are consistent themes in MacCormick's work,[9] as is, more generally, an examination of the relationship between legal reasoning and practical reason. In turn, Lamont acknowledged MacCormick's assistance, saying, in the "Acknowledgements" to *Law and the Moral Order*, that MacCormick and Richard Tur (at the time, a lecturer in jurisprudence at the University of Glasgow) had "both read the whole script in two successive drafts and advised on general presentation and inclusion of legal material".[10] And Lamont then added: "Indeed, it might with some justification be said that this is about as near to being a joint work as it could be while remaining under the name of a single author." The Lamont archives at the University of Glasgow reveal that MacCormick and Tur had provided Lamont with

---

[5] Broadie refers to Lamont as an "idealist", but does not elaborate further: see A Broadie, *A History of Scottish Philosophy* (2009) p 324.

[6] See N MacCormick, "Dr W D Lamont" *The Times*, 20 November 1982.

[7] See MacCormick in M E J Nielsen, *Legal Philosophy: 5 Questions* (2007) p 172. MacCormick cited Lamont as the inspiration for his exploration of the similarities between Lord Stair's *Institutions* (2nd edn, 1693) and John Locke's *Two Treatises of Civil Government* (1690) in "Law, obligation and consent: reflections on Stair and Locke" in *Legal Right and Social Democracy: Essays in Legal and Political Philosophy* (1982) ch 4. Further, in delivering the Stevenson Lecture in Citizenship at the University of Glasgow on 18 January 1994, MacCormick acknowledged that his ideas about "universality" and "self-realisation through autonomy" owed a "great debt" to Lamont: see N MacCormick, "What place for nationalism in the modern world?" in H L MacQueen (ed), *In Search of New Constitutions* (1994) p 95. It seems that this influence continued, if more intermittently and more personally, at a later stage in MacCormick's career, for Lamont's archives at the University of Glasgow contain a number of important letters from MacCormick to Lamont, including some in which MacCormick responds to Lamont's advice on the former's involvement in politics (Lamont advises against such involvement).

[8] MacCormick, "Dr W D Lamont" (n 6).

[9] See N MacCormick, "Adam Smith on law" (1981) 15 Valparaiso ULR 243, and *Practical Reason in Law and Morality* (2008).

[10] *Law and the Moral Order*, p x.

considerable feedback on an earlier draft – but, even so, Lamont was surely being (characteristically) over-generous and modest here: the book was definitely his own. According to MacCormick, it was this same trait of character that was on display in Lamont never telling his students that prior to returning to Glasgow to lecture philosophy (as a senior lecturer and then reader), he had been offered, while lecturing in Cairo in 1946, the Chair of Moral Philosophy at Glasgow.[11]

Lamont's relations with the Law School at Glasgow were not, however, confined to discussions with and feedback from its members – Tur, for the 1981 book, and Harold M'Intosh (then lecturer in jurisprudence) and John Boyd (then Professor of Mercantile Law) for the 1946 book. Lamont also read and drew on their scholarship, in particular, Gloag and Henderson's *Introduction to the Law of Scotland* (various editions). In doing so, Lamont was at once in the minority of contemporary moral philosophers to engage with law and legal scholarship, and at the same time, part of a tradition of Scottish moral philosophy from the eighteenth century, during which Glaswegian professors of moral philosophy, and in particular Gershom Carmichael (Professor of Moral Philosophy from 1727 to 1729), Francis Hutcheson (1729 to 1746), and then Adam Smith (1752 to 1764) also engaged with and contributed significantly to jurisprudence.[12]

Lamont drew on law and legal scholarship on the back of a particular methodological commitment, ie a vision for moral science, which was perpetually on the lookout for evidence of the practice of (moral) judgement (as noted above, Lamont also drew on economics). As "scientific" as he was, Lamont did sometimes have to work under extraordinary limitations: *The Principles of Moral Judgement* was published in 1946, and, having served in the Clyde River Patrol and as a naval intelligence liaison officer from 1939 to 1942, Lamont spent the remaining years of the war as Professor of Philosophy at Cairo University (1942–46). Whilst in Cairo, Lamont had limited access to common law legal materials – indeed, he had brought with him just the one volume of the *All England Law Reports* (1942, volume 1). Accordingly, all of the examples of case law that Lamont analyses in the 1946 book come from this one volume of reports. A hard-nosed critic might argue that that was not particularly "scientific" – but a more sympathetic spirit would say that, in this case, the randomness of the data trumped its narrowness.

One final biographical comment: Lamont himself, though born in Canada (on Prince Edward Island), was a student at Glasgow, obtaining an MA in 1925. His subjects were: logic and history (first year); english,

---

[11] See MacCormick, "Dr W D Lamont".
[12] See D M Walker, *A History of the School of Law, The University of Glasgow* (1990) pp 27–28.

moral philosophy and geology (second year); and higher moral philosophy and political economy (in his third year). Having won the Edward Craig Medal, he went on to complete a DPhil (under John Macmurray) at Oxford, though he was clearly spending considerable time at Glasgow during that period, beginning teaching in Glasgow already in 1926 as an assistant in moral philosophy. Discounting the years he was in service and in Cairo (as well as the three years he was Principal of Makerere College, Uganda, from 1946 to 1949), Lamont taught moral philosophy at Glasgow for thirty-two years. MacCormick must not have been the only legal philosopher or lawyer influenced by Lamont and his gregarious blend of moral philosophy, law and the social sciences.[13]

The plan for this chapter is as follows: in the first part, I will offer a summary of Lamont's moral science, including both his methodology and the manner in which he engaged with the law; in the second part, I will put Lamont's contribution in perspective, and, in the process, sketch out what I propose to call a "science of situated judgement".

LAMONT'S MORAL SCIENCE

The very first line of Lamont's *The Principles of Moral Judgement* provides a clear indication of his methodological commitments: "The best short description of ethics", he writes, "is to say that it is one of the mental and social sciences, and that its specific field is the study of moral ideas."[14] To get at the ideas, we need to understand the "standards or principles upon which moral judgements are based".[15] As Lamont knows, however, we can approach the study of those standards or principles in two different ways: first, we can ask what standards or principles we ought to use; and, second, we can ask what standards or principles we actually do use. Lamont's chosen approach is the second, and here he comes up against a question which was to pursue him for his entire career: if moral philosophy was to be a science, and this science involved examining the judgements (which he also called "attitudes or states of mind"[16]) which people actually make, then where do we find evidence of these judgements? What is the data of this moral science? Where are its "observable facts"? Or, as Lamont put it at one point, "What evidence can we get to show what are the moral convictions of men [sic] in general?"[17]

---

[13] For a basic biographical sketch in support of the above, see *http://www.internationalstory.gla. ac.uk/person/?id=WH25194* (last accessed 18 February 2014).

[14] *Principles of Moral Judgement*, p 1.

[15] *Principles of Moral Judgement*, p 5.

[16] *Principles of Moral Judgement*, p 16.

[17] *Principles of Moral Judgement*, p 22.

Lamont identifies a number of possible sources, including introspection, a process of cross-examination of subjects faced with a particular moral dilemma (here Lamont draws on Jean Piaget's interviews of children), and – this being where his contribution is particularly valuable for present purposes – "systems of social institutions, laws, and customs which have had a more or less continuous development over a considerable period of time". Indeed, Lamont characterises this source as "the most reliable" of all the others.[18] Law, in particular, if favoured by Lamont for the following reason:[19]

> Systems of law are slowly built up through men's reactions to and judgements upon concrete situations in life; and, in so far as they can be said to offer a clue to moral ideas at all, it is obvious that they will be of special value as affording insight into the common moral consciousness.

Lamont makes this endorsement with a caveat: he asks us not to suppose "that the contents of the law are, in every particular case, a guide to the contents of the common moral consciousness", and to also keep in mind that "even when the legal and the moral coincide, we are in touch with only a part of morality, which extends over ground that law does not traverse".[20] Nevertheless, says Lamont, law and morality are "intersecting circles", with a great deal of overlapping content, and this, he conjectures, is because "moral ideas and legal codes exert a strong influence upon each other".[21] For Lamont, the impact of moral ideas is one of the most important engines of legal change, and this is so in the context of four sources of law: first, judge-made law, where judges' decisions are guided by certain principles of equity and justice; second, legislation, at least some of which is introduced as a result of changes in "the body of convictions, held by society and by groups within society, as to what is right from wrong" (the examples here include the abolition of slavery, reforms in the electoral system, and control of working hours and conditions); third, custom, which is "not indifferent to social opinion on questions of right or wrong"; and fourth, "the great mass of conventions and agreements which individuals voluntarily make with each other", which contain "rules of behaviour, of give and take" concerning what the parties "feel to be expedient, reasonable and just in the circumstances".[22] Lamont is perfectly aware that the law may often lag behind public conviction, and "therefore embody the conscience of the past rather than that of the present",[23] but as long as one is aware of this,

---

[18] *Principles of Moral Judgement*, p 27.
[19] *Principles of Moral Judgement*, p 27.
[20] *Principles of Moral Judgement*, p 28.
[21] *Principles of Moral Judgement*, p 28.
[22] *Principles of Moral Judgement*, p 30.
[23] *Principles of Moral Judgement*, p 31.

it ought not to be a methodological obstacle – further asserting that it is sometimes the other way round, namely that sometimes "the law, as it exists at any given time, will tend to form a considerable part of the content of the individual moral consciousness".[24]

Having set out the method, Lamont gets on with the business of describing the principles (of moral judgement) to be found within custom and law. He does so in four rich chapters (2 to 5) of the book. Of these, chapters 3 to 5 are the heart of the book, and also the most telling for present purposes, for it is in these chapters that, at least in part by drawing on the law, Lamont articulates what he calls "the morality of social justice".[25] Lamont divides this morality into three branches, corresponding to those three chapters: first, rights, duties and obligations (chapter 3); second, the idea of the good (chapter 4); and, third, the idea of justice (chapter 5). The basic thesis is that duties and obligations are consequent upon rights. Rights, in turn, protect the interests of persons. Understanding the idea of the good allows us to identify which interests are protected by rights (for not all interests are so protected) – and it thereby gives us the content of the duties and obligations we have. In addition to the content of duties and obligations, there is also what Lamont calls "the formal principle of obligation",[26] ie a principle that explains why we (on the whole) fulfil our duties and obligations – this principle being, in short, that of justice, which Lamont defines as having to do with "respect for persons as such, involving the notion of their liberty and equality as subjects-of-ends".[27]

For present purposes, what is more significant than the overall thesis is the manner in which Lamont draws on the law, ie the way in which he looks to the law, and what he understands[28] it to demand and protect, in order to shape his thesis about how moral judgement works. In other

---

[24] *Principles of Moral Judgement*, p 31. On this aspect of the relationship between law and morality, see T Honoré, "The dependence of morality on law" (1993) 13 OJLS 1, and J Finnis, "Law as Co-ordination" (1989) 2 Ratio Juris 97.

[25] To the extent that Lamont presents his analysis as a progression from customary morality (treated in Chapter 2), through to the morality of social justice (Chapters 2 to 5), and finally ideal morality (in Chapter 6), this is unpersuasive, and indeed jarring to a contemporary readership.

[26] *Principles of Moral Judgement*, p 132.

[27] *Principles of Moral Judgement*, p 132. At a later point in the book, he gives a more formal definition of justice: "The principle of Justice may, therefore, be defined as: The Equitable recognition of Liberty and Merit" (p 161). I do not discuss this principle of justice any further here as the data upon which Lamont bases his conclusions are not primarily legal (instead, he looks to Piaget's experiments, political speeches and parliamentary debates).

[28] To reiterate, in case it is not clear, my focus here is not on whether Lamont is accurate about the law or legal scholarship – it is on the manner in which he approaches the law and legal scholarship.

words, Lamont does not first articulate a general and abstract theory of, say, the good, or of justice – instead, he looks at particular instances of what the law demands or protects, and proceeds from there to articulate the workings of moral judgement. Indeed, the very need (in an account of moral judgement) for an idea of the good and the principle of justice arises from the way in which he understands the rights, duties and obligations enshrined in the law.

Lamont's starting point, then, is to understand rights, duties and obligations, and to do this he looks to the concrete example of promise-keeping. In keeping with his method, he looks to "the law of contract as setting out an actual system of rights and duties with regard to promise-keeping".[29] Happily, for present purposes, it is also here that Lamont draws most on Gloag and Henderson.[30]

Throughout his discussion of some of the basic principles of the law of contract, Lamont identifies the following golden thread: the protection of the interests of persons. This insight is the foundation of his account of moral judgement. He defines an interest as "[a]n object of conation", by which he means "an end, an object of desire or will, or something aimed at".[31] Not every interest is protected by the law, and so Lamont creates a special category of interests pursued that are neither commanded nor prohibited by law (which he calls "spheres of autonomy"). Once an interest is protected by the law, Lamont calls it a "right". To put it more schematically: a right is "[a] sphere of autonomy to which are annexed legal demands upon the behaviour of other conative beings".[32] Rights, in turn, are divided by Lamont (again, on the basis of his understanding of the law) into two kinds: first, real rights, which are spheres of autonomy "to which are annexed legal demands upon the world at large", and second, personal rights, which are spheres of autonomy "to which are annexed legal demands addressed to a specific person or persons".[33] The different duties and obligations that we have come from either real rights or personal rights that persons enjoy in particular legal systems.

Let us go back to Lamont's discussion of the principles of contract law. Lamont begins by observing that in many legal systems – including Scotland – there is a presumption that an obligation has been created whenever a promise is made.[34] He adds that the law takes no interest in

---

[29] *Principles of Moral Judgement*, p 63.
[30] The internal footnotes Lamont has to Gloag and Henderson are not reproduced here – but Lamont is certainly generous in his attribution.
[31] *Principles of Moral Judgement*, p 72.
[32] *Principles of Moral Judgement*, p 78.
[33] *Principles of Moral Judgement*, p 78.
[34] *Principles of Moral Judgement*, p 63.

"trivial disputes", and his way of explaining this is to say that a promise
to accompany a friend to a concert, as distinct from a promise of £100,
will not be entertained by the law, first, because "in the first case there is
not, while in the second case there is, some chance of assessing gain and
loss with respect to the interests of the 'promisee'", and second, because
"the former promise is so trivial that the taxpayer can hardly be expected
to take any profound interest in the dispute".[35] His general conclusion
from this is that "promissory obligations derive their significance from the
interests of the persons concerned".[36]

Lamont finds further support for the idea that duties and obligations
in this context are about the protection of interests in the principle that
for something to count as an enforceable promise what is important "is
not whether the statement is made in his [sic; the promisee's] presence
or directly to him, but whether I am aware that his interests are directly
affected and whether I intend him personally to count on my behaviour
in planning his own conduct with respect to those interests".[37] The
example Lamont gives here is that of the difference between a witness
to a signature to a contract (which precisely is not a promise) and that of
"a promise to give a subscription to a charitable society", which may be
enforceable "though not made to the society itself nor to anyone acting as
agent for it" – the crucial thing being that the promisor's assertion is one
that is "made in the knowledge that a particular person or group is likely
to act in anticipation of this behaviour, the promisor binding himself to
secure in this respect the interests of the promisee".[38]

Lamont goes on to note the various contexts in which the
"presumption" he identified that promises are to be honoured can be
rebutted, including circumstances which render contracts both void and
voidable. These include lack of legal capacity; defect in the form of the
agreement; consent being obtained irregularly (eg by fraud or duress);
and illegality. Here, again by looking at the law, he rejects the idea that
these circumstances can be explained on the basis that in them persons
are confronted by greater obligations than the obligation to keep the
promise. This is particularly clear in the case of lack of legal capacity,
for "the nullity of a child's agreement is not inferred from some other
'obligation' incumbent upon the child", but is instead based on the
assumption that the child "is incapable of wise judgement, and that he is

---

[35] *Principles of Moral Judgement*, p 64.
[36] *Principles of Moral Judgement*, p 64. This is perhaps a less persuasive analysis (and example) for
    one might question whether there is equivalence between the (difficulties in assessing) the
    interest of the promisee and the interest of the taxpayer.
[37] *Principles of Moral Judgement*, p 65.
[38] *Principles of Moral Judgement*, p 65.

to be protected from consenting to his own serious disadvantage and to the frustration of the interests of those closely related to him".[39] Even in the context of illegality, where the "greater obligations" characterisation may seem to have most bite, it is the protection of interests which really seems to be doing the work, as is clear from two specific rules, eg "the rule against illegal restraint of trade, and the rule that a man cannot, by testamentary deed, defeat the claims of his wife and children upon his estate".[40] Lamont's conclusion here, too, is that "when the breaking of a promise is permitted or commanded by the law, the governing principle seems to be the care for personal interests".[41]

Lamont finds the same principle underlying remedies for breach of contract. Thus, for instance, the determinant of whether specific performance or damages will be awarded "will depend, not only upon the actual situation arising from the breach, but also upon the effect of the remedy upon the major interests of all the persons concerned".[42] So even if the party in question wishes or desires specific performance, this will not be ordered "where it would involve the parties in close personal relationships and where it is felt that forced compliance would be worse than none"[43] – again, presumably because that would be against their interests. What the law demands or excuses, then, is explicable on the basis of its ultimate prioritisation of the interests of persons. From this Lamont concludes that, at least in so far as we draw on the law as our data for moral science, moral judgement is intimately connected to the protection of interests.

So far so good, but how can we identify which interests the law protects? Is there anything more that we can say about the kind of interests in question? As Lamont phrases it, "On what principle, then, do we select the kind of interest which we think ought to be protected?"[44] Here is where Lamont's analysis of the idea of the good comes to the fore. His analysis sticks to his method of looking at the practice of moral judgement, and thus at concrete examples of judgements where the idea of the good is appealed to. He finds that although *a* good is essentially an interest – he calls it in this context "an end ... some object or state of affairs desired by a conative subject" – *the* good, or "the conception of total good", refers to the overall coherence, or harmonious unity, of various different kinds of goods (or ends) that a person may have.[45] The different ends in question

---

[39] *Principles of Moral Judgement*, p 66.
[40] *Principles of Moral Judgement*, p 67.
[41] *Principles of Moral Judgement*, p 67.
[42] *Principles of Moral Judgement*, p 68.
[43] *Principles of Moral Judgement*, p 68.
[44] *Principles of Moral Judgement*, p 96.
[45] *Principles of Moral Judgement*, p 119.

are: neutral (which does not refer to a particular person, but rather, say, a state of affairs), self-regarding, other-regarding, and mixed ends (in the sense of both other- and self-regarding).

Lamont turns to and defends the idea of the good in coherence terms because he wants to avoid the extreme version of both objectivist and subjectivist accounts of the good, and especially the theory of intrinsic goodness. Interestingly, he finds the resources for dismissing intrinsic goodness, and defending the coherence view, in a legal judgement. Analysing the court's evaluation of the defendant's reasoning in *Crofters' Hand Woven Harris Tweed Company Ltd v Veitch*,[46] Lamont comes to the conclusion that "a genuine good-as-means [as opposed to good-as-end] judgement upon an act must regard that act (whether mistakenly or not) as necessary for the promotion of an ulterior interest; otherwise the injury is not being judged by the agent to be good-as-means but is being accepted as an end".[47] As Lamont characterises it, the issue in the case was whether the defendant and his associates acted with the end of injuring the plaintiff (which would have been unlawful) or whether they acted in that way as but a means to the pursuit of an otherwise lawful end. The crucial point for Lamont is that in the latter case – where one does something injurious to someone else, but only as a means in the pursuit of an otherwise lawful end – the end is not somehow "intrinsically good". This avoids the difficulty of saying that in order for there to be a judgement-as-means, one must assume that the end to which it is related is good in itself. Those who make this argument – that for any of our judgement-as-means to make sense, there must be intrinsically good ends – misunderstand the character of judgement-as-means judgements, for, as in the legal judgement above, the end in question need not be good in itself, but, for instance, simply lawful. Lamont's conclusion is that if an end – the means to which are pursued by a subject – is to be judged as good, it must be not because it is intrinsically good, but because of its relations with some other end or ends of the subject.[48] Or, as he puts it himself: "So far as I can see, the judgement that a thing is good as an end ... is made on whatever end is thought to fit into a pattern of ends of the same subject."[49] The legal judgement above did not so much yield this conclusion, as it made it possible – for it allowed Lamont to see and show that an end need not be good in itself in order to justify a particular means judgement.

[46] 1942 SC (HL) 1. The case is also reported in [1942] 1 All ER 142 – from the one volume of reports he had with him!
[47] *Principles of Moral Judgement*, p 111.
[48] See *Principles of Moral Judgement*, pp 112–13.
[49] *Principles of Moral Judgement*, p 113.

Readers may be forgiven for thinking that what Lamont is doing here is using the law to buttress theoretical intuitions Lamont already had before he encountered the data, eg that there is no such thing as intrinsic goodness, or that he is using the law to solve certain problems in moral philosophy (eg finding a middle path between extreme versions of objectivism and subjectivism in ethics). But this would be uncharitable: for all we know, Lamont's way of proceeding was to begin with careful reading and analysis of the data (including not only legal judgements, but also judgements made in political speeches, and in answers to questions from psychologists, etc), going on to draw from that analysis general characteristics of how moral judgement works, including the principles it is based on or implies. Of course, one could argue that the principles he takes moral judgement to be based on or imply are indeed principles that he would also normatively endorse (there is a Kantian ring to them which sounds louder in subsequent books), but it would be unfair to presume that he was but searching for evidence to support his intuitions, rather than forming his intuitions as he processed the data.

Sufficient flavour should now have been given of Lamont's use – in his first book, *The Principles of Moral Judgement* – of law as the data of the practice of moral judgement. Approximately ten years later, in his next book, *The Value Judgement* (1955), Lamont insisted on a strict division between two different kinds of judgement: the value judgement, and what he now called the moral judgement. The former involved the assertion that something is good or bad, or better or worse than something else, while the latter is expressed in terms such as "duty", "right", "obligation", "justice" and "imperative". Further, whereas evidence for the latter can be found in "the juridical order" (or law), evidence for the former is found in "the economic order".[50] At one point, Lamont notes that both economics and law ought to be engaged with by the moral philosopher interested in understanding judgement: "the theory of moral judgement will be most fruitfully pursued if we begin with the study of 'legal judgement', just as the theory of the value judgement is best approached through study of the analysis made by the economist".[51] As its title indicates, Lamont's second book focuses on analysing valuation within economics, and thus lies outside the scope of the present chapter.[52]

Lamont returns to the issue of the place of law in the study of moral judgement in his last book, *Law and the Moral Order* (1981). Although short (approximately 100 pages), the book is wide-ranging, including a theory of

---

[50] *The Value Judgement*, p xi.

[51] *The Value Judgement*, p 297.

[52] Lamont does include a short chapter in which he sketches a picture of moral judgement, but this does not cover new ground.

practical reason and an analysis of responsibility and punishment. Missing is a methodological chapter,[53] and the few methodologically explicit phrases that can be found speak less about the data needed for a moral science, and more about the need for moral philosophers to "keep in touch with real moral issues often forgotten amid the pleasures of academic debate".[54] Indeed, it is on this more practically-oriented footing that Lamont now calls for a "partnership between jurisprudence and ethics",[55] or, in the alternative, studying "jurisprudence in the service of ethics".[56]

Nevertheless, many of the features found in the first book also appear here. Intrinsic goodness is once again criticised. The focus is squarely on individuals and their "valuations" – as in his previous works, Lamont avoids (at least to begin with) the abstractions and idealisations of talk of the good and the just, and prefers to focus on practical moral attitudes of ordinary people. And he turns, once again, to the law for evidence of those practical moral attitudes, characterising "the positive law" as part the normative order, and indeed that part of it that has "been most systematically expounded".[57]

Perhaps the most striking difference between this last book and the first two is the explicit endorsement of, and extensive reliance on, Kant. For example, Lamont asserts that "there is nothing in the whole of modern ethical theory comparable to the *Groundwork* [*of the Metaphysics of Morals*] for its insight into the proper approach to the theory of morals, for its grasp of the fundamental principles of moral judgement, and for its insistence on their being rooted in our rational nature".[58] The basic intuition that the formal principle of obligation – the reason why we obey (eg comply with certain duties that derive from rights) – is respect for persons-as-ends was already there in *The Principles of Moral Judgement*. What appears with much greater emphasis in this book is the role of universality – as Lamont puts it now, "respect for the pure form of normative or juridical law has its source in respect for persons universally".[59]

Drawing so heavily on Kant may come as a surprise, given Lamont's methodological commitments to moral science. In fact, however, Lamont has an interesting approach to reading Kant. In a short but insightful appendix "On the Necessary Connexion between Law and Morality", Lamont addressed MacCormick's concerns – articulated in his *Legal Reasoning and*

---

[53] Previous drafts of the book, available in the University of Glasgow Archives, indicate that a methodology chapter was conceived, and some notes made towards it, but eventually not included.

[54] *Law and the Moral Order*, p xxviii.

[55] *Law and the Moral Order*, p xxviii.

[56] *Law and the Moral Order*, p 79.

[57] *Law and the Moral Order*, p xxviii.

[58] *Law and the Moral Order*, p 55.

[59] *Law and the Moral Order*, p 64.

Legal Theory (1978)[60] – that "Kant's ethics fails to 'make sense in the real world'".[61] Lamont could not disagree more. What Kant was really trying to do, says Lamont, is elucidate "the moral thinking of ordinary people".[62] The following passage is worth citing in full:[63]

> It [Kantian ethics] presents us with a theory of moral reasoning which certainly makes sense in the real world. The clue to the practical relevance is in his conception of a "maxim". Beginning with a down-to-earth desire for some end in certain circumstances and requiring certain means for its realisation, a person will make explicit the maxim he proposes to follow – I shall pursue this end x by these means y in these circumstances z. The moral question arises when he asks whether he could universalise the maxim, affirming the right or duty of every person everywhere to pursue such an end by such means in such circumstances. Could he will that in this instance all like cases should be treated alike? This is analogous to the issue placed before a judge. The moral agent (like the judge), having been bred in the ethos of a certain society, and now faced by an issue directly involved with day-to-day values, employs the same test of universalisability as that applied by the judge to any rule proposed to him as the basis of a decision. In short, the meaning of autonomy in Kantian ethics is not (as he so frequently suggests) the capacity of a rational will to take decisions uninfluenced by mundane values and traditional norms; it is the capacity to take responsibility for a final decision, those values and norms having been taken into account. This is the autonomy intrinsic to the judicial office; and that is why a work on "legal reasoning" [like MacCormick's 1978 book, which Lamont was earlier discussing] can be so illuminating for the student of ethics.

There is certainly a whiff of moralising in this passage, the implication being that the exercise of autonomy (in the sense of taking responsibility for the selective endorsement of rules one has inherited through one's culture or family) is a sign of the moral development of an individual – a topic that has been a favourite in contemporary moral philosophers following Kant.[64] But that is not what I would like to emphasise about this passage: what I find important and moving about it is Lamont's eagerness to read Kant as a philosopher of ordinary, everyday moral judgement, and, equally, his desire not to place the (moral) reasoning of judges on a pedestal. In this he was faithful to his original project, namely that of drawing on the law, especially in the form of the reasoning of judges as articulated in published decisions, as data for a science that attempts to understand the practice of moral judgement.

---

[60] MacCormick continued to wrestle with the place of Kant in his account of the moral and legal life, especially in his model of practical reason. He must not have been too persuaded by Lamont's interpretation, for in his last book, *Practical Reason in Law and Morality* (2008), he returned to the project of making Kant more realistic (via Adam Smith).

[61] *Law and the Moral Order*, p 113.

[62] *Law and the Moral Order*, p 113.

[63] *Law and the Moral Order*, p 113.

[64] One prominent example is the work of Christine Korsgaard.

TOWARDS A SCIENCE OF SITUATED JUDGEMENT

In this second part of the chapter, I propose drawing out some lessons that legal theorists may learn from Lamont's methodological commitments. In brief, my argument is as follows: legal theory ought to work more in tandem with moral science, and thus study the practice of judgement. In this respect, legal theory can learn a great deal from Lamont. But this study of the practice of judgement ought to be accompanied by a sociological sensibility, ie recognition that the practice of judgement is a situated one, conducted in particular social contexts, and thereby requiring legal theory to be cognisant of the different ways in which that social dimension can be conceptualised. In this respect, Lamont's legacy needs to be supplemented with greater awareness of the sociality of judgement: that our practices for evaluating each other need to be understood in the context of, for example, certain long-term relationships, or certain networks, groups or communities. What we conventionally (from the internal point of view of a legal official) think of as legal here can continue to play a role as a source of data for our science of situated judgement. But we should also broaden our enquiry to other forms of expression, studying the character of evaluative language (the standards we use to evaluate each other) in a range of different social arrangements, which will often include studying the changes and continuities in that language. This endorsement of a (historical) sociology of evaluation will inevitably mean being less insistent on identifying allegedly universal markers of "legality". But it will not mean moving away from the arguably normative concerns of legal theory, and in particular, the importance of limiting and channelling the exercise of power. My feeling is that this science of situated judgement will be particularly useful in new contexts of regulation, such as the transnational. Let me now briefly elaborate on this highly-condensed summary.

There are a number of impressive features of Lamont's work. An outstanding one is his openness to fields of scholarship and practice all too often ignored by moral philosophers, especially law and economics. To this it should be added that Lamont does not confine himself to those two fields, but also draws on material which is historical (orations), political (parliamentary debates) and psychological (interviews with children). This willingness to look in multiple sources for evidence of the way people evaluate (especially each other) is refreshing and useful. The second feature is related to this: the manner in which Lamont approaches these sources. He lets them set the parameters within which he does his analytical work. In other words, Lamont does not shy away from analysing, and especially rationally reconstructing the themes and patterns he sees emerging from these sources, but he does so with respect for what the sources indicate:

he is faithful to the distinctions drawn by the law, for example, and he is careful to pay attention to the precise language used, again in the law, but also in orations and parliamentary debates. Having said this – and this is the third feature – Lamont does know in a general sense what he is looking for: evidence of the practice of judgement. He knows that he is looking for the use of evaluative language, for evidence of the taking of an evaluative stance towards someone (including oneself) or some state of affairs. There is much to take from these methodological commitments.

Nevertheless, there are some drawbacks of Lamont's approach. The most obvious and serious is the lack of any theorisation about the social dimension of the practice of judgement. At first blush, this may seem like an unfair comment: after all, by looking to law and economics, and by explicitly stating that moral science ought to work in tandem with the social sciences, Lamont could be seen to be immersed in the sociality of judgement. What is missing, however, is any concentrated, reflective engagement with the different ways in which one might conceptualise the social contexts in which judgement occurs. Even when it comes to the law, Lamont focuses almost exclusively on the practice of judges, and he isolates and analyses one particular judgement. Further, in his last book, Lamont is explicitly individualist: the individual, he asserts, is the appropriate locus of judgement (or valuation, as he puts it in the last book). Where he does speak of "society", he demonstrates a rather monolithic idea of the concept – as if there was always one homogeneous community of shared norms and values. There are at least two specific problems with this lack of engagement with the social: first, we may be missing specific features of the practice of judgement in particular social contexts; and, second, we may be missing potentially valuable sources of the evidence of the practice of judgement, which we would locate if we framed our social context in different ways.

The drawbacks of the tendency – prevalent not only in moral philosophy, but also moral psychology – of focusing on an individual act of judgement, isolated from any social context as well as the life of the individual in question, are of course not new. Scholars as varied as G E M Anscombe, Iris Murdoch, Alasdair MacIntyre, Charles Taylor and Bernard Williams all criticised the narrowly individualist and decisionist character of much of moral philosophy. Murdoch, to give but one example, spoke of the need for understanding moral life as it continually goes on, and develops (or at least changes) over time, rather than focusing on the instance of a decision about what one ought to do.[65] More recently, in the context of moral psychology (as well as other naturalistic approaches to the study of morality), Gabriel Abend has criticised the almost exclusive

---

[65] See I Murdoch, *The Sovereignty of Good* (1970).

focus in the literature on "an individual's judgement about the rightness, appropriateness, or permissibility of an action made in response to a stimulus at a particular point in time".[66] Abend's argument is in fact critical not only of the individualism and decisionism of much of the literature, but also its focus on judgement – though this has to be understood to mean specifically the features of moral judgement found in the literature he criticises.[67] In other words, it is important for me to clarify that "judgement" as I use it in this chapter is not confined to isolated moments of decision, but to a wide range of the uses of evaluative language, as found in a wide range of sources. Thus, this includes the use of the language of being and character; talk of things we find valuable, worthy; objects of hope and admiration; talk of vice and virtue, and the use of such language in questions posed, thoughts articulated (eg in diaries, on blogs), and narratives (personal and cultural).[68]

Studying moral life social scientifically – in other words, practising the sociology of morality – is of course not new. There is, however, recent scholarship on what is being called "the new sociology of morality".[69] This is precisely an approach that is sensitive to different kinds of sociality, including, very importantly, the presence of fragmentation and conflict amongst evaluative languages. As Steven Hitlin and Stephen Vaisey say, in the old version, morality was "synonymous with conformity".[70] The new approach argues that "[m]orality belongs more to cross-cutting groups and less to society as a whole",[71] though one should add here that "groups" are by no means some kind of basic social element – one has, instead, various possible ways of conceptualising the social, including relationships (long

---

[66] G Abend, "What the science of morality doesn't say about morality" (2013) 43 Philosophy of the Social Sciences 157 at 158.

[67] These features are: "1. A moral judgement is made by and is an attribute of one individual. 2. It's made in response to a specific stimulus. 3. The stimulus is an imaginary situation and question about it. 4. The judgement is about an action (rather than, say, a person or state of affairs). 5. A moral judgement is a statement (indicative mood). 6. It is in essence an utterance or speech act (even if not in fact uttered). 7. It makes use of 'thin' ethical concepts only (okay, appropriate, permissible, acceptable, wrong, etc). 8. It's fixed, settled, verdict-like. 9. It's clear (not conceptually or semantically muddled, incoherent etc). 10. It's made a specific, precise, discrete point in time." (See Abend (n 66) at 162–63.)

[68] Abend (n 66) at 159. In other work, Abend also argues that it may be insufficient to rely on what people say – however wide the range of evaluative talk, and however rich one's range of sources where one looks for it. For Abend, some level of "participant observation" is "unavoidable" (see G Abend, "What's new and what's old about the new sociology of morality", in A Hitlin and S Vaisey (eds), Handbook of the Sociology of Morality (2010) p 581). Abend may be right in this, but to keep the project manageable, I suggest focusing on the use of evaluative language.

[69] S Hitlin and S Vaisey, "The New Sociology of Morality" (2013) 39 Annu Rev Sociol 51.

[70] Hitlin and Vaisey (n 69) at p 53.

[71] Hitlin and Vaisey (n 69) at p 53.

and short term), networks, communities, cultures, and much else besides. This new sociology of morality casts a wide net in terms of sources, looking at "narratives, identities, institutions, symbolic boundaries, and cognitive schemas",[72] and it is interested in "how people pursue long-run 'strategies of action' than in how they make choices one at a time".[73]

A particularly interesting contribution in this context is that of Lamont's namesake (no relation, as far as I am aware), Michèle Lamont. In a recent paper, she calls for a "comparative sociology of valuation and evaluation", with a focus on (e)valuation as social processes.[74] By (e)valuation, Lamont means both giving worth or value to something ("valuation") and "assessing how an entity attains a certain type of worth" ("evaluation").[75] The range and richness of the concepts Lamont draws on is impressive – for instance, she advises we study categorisation dynamics (where people determine in which group a certain entity, whether object or person, belongs) and legitimation (where, for instance, a certain text is said to be part of a canon).[76] Importantly, M Lamont also asks us to be sensitive to what she calls "heterarchies", or the "multidimensionality, or plurality of criteria/ grammars of valuation and evaluation".[77] In terms of the social dimension of these (e)valuation processes, Lamont says the following:

> What makes (e)valuation a social and cultural process is that establishing value generally requires (a) intersubjective agreement/disagreement on a matrix or a set of referents against which the entity (a good, a reputation, an artistic achievement, etc) is compared, (b) negotiation about the proper criteria and about who is a legitimate judge [often involving conflicts and power struggle], and (c) establishing value in a relational (or indexical) process involving distinguishing and comparing entities[.][78]

The sensitivity that Lamont shows here to both plurality of evaluative languages, as well as conflict and negotiation between them, including the struggle for power and domination, clearly makes her approach attractive for a legal theorist. Further, M Lamont's change in nomenclature – her characterisation of her approach as a sociology of (e)valuation, rather than a sociology of morality – is also, from the perspective of this chapter, to be preferred. To characterise something as "moral" is, after all, to place it on a certain pedestal, or to claim for it a certain level of allegiance (if not

---

[72] Hitlin and Vaisey (n 69) at p 54.
[73] Hitlin and Vaisey (n 69) at p 55.
[74] M Lamont, "Toward a comparative sociology of valuation and evaluation" (2012) 38 Annu Rev Sociol 201.
[75] See M Lamont (n 69) at 205.
[76] See M Lamont (n 69) at 206.
[77] See M Lamont (n 69) at 207.
[78] See M Lamont (n 69) at 205 (references omitted).

universality, or superiority as a standard) that may keep from view other softer, less demanding, less-status-seeking standards. In other words, as conceptualised here, studying the practice of situated judgement ought to include the full range of normative phenomena, from conventions thought of as largely arbitrary (but still with normative weight) to norms and values that are highly stable and used regularly to make judgements.

Happily, in the context of this chapter, this science of situated judgement would also echo the methods and ambition of the philosophers of the Scottish Enlightenment, and in particular Adam Smith, Adam Ferguson and John Millar, all of whom combined what modern and contemporary scholarship carved up into specialisations, namely sociology, morality, and jurisprudence. The recasting of Smith here is of special importance, seeing him not as a theorist of the liberal individualist tradition, but rather as an interactionist – someone who understood moral and legal ideas and institutions to be the outcome of the dynamics and needs of social interaction.[79] An important feature of these scholars was attention to and interest in history, and this diachronic dimension would also be important – indeed, I see it as being part of the activity of conceptualising the social, which would necessarily include interaction over time. In other words, studying the situated practice of judgement will necessitate paying attention to change and continuity in the use of evaluative language in a variety of different social relationships/networks/communities (etc).

What, it might be asked, does this all have to do with law? Where is the legal in this grand-sounding science of situated judgement? Proceeding in the way suggested above – namely identifying, and tracking changes and continuities, in the use of evaluative language in a range of different social contexts – means that one does not truncate the enquiry before it has begun. Truncating the enquiry would occur if one was to begin – as legal theorists are wont to do – with identifying and settling on criteria of legality, most usually from the perspective of the legal profession (reconstructing the alleged internal point of view of the legal official), and going on from there to focus exclusively on the allegedly unique legal materials identified by those criteria. By casting the net widely, as suggested above, one can include in one's view a range of evaluative language, including that which appeals to terms and concepts recognised by the profession. One can then, for example, compare *when* that professionally-

---

[79] For readings of Smith sympathetic to this position, see, eg, Richard Gunn, "From Smithian sympathy to Hegelian recognition" (2009), available at *http://richard-gunn.com/pdf/3_smithian_sympathy.pdf*; Richard Gunn, "Scottish political theory: from natural law to common sense" (2010) available at *http://richard-gunn.com/pdf/4_scottish_pol_theory.pdf*; and Vivienne Brown, "The dialogic experience of conscience: Adam Smith and the voices of stoicism" (1993) 26(2) *Eighteenth-Century Studies* 233.

recognised legal language is used – when it is appealed to rather than, say, terms and concepts not recognised as appropriate grounds of judgement in courts and tribunals (talk of virtues and vices, for example, or moral fables, or social customs, and so on). Thus, the legal approached in this sense of the professional's internal point of view can remain, but does not ground or dominate the research. Instead, one examines the purposes to which such language is put – eg does it come to be used when other avenues have been exhausted, when the potential for agreement seems bleak and a decision is required?

But the legal can come into the picture in another way. One can think of the legal as that which constrains and channels power. First, it divides it (separating certain powers from each other), and requires its exercise to be made on the basis of, and reviewable by virtue of, certain publicly accessible standards articulated in advance; and second, it directs it, by guiding its exercise (whether it be legislative or adjudicative in character) with certain more or less specific values (such as equality and liberty, or reasonable care and diligence). In light of this, one can, through the science of situated judgement, pick up on the dynamics of power in a more comprehensive and disciplined way. One can, in short, track the use of evaluative language in a variety of different social contexts where the exercise of power is at stake: when someone is trying to gain the legitimacy to issue norms or decisions, and when someone else is responding to that, criticising it, undermining it or supporting it.

Although providing a specific example of this science of situated judgement is outside the scope of this chapter, I would surmise that a promising context for it would be transnational regulation and governance. In this context, beginning by pinning down criteria of legality would be distinctly unhelpful: there are, for a start, few officials, at least not in the traditional state-centric sense, eg there is no "transnational bar", there are few if any examples of established and recognising transnational norm-issuing bodies, etc. By contrast, there is frequent and dense use of evaluative language, by a wide range of social actors in a wide range of different social relationships, many of whom are clamouring to have their standards become dominant. Transnational transactions conducted via, for instance, eBay and other similar private companies, are informed by the use of evaluative language in the form of reputation-tracking of sellers, seller feedback, standards issued by eBay itself, standards issued by a range of other bodies, discussion on various social media, blog posts on what is appropriate and not from both the perspective of the buyer and the seller in such transactions, and so on. Studying the change and continuity in the use of evaluative language amongst the persons involved in these commercial networks would help identify sites of agreement and disagreement on the standards to be used in evaluating behaviour in this context. Tracing the origin of those particularly stable standards would also help identify those exercising power. This attention to detail would no doubt be a slow and laborious process, but it would also help reveal what is at stake in this context in a way that immediate focus on what is or ought to count as legal arguably would not. Of course, I make these comments tentatively, for any conclusions to this effect would require such a study to be carried out and speak for itself.

CONCLUSION

I have tried in this chapter to articulate the methodological commitments to be found in the work of W D Lamont, and especially to offer a taste of the way in which he approached the law. He did so as data for what he thought of as moral science or, differently, as the science of moral judgement. Following the exposition, as brief as it was, of Lamont's approach, I attempted to reconstruct what I took to be its most appealing attributes and, together with some additional features, offered a sketch of a science of situated judgement. In doing so, I have no doubt made my proposal vulnerable to the charge of hopeless ambition. My defence is that ambition is precisely what is often missing from today's legal theory. It takes ambition to look for ways in which law is part of the evaluative fabric of social life. Lamont approached this project from a different angle – as a moral philosopher, he sought to include the law within his ambit of the study of moral judgement. As legal theorists, we can learn from him – and from the work of the scholars of the Scottish Enlightenment – and broaden out our enquiry, away from criteria that allegedly protect "the law" as the object of our scholarship, and return us to the vital task of understanding how, when, and why we evaluate each other, with what impact on the quality of social interaction.

Muir v Glasgow Corporation: The Case of the Dropped Urn

William W McBryde

THE TRILOGY

It used to be said that the modern law of negligence, in the United Kingdom and the Empire, was established by a trilogy of Scottish cases decided by the House of Lords in just over a decade: *Donoghue v Stevenson;*[1] *Bourhill v Young;*[2] and *Muir v Glasgow Corporation.*[3] Otherwise known as the case of the snail in the bottle, the case of the pregnant fishwife, and, somewhat misleadingly, as the case of the children's tea party (which ignores the fact that at least some of the children who were injured drank milk not tea). *Donoghue v Stevenson* is known throughout the English-speaking legal world. *Bourhill v Young* remains the start of any discussion of liability for nervous shock. The background to both these cases, including the people involved, has received analysis.[4] But *Muir v Glasgow Corporation*, apart from some references to Lord Macmillan on reasonable care, tends to be in the shadow of its more famous predecessors. Yet any search of recent cases in the Court of Session on negligence will demonstrate that the speech of Lord Macmillan on reasonable foreseeability is one of the most often referred to *dicta*. Outside the lecture theatre and the exam hall, cases with debatable or uncertain issues on the existence of duty of care or liability for nervous shock are unusual. Reasonable foreseeability arises as a potentially live issue in most common law negligence cases. *Muir v Glasgow Corporation* does encapsulate important parts of the law on negligence. Like many good cases it involved a story of a place, of people, some mystery and a portion of human misery.

---

[1] 1932 SC (HL) 31.
[2] 1942 SC (HL) 78.
[3] 1943 SC (HL) 3.
[4] W W McBryde, "*Donoghue v Stevenson*: the story of the 'snail in the bottle' case" in A J Gamble (ed), *Obligations in Context: Essays in Honour of Professor D M Walker* (1990) p 13; reprinted with minor revision in P T Burns and S J Lyons (eds), *Donoghue v Stevenson and the Modern Law of Negligence, The Paisley Papers* (1991) p 25; E Reid, "The snail in the ginger beer float, *Donoghue v Stevenson*" in J P Grant and E E Sutherland (eds), *Scots Law Tales* (2010) p 83; W W McBryde, "*Bourhill v Young*: the case of the pregnant fishwife" in D L Carey Miller and D W Meyers (eds), *Comparative and Historical Essays in Scots Law: A Tribute to Professor Sir Thomas Smith QC* (1992) p 66.

THE FACTS

King's Park

On the south side of Glasgow there is a large public park now known as King's Park with a history traceable to a royal confirmation from Robert II dated 1373.[5] A new mansion was built in the park in 1806 and wings were added in 1823 when the area was owned by the Gordon family who acquired their wealth in the West Indies trade and after whom Gordon Street beside Central Station is named.[6] The mansion house and its policies were acquired by the builder John Mactaggart in 1930 who then gifted them to Glasgow Corporation. At that time the park was named King's Park, the name also given to the surrounding suburb, but the mansion house retained its original name of Aikenhead House.

The Corporation were grateful for this magnificent gift and decided to recondition the house as a museum and a tea room.[7] There was a formal opening on 1 May 1936. The contents of the museum included period dresses from about 1700 to the middle of the Victorian era, sixteenth- and seventeenth-century furniture lent by Sir William Burrell, and portraits from Mary Queen of Scots to Queen Victoria.[8] The south wing of the house was converted into a kitchen and two tea rooms. Access to those areas was from outside up steps (which, or a version of which, still exist), through doors and along a narrow corridor beside a counter and showcase which formed a small shop. Plans with measurements were part of the papers in the subsequent litigation. At that time it seems that a former access to this area from the museum had been blocked off.

The house is in a dip in the park. The ground rises to the west and a few hundred yards from the house where there is now a swing park there was a shelter[9] with a boiler to provide hot water which the Corporation sold at 2d per gallon, a practice which it adopted in other parks. An aerial photograph of the shelter and the house, showing the path

---

[5] R Dell, "King's Park's roots stretch 600 years" in *Fifty Years of King's Park 1925–1975*, Mitchell Library, Glasgow AGN 826.

[6] H MacIntosh, *Origin and History of Glasgow Street Names* (1902).

[7] J Eggleton, "A commentary" in *Glasgow's Art Galleries and Museums* (1936) p 53: Mitchell Library, DTC.7.16.

[8] Eggleton (n 7) p 55.

[9] Shown on the Ordnance Survey map of March 1953: 1:1250; plan NS 5960 SE. It seems that the area was, or was close to, a pheasantry in 1913: OS map 1913: 1:2500: Lanarkshire Sheet x.7. The 1953 map also shows the hutted camp which was part of the wartime activity. There was another shelter in the park but James Taylor in evidence referred to a shelter "at the top of the hill" and the urn being carried "down to the bottom of the hill". Inspection of the ground shows that the larger shelter to the SW of the mansion house, which had a water supply (a drinking fountain is marked on the map), is most likely the shelter being referred to and where the play park now is.

between them and the trees, taken by the RAF in 1950 is available on the internet.[10] The park is now full of mature trees and some relatively recent planting.

The picnics

The fifteenth of June 1940 was a wet Saturday afternoon in Glasgow: a very wet day. It was also a traumatic day in the rest of Europe. It was the day German troops occupied Paris and Russia invaded Lithuania. France was to surrender a week later. Malta was being bombed. It was nearly a year before the Luftwaffe would blitz Clydebank but thoughts of war would not have been far from people's minds. Ten days previously the *Daily Record*[11] had reported on the escape from Dunkirk and on Churchill's famous speeches, "We shall never surrender" and "We shall fight them on the beaches". Soon the Battle of Britain was to commence. Because it was wartime those planning picnics in a park would not have known it was going to rain. They could have scoured the pages of the *Glasgow Herald* or Friday's *Evening Times* without finding a weather forecast. During the war the Met Office ceased publication of weather forecasts to prevent these assisting the enemy. But without the rain the accident would not have happened.

A picnic was a respite from stories of conflict for the adults and children of the West End Municipal Tenants' Association of Rutherglen who in their hundreds were having their annual outing. There were other parties. For the children of Milton Free Church, in Rose Street on the north side of Glasgow, a Sunday school picnic was a chance to escape the thoughts of an uncertain future and to do something normal – rain or no rain. From the church thirty or forty adults and children gathered in King's Park for an open-air picnic. They had their cakes with them. They were prepared with their own urn to make tea using the boiling water provided by Glasgow Corporation in the park. But there was a problem apart from the rain. The Free Church party were not there early enough. When they arrived the shelter in the park was already occupied mainly by the West End Tenants' Association from Rutherglen. Some 900 had come from Rutherglen, adults and children. The shelter only held about 100. The rest of the Rutherglen party took what respite from the rain they could under the large trees in the park.[12]

---

[10] On the website of the Royal Commission on the Ancient and Historical Monuments of Scotland: scanned image 1024377: *http://www.scotlandsplaces.gov.uk/recordrcahms/172598/glasgow-325-carmunnock-road-kings-park-aikenhead-house-walled-garden/rcahms?item=1024377#carousel.*

[11] Wednesday, 5 June 1940.

[12] The House of Lords Record Office, London, have the notes of the evidence and other papers which are an important source for the details of the case: HL/PO/JU/4/3.

The Sunday school teachers had a dilemma. They were faced with the problem of everyone including children getting wet, the food also. The mansion house did have two tea rooms but there was a further difficulty. In the tea room you were not allowed to eat your own food and drink your own drink. The manageress of the tearoom, Mrs Emily Alexander, who was in her late fifties, was, however, a kind soul. For the first, and probably only, time she invented a charge for the use by the church party of the tea rooms and gave permission for them to carry in their own tea and cakes. Instead of using the kitchen attached to the tea rooms the hot water for the tea was to be carried from the shelter in the park. Why the kitchens were not used is not known but, perhaps, this was going a step too far without a further charge. The hot water had to be carried in the urn which the church had brought with them. Many a modern law student may have pondered the litigation which followed without, perhaps, contemplating that at this time some children on a picnic drank tea. The Rutherglen party drank milk; 900 half bottles of milk had been delivered to the park from East Kilbride Dairy Farms. If the church had followed that approach, or if the logistics of carrying boiling water for a distance into a building had been thought through, the accident would not have happened.

The distance from the shelter, where the boiling water was supplied, to the tea rooms in the mansion house was several hundred yards. The urn to be carried was not large but its shape was almost as tall as it was wide: 16 inches high and 18 inches wide. Nor was it completely filled with boiling water or tea, at most 6 gallons or, in modern measure, just over 27 litres. That was over a pint of tea for each adult and child, so plenty to drink. The movement of the fluid in the container potentially made it awkward to handle. At least from the shelter to the mansion house it was a downhill journey. You can even now walk the route. But the entrance to the tea rooms had a further problem. There were steps to climb, corners to turn, and a corridor to pass through and the corridor was narrow – about 3 feet 3 inches at its far end. What was worse was that the corridor also functioned as part of a shop selling ice cream and sweeties. On a rainy day this was filled with excited children, pushing and shoving to get to the counter, and not all waiting for their turn.

The urn was filled with tea in the shelter and carried down the slope to the mansion house with a boy carrying the cakes. At first the church officer George McDonald and a boy named Murray carried the urn and James Taylor, aged about sixteen, carried the food. Then Murray asked for a change and Taylor took over carrying the urn by the front handle, with the church officer holding the rear handle. The party entered the corridor forming part of the shop following Murray, who had been shown the way. At the end of the corridor, while about to leave the shop area, Mr McDonald let go of the urn. Why we do not know. At the subsequent proof he was not called to give evidence. Nor did anyone appear to witness him dropping the urn. James Taylor said in evidence that Mr McDonald stated that the children bumped his arm. The consequences of the urn dropping to the ground were, however, serious.

The lid of the urn came off and the hot fluid splattered onto at least six children in the shop. These children all had addresses in Rutherglen or Cambuslang. Some of them[13] were probably part of the Rutherglen Tenants' Association party, despite the impression sometimes given that it was the Free Church Sunday school party which was injured. Eleanor Muir's family story was that she and her sister were part of a Sunday school outing from the West Parish Church, Rutherglen which was, and is, a Church of Scotland church.[14] All this had the consequence, as Lord Carmont later pointed out,[15] that the bearers of the urn had no authority to clear the shop of children.[16]

Six children, all girls, were injured. Eleanor Muir had come from her new council house[17] at Glencairn Drive, Rutherglen, along with her sister Agnes (always known as "Nan"). Eleanor was the youngest of a family of five children and two adults living in this four-bedroomed house with its neat garden.[18] Martha Chalmers lived in similar property in Gilmour Crescent which is a very short walk from Glencairn Drive. Charlotte Toner and Theresa Haughey were neighbours in Toryglen Road, just round the corner from Gilmour Crescent. The addresses are close to each other but it does not follow that all the children knew each other. Eleanor Muir does not now remember any of them except, of course, her sister. May Yardley lived in the neighbouring area of Cambuslang.

---

[13] In evidence William Muir, Agnes Muir, Hannah Chalmers, George Yardley and Theresa Haughey (who said she was with her neighbour Charlotte Toner) referred to "the outing"; Charlotte Toner to the "West End Tenants' Association outing" and Hugh Haughey to the "West End Tenants' Association picnic". Given the addresses in council houses at the West End of Rutherglen the balance of probabilities is against them being part of a Free Church party coming from the other side of the river Clyde. May Yardley lived in Cambuslang and may not have been part of any of the groups mentioned.

[14] The church formed a union with Wardlawhill Church in 2007: Rutherglen West and Wardlawhill Parish Church of Scotland: Report and Financial Statements for the Year Ended 31 December 2007, p 5: *http://www.westandwardlawhill.org/pdf/2007finrep.pdf*.

[15] 1942 SC 126 at 137.

[16] Although in the House of Lords Lord Thankerton thought this point was immaterial: 1943 SC (HL) 3 at 9.

[17] The area was developed for council housing around 1936. The Rutherglen Heritage Centre in Rutherglen Library adjacent to the Town Hall has maps showing the development of the area. The 1940–41 valuation rolls for Rutherglen Burgh show details of the tenants: NAS, VR76/39.

[18] Apart from his family her father William Muir's main interests were gardening and football.

When the urn was dropped children screamed and rushed to the door pushing Agnes Muir with them. There was panic. Most of the injuries were scalds to legs and feet. But four-and-three-quarter-year-old Eleanor Muir was the most seriously affected. She suffered burns to her buttock, abdomen, both legs and her left arm. She spent six weeks in hospital and it was alleged that at the early stage there was a danger of her losing her life. She spent a further two weeks in a convalescent home. She was left with large, permanent scars and some effect on her behaviour. The other children had burns to legs and feet and shock and were treated as outpatients at hospital or by their GPs.

THE PROCEEDINGS

The claims

Children aged from four to thirteen went on a picnic and came back scalded – in one case with injuries which might have lifelong traces. Any accident to children produces very human responses. Amongst these is the desire to claim compensation for the injuries. No one suggested that the children had been at fault.

At some stage the parents of the children contacted the one solicitor and claims were intimated to the Corporation of Glasgow. The minutes of the Parks Committee of the Corporation[19] record that on 7 August 1940 Mr John Carty,[20] solicitor, 462 Paisley Road, Glasgow, intimated claims against the Corporation by (1) William Muir on behalf of his two daughters, Eleanor and Agnes; (2) John Toner on behalf of his daughter, Charlotte; (3) Hugh Haughie (in the court papers spelt "Haughey") on behalf of his daughter Theresa; and (4) James Chalmers on behalf of his daughter "Mattie" (later called "Martha"). These were all the Rutherglen group. May Yardley from Cambuslang is not mentioned at this stage.

The Parks Committee heard a report from the Director of Parks and agreed that liability should be repudiated. The committee minutes for the period show many other similar claims intimated for Glasgow parks, for example, when children fell off swings or stepped on glass. The "claims culture" is not a feature only of the late stages of the twentieth century. The Parks Department were used to claims and to rejecting them. On this occasion, however, the result was litigation.

---

[19] Minutes of the Corporation of Glasgow, May 1940 to November 1940, print no 19, p 1981.

[20] Admitted as a solicitor in 1936 having served a three-year apprenticeship in Glasgow. He graduated BL from Glasgow University in 1936. See NAS, CS 46/1936/9/41. He died aged fifty-two of tuberculosis and heart disease while in Culduthel Hospital, Inverness, on 6 October 1962. The hospital had a history as a TB sanitorium. It closed in 1989. The building is now private flats.

A solicitor, Herbert Macpherson, 14 Stafford Street, Edinburgh, and counsel were instructed, and a summons drafted and signeted on 10 December 1940, a commendably short period after the accident. By this time May Yardley was added to the claimants. The summons was posted that evening at Hope Street Post Office, Edinburgh, to the Corporation at the City Chambers in Glasgow. Thus this famous case commenced.[21] On 13 December the Corporation instructed Simpson & Marwick WS who sought medical reports from Dr Forrest of the Victoria Infirmary on four of the children (there being no averments that the other two attended the Infirmary). Defences were lodged.

Aikenhead House

While the lawyers were communicating something else was happening in King's Park. On 5 July 1940 the town clerk intimated to the Parks Committee that the military authorities had requisitioned Aikenhead House for military purposes.[22] This requisition continued throughout the war until, in 1946, the War Department intimated it was willing to de-requisition the house with the exception of the area forming the site of the guns operation room.[23] There followed various problems with the house and adjacent wartime buildings, including squatters, and demolition of wartime huts, although by 1948 the Corporation were discussing de-requisition compensation. The house was not released from the War Department's control until the 1950s but adjacent buildings were continued in use for civil defence purposes. The house was later used as a store for the Burrell Collection and in the early 1970s it had a conservation laboratory.[24] Subsequently the house was restored and converted into fourteen private luxury flats, its present use. Being a listed building the exterior was preserved. The restored building was opened on 7 March 1986. This was possibly the first time the Council had allowed part of its parks to be used for private housing.

There were minor effects of the requisition on the subsequent litigation. The tea rooms disappeared only a few weeks after the accident, never to return. When the pursuers' engineer, Thomas Lucas, inspected the site he was able to see the marks on the floor where the shop counter had been, although he was unable to access the whole house. Mrs Alexander had been

---

[21] NAS, *William Muir & Othrs v The Corp of the City of Glasgow* CS 46/1944/1/15. This is confusingly catalogued as a decree of absolvitor but it is the whole of the original process. The error may explain why some years ago the author was informed in writing that the process did not exist in the National Records.

[22] Minutes of the Corp of Glasgow, May 1940 to November 1940, print no 18, p 1869.

[23] Minutes of the Corp of Glasgow, Parks Committee, 3 April 1946, print no 12, p 950.

[24] The Mitchell Library, Glasgow, has an incomplete collection of the annual reports of Glasgow Art Galleries and Museums which gives some of the history as do the minutes of various committees of Glasgow Corporation.

manageress of the tea rooms and shops since 1936 when the Corporation opened the building but, although she still maintained that was her job when she gave evidence in May 1941, this may not have been fully accurate.

The pleadings

The seeds of future problems arose the moment that summons was posted. There were six pursuers – three fathers as tutors of girls aged under twelve and three girls, aged twelve or more, with the consent of their fathers as curators. Eleanor Muir had injuries which might have justified a Court of Session action. The sum claimed for her was £1,000. But the sum sued for the other children was £75 each. The potential danger in this was hinted when May Yardley, aged seven, gave evidence. She said her feet were burned. She did not feel sore. She was not taken away in the ambulance. She had bandages on her feet for two weeks. Her feet did not hurt her. She told the court, no doubt proudly, that she did not cry. In cross-examination there was only one question "Was it just a wee burn you got?" Her answer was "Yes". Litigating can create liability for legal expenses (jointly and severally with others) if the case is lost. Litigating in the Court of Session with the potential for a proof, and appeals, involves risk. Was the injury worth that risk? Should all those families have been advised to sue along with the Muirs? That difficult issue is discussed later.

More critically did the pursuers have the correct defender? The Corporation owned and managed the park with its tea rooms. The accident happened on their property. They employed Mrs Emily Alexander, the tea room and shop manageress. The Corporation also had money. Liability, however, depended on the fault of the Corporation. The pleadings claimed that Mrs Alexander had been at fault.

Glasgow Corporation managed its parks through its employees and agents. In this case there was a park attendant although he was given the rather grand title of curator. There was Mrs Alexander. But there would have been others: the waitress who was helping Mrs Alexander (which suggests that the tea rooms were open for normal business); the cleaner who may have left a slippery corridor; the maintenance engineer who, it could be speculated, may not have spotted a protruding floor board or a hole in the floor. There might also have been a question as to whether the narrow entrance to the tea rooms was a safe design. Who was negligent and what did the negligence consist of? That was the problem for the pursuers. In our system of written pleadings the court is restricted to the fault averred by the pursuers. It would be unfair to the defenders if they were to be surprised by another ground of liability of which they had not had notice. A reparation action is not a public enquiry into the truth of what happened.

The ground of fault alleged was that Mrs Alexander failed to exercise reasonable care for the safety of the children. In particular it was her duty "not to allow persons to enter the shop carrying the said urn of hot tea and to prohibit them from doing so while the shop was crowded with children as it was".[25] There were subsequent averments that there should have been steps to protect the children by clearing a space. The case was based solely on the Corporation's vicarious liability for their servants which meant Mrs Alexander, and on her failure to clear the passage. So the pursuers restricted their case to one very particular ground of alleged fault by one individual. This is the type of case which defenders can find relatively easy to attack in the sense that if they show that the accident could have been caused by some other factor – and they have several to choose from – the pursuers may fail in their onus of proving their averments on the balance of probabilities.

Because Mrs Alexander gave evidence in the proof we have some idea of what she thought and some things can be imagined. She was caring – she worried about the problem that the Sunday school party faced in the rain. She was conscientious. She was inventive. She produced a unique solution to a problem. She was bold. She changed the rules. But she did not know when the tea urn was to arrive. She had her back to it getting ice cream from the fridge when the urn arrived. The children were her customers, but she was not in charge of them. She had no authority over either the Free Church party or the Rutherglen party. She might reasonably have expected that those who were in charge would control the children or, at least, try to. Above all, she was not responsible for the transport of the urn from one place to another. Why did the church people not make sure the route was safe? Without a detailed analysis of the law it may be obvious that a case based solely on her fault had some problems.

The obvious causes of the accident were (1) the decision by the church officer, Mr McDonald, to proceed through a crowd of excited children with an urn two-thirds full of liquid hot enough to scald; and (2) his failure to keep a grip on the handle and to let the urn fall. But neither he nor the Free Church were parties to the action. Nor indeed did he give evidence which raises other questions. Why did he let the urn fall? We do not know. The absence of evidence of the cause became a serious obstacle for the pursuers.

The procedure roll

The case proceeded in the normal way with the record being closed on 5 February 1941. It went to a procedure roll hearing before Lord Robertson on 21 February. The defenders, as was usual, had taken a plea to the relevancy

---

[25] Closed Record, Cond 3 (NAS, CS 46/1944/1/15).

of the pursuers' averments. Their aim would have been to have had either dismissal or a proof before answer. Above all to avoid the case proceeding to a proof, which would have meant a civil jury trial with a potential for sympathy for injured and innocent children claiming from a local authority.

Lord Robertson issued his opinion on 7 March 1941.[26] He thought that the pursuers' averments had to be considered on the basis that there was no claim that the spilling of the tea was due to the negligence of the two persons carrying the urn. He had difficulty with saying that the pursuers' averments were specific enough on whether there had been a breach of duty, weighing up the element of danger, the likelihood of an accident and its possible consequences. He was much concerned with the seriousness of the danger and the averments limited to the size of the urn and the nature of its contents. On the other hand he thought that the proper course was a proof before answer.

The proof before answer

The case went to a proof before answer in Lord Robertson's court on 29 May 1941. Counsel for the pursuers were Mr Duffus KC and Mr James Walker. The defenders were represented by Mr Blades KC and Mr George A Montgomery. The minute of proceedings show that the pursuer led fourteen witnesses starting at 10.50 am and finishing at 2.25 pm with a break of eighty minutes for lunch. The defenders led two witnesses and finished their evidence at 3 pm. By 3.55 pm submissions had been made and Lord Robertson made avizandum. The total time occupied was about four hours. Modern reparation proofs are not as quick.

Lord Robertson issued his opinion on 6 June 1941. He found for the defenders. The pursuers had failed to establish the cause of the upsetting of the urn. That being so they had failed to establish the negligence of the defenders. *Res ipsa loquitur* was rejected. The only person who gave any evidence of how the accident happened was Taylor. Lord Robertson was strongly critical of the fact that it suited neither party to call McDonald, the church officer, as a witness. He considered various possible causes of the accident but none of these had been proved. He assoilzied the defenders. He did not, as in modern practice, make any finding of the damages which would be due if liability had been established.

The reclaiming motion

The pursuers reclaimed[27] against the interlocutor of the Lord Ordinary to the Inner House of the Court of Session. The case was heard before four

---

[26] *Muir v Glasgow Corporation* 1941 SLT 163.
[27] Often wrongly called an "appeal" but for historical reasons the Division is technically rehearing a case already before the Court of Session.

judges of the First Division on 16 and 17 October 1941. They were Lord President Normand, Lord fleming, Lord Moncrieff and Lord Carmont. About three weeks later, on 7 November 1941, their Lordships recalled the interlocutor of the Lord Ordinary, with the Lord President dissenting. The case was continued for a hearing on the quantum of damages.[28]

Any criticism of the way the pursuers presented their case has to be tempered by the fact that they won before the First Division. None of the majority of the judges cited any case law in their opinions or expounded at length on the law. They decided the case on its particular facts. The majority took the view that there was an obvious danger in allowing an urn with hot tea to be carried through a narrow corridor full of children. This procedure had been authorised by Mrs Alexander who had not taken steps to make sure that the confined space was clear during the short period of transport of the urn through the shop. The failure of these judges to analyse the standard of care on Mrs Alexander, and what that involved, was a fundamental weakness in their approach.

Lord President Normand dissented and thought that the case raised an issue of general importance. The start of his opinion indicated his direction of thinking. In the second paragraph he acknowledged that Glasgow Corporation owed a duty of care for the safety of the children who were invitees[29] of the defenders. Also a duty of care was owed to the two men carrying the tea, who were also invitees. If one party was permitted to perform some act which was attended with danger to the other party there was a duty to take precautions against the permitted danger. "But," he said, "if the authorised act is one which is not obviously attended with any danger to others if it is performed with ordinary care and skill, the occupier has no duty to take precautions, and he will not be liable if injury follows whether from the negligence of those who performed the authorised act or from some mischance not attributable to their negligence."[30] By approaching the case this way he was going beyond the more simple approach of his fellow judges in seeing an obvious danger. He was considering what would happen if the act was performed with ordinary care and skill. This turns the spotlight on those carrying the urn. If they were negligent that affected the liability of the Corporation. Lord Normand was still referring to cases of obvious danger, which was an inaccurate way to view the law. Whether

---

[28] 1942 SC 126.

[29] Until the Occupiers' Liability (Scotland) Act 1960 the duty of care owed by an occupier of premises to those who came onto the premises depended on whether they were invitees, licensees or trespassers. This categorisation, forced on Scots law by *Dumbreck v Addie & Sons (Collieries) Ltd* 1929 SC (HL) 51 and current at the time of *Muir's* case, was abolished by the 1960 Act. The duty towards an invitee was a duty of taking reasonable care that the premises were safe: *Dumbreck* at 55 per LC Hailsham and at 59 per Viscount Dunedin.

[30] 1942 SC 126 at 141.

a danger is obvious or not involves categorisation and is a different, and less flexible, standard than a requirement to take reasonable care in the circumstances. He followed the view of the Lord Ordinary that the accident could only have been caused by the negligence of the men carrying the urn or by an unforeseeable mischance. Furthermore, on the facts he did not think there was an obvious danger. Something turned on the evidence of Taylor that he had asked the children to stand aside and they did so and that Mrs Alexander would not know about the details of the urn and what it contained.

With hindsight a remarkable aspect of the views of the Court of Session judges is what they did not say. The essence of the case was the actions of Mrs Alexander. There is not any reference to the standard of reasonable care on her. A question which should have been asked is what she should have reasonably foreseen? Rather than, for example, Lord Carmont's standard of "what she should have made herself acquainted with in those circumstances".[31] Reasonable foresight is not explicity discussed. Nor is there any reference to the law expounded in *Donoghue v Stevenson* or *Bourhill v Young*. It is as if some judges and counsel in the Court of Session were unaware of the general importance of these relatively recent cases.

The reactions to the decision of the First Division

Glasgow Corporation were not pleased by the decision of the First Division which had three immediate consequences.

(1) They agreed damages with the pursuers. A joint minute was signed by James Walker and George A Montgomery, advocates, and lodged in process on 21 November 1941.[32] Authority was interponed to the joint minute by the First Division on 2 December 1941. The joint minute agreed damages for Eleanor Muir of £400. Martha Chalmers, Charlotte Toner, and Theresa Haughey had agreed damages of £25 each. The sum for Agnes Muir and May Yardley was £10 each, not a lot for a Court of Session action.

(2) The Parks Committee of the Corporation ordered its Director to give instructions to tea rooms in public parks to discontinue the practice of supplying boiling water to picnic parties, pending a decision of the House of Lords.[33] It seems that to the Corporation the case was about the supply of boiling water.

---

[31] 1942 SC 126 at 137.
[32] NAS, CS 46/1944/1/15.
[33] Glasgow Corp Parks Committee Minutes, 24 December 1941, print no 5, p 453.

(3) The Corporation gave authority to the town clerk to appeal to the House of Lords. The appeal was heard in the House of Lords, just over a year later, on 28 and 29 January 1943 before Lords Thankerton, Macmillan, Wright, Romer and Clauson.

The House of Lords appeal

On 16 April 1943 the House unanimously allowed the appeal.[34] The speeches provided the opportunity for their Lordships to set out the standard of care imposed on Mrs Alexander. It is these statements which give the case its long-lasting importance. Although giving the second speech it is Lord Macmillan's views which are now much quoted.

The correct starting point in analysing the legal effect of the facts was the concept of reasonable care. This had been explained by the House of Lords the previous year in the famous Scottish case of *Bourhill v Young*.[35] Amazingly it does not seem that either the appellant's counsel or the respondent's counsel referred to this case before the House (or in the Court of Session). The legal arguments were around older, mainly English, cases about operations with attendant danger. Their Lordships, however, were not deterred. Lords Thankerton, Macmillan and Wright started their legal analysis by reference to *Bourhill's* case. They had all been judges in *Bourhill*.[36] Lord Wright went further[37] and quoted Lord Atkin in *Donoghue v Stevenson*: "You must take reasonable care to avoid acts or omissions which you can reasonably foresee would be likely to injure your neighbour."[38]

Lord Macmillan's speech contains the core of the modern law of negligence. He set out the law in his first, rather long, paragraph before applying this to the facts.[39] It would be tedious to quote it all but, in summary, he made the following points:

(1) The degree of care for the safety of others which the law requires varies with the circumstances. Those who engage in inherently dangerous operations may have to take extra precautions.

(2) There is not liability for every injury caused by our conduct: "In Scotland, at any rate, it has never been a maxim of the law that a man acts at his peril."

---

[34] 1943 SC (HL) 3.
[35] 1942 SC (HL) 78.
[36] The two other judges were Lord Russell of Killowen and Lord Porter.
[37] 1943 SC (HL) 3 at 13.
[38] 1932 SC (HL) 31 at 44. This case was not mentioned by any judge in the Court of Session.
[39] 1943 SC (HL) 3 at 10.

(3) "Legal liability is limited to those consequences of our acts which a reasonable man of ordinary intelligence and experience so acting would have in contemplation."

(4) The standard is the foresight of the reasonable man. This is both objective and subjective. It is objective because it ignores the unduly timorous: those who "imagine every path beset with lions". It ignores those who at the other extreme are over-confident. But there is a subjective element in that a court looks at what the reasonable man would have foreseen in the particular circumstances.

Lord Thankerton summed up his view of the law with the sentence: "In my opinion, it has long been held in Scotland that all that a person can be bound to foresee are the reasonable and probable consequences of the failure to take care, judged by the standard of the ordinary reasonable man."[40] Lord Wright similarly said that the question was not "what Mrs Alexander actually foresaw, but what the hypothetical reasonable person in Mrs Alexander's situation would have foreseen".[41] Lord Clauson had similar views.

Even if the House of Lords had held Mrs Alexander negligent, the case would still be important in the law because of the method of judicial analysis and the statements of the law. After the trilogy of cases, *Donoghue v Stevenson*, *Bourhill v Young*, and *Muir v Glasgow Corporation*, one could not have been left in any doubt that the correct starting points in the application of the law were to consider the existence of a duty of care, and then the breach of that duty by failing to exercise the standard of care of the reasonable man, who would have reasonable foresight, but only *reasonable* foresight, in the particular circumstances.

Applying the law to the facts in this case their Lordships found Mrs Alexander had no reason to anticipate that a carefully carried urn would pose a danger to the children. She was not "an insurer against any risk of danger from the tea urn".[42] The failure of the pursuers to establish why Mr McDonald let go of the urn was a problem. Lord Romer found the lack of evidence on how the accident happened a barrier to deciding what was within the reasonable contemplation of Mrs Alexander.[43] Lord Macmillan referred to the difficulty of showing that Mrs Alexander ought reasonably to have foreseen an event the occurrence of which was unascertained.[44] Lord

---

[40] 1943 SC (HL) 3 at 8.
[41] 1943 SC (HL) 3 at13.
[42] 1943 SC (HL) 3 at 9 per Lord Thankerton.
[43] 1943 SC (HL) 3 at 18.
[44] 1943 SC (HL) 3 at 11.

Thankerton mentioned some physical failure on the part of Mr McDonald which neither he nor Mrs Alexander could have foreseen.[45] The absence of Mr McDonald from the witness box was always going to pose a problem for the pursuers, not least because the suspicion might be that he was the negligent party.

There was one factor potentially in the pursuers' favour. The Corporation had called only two witnesses, one of whom was Mrs Alexander. In cross-examination she said that if she had been given warning of the arrival of the urn she would have cleared the children out. This had impressed Lords Moncrieff and Carmont as tantamount to an admission of fault on her part.[46] It is always satisfying to a cross-examiner to have a defender's witness admit that there was something they could have done to prevent the accident, particularly when that is the ground of fault averred in the closed record. But in the House of Lords Lord Macmillan treated this as "natural expressions on her part of wisdom after the distressing event".[47] In the end the pursuers were seeking to impose on the Corporation a higher standard of care than the law exacted.

The House held that the appeal should be allowed and the judgment of the Lord Ordinary restored. Following normal procedure the Corporation made an application to the First Division of the Court of Session to apply the judgment of the House of Lords. By interlocutor of 13 October 1943 the Division recalled its earlier interlocutors and adhered to Lord Robertson's interlocutor. There was a minor procedural flourish because the date of Lord Robertson's interlocutor in favour of the Corporation was wrongly stated and the pursuers attempted to rely on this error. The First Division would have none of it and Lord President Normand corrected and initialled the interlocutor sheet. The First Division also found the pursuers jointly and severally liable in the expenses of the action in the Inner House along with the account of expenses in the Outer House and also the sum of £456 7s 6d being the amount of unpaid costs certified by the Judicial Taxing Officer of the House of Lords.

The effects of the decision of the House of Lords

The *Glasgow Herald* on Saturday, 17 April 1943 reported the result of the case under the headline "Glasgow Tearoom Accident". Mr McDonald, Mr Taylor and Mrs Alexander were named. The Parks Committee met on 12 May and were informed of the decision of the House of Lords by the town clerk. The Committee decided to cancel its previous instruction to

---

[45] 1943 SC (HL) 3 at 9.
[46] 1942 SC 126 at 135 per Lord Moncrieff and at 138 per Lord Carmont.
[47] 1943 SC (HL) 3 at 12.

discontinue the supply of boiling water to picnic parties in public parks. The practice of supplying boiling water was again authorised.[48]

The Corporation proceeded to tax[49] the account of expenses and on 11 November 1943 the First Division, headed by Lord President Cooper, approved the auditor's report and decerned against the pursuers for the sum of £255 11s 5d. For these sums and the sums found due in the House of Lords the Corporation proceeded to extract a decree.[50] This shows a serious resolve to enforce the total claims for expenses of about £700 against the pursuers. What happened next is not known. It may be, although it is doubtful, that some attempt might have been made to have some of the pursuers who sued as tutors to pay the sums due by instalments (the three children who sued with the consent of curators would, presumably, have no assets).

LESSONS FROM THE CASE

It is possibly the case that the pursuers did not understand why they lost. The children went to a picnic in a public park and six of them returned injured. But no one was found liable to pay compensation. Instead the pursuers were liable to pay money to the Corporation. Any practitioner who has to explain this to clients knows the pain involved.

The case could be used to this day to teach and discuss the law even although it belongs to a different era. The evidence led by both parties did not conform to modern standards. There was the absence of critical witnesses, particularly Mr McDonald, but also the Sunday school teachers who had made the arrangements with Mrs Alexander for the use of the tea rooms. What was said, promised or agreed? The brevity of the examinations in the witness box, while commendable in some ways, does leave questions unanswered. This is startlingly obvious with the medical evidence. Only one doctor gave evidence – Dr James Carnduff – who was Eleanor Muir's GP. He first saw his patient about the end of October 1940, that is, over four months after the accident. He gave detailed evidence about the scars on Eleanor's body, measured the previous day, but he was waiting for physicians to examine her to explain an unusual temperature. The account of expenses shows that Simpson and Marwick, for the defenders, had procured medical reports on all the children and just prior to the proof instructed another medical report on Eleanor Muir. The results were not given in evidence. Nor were there hospital records or reports from those who treated the hospital patients.

---

[48]   Glasgow Corp Parks Committee Minutes, 12 May 1943, print No 16, p 865.
[49]   Ie to have the amounts claimed checked as reasonable and certified by the auditor of court.
[50]   Register of Acts and Decrees, 13 January 1944.

In the averments in the closed record there are not any statements about any future effect on Eleanor Muir other than that she would be permanently disfigured. Her GP, Dr Carnduff, in evidence, tended to discount any long-lasting impact unless she became an actress "or something like that". This overlooked the effect on a young girl of scars which would show when wearing a swimming costume or taking part in sports. It made no attempt to predict adverse, and lifelong, psychological effects.

The case can be used to show the difference between a *causa sine qua non* and a *causa causans*, a point mentioned by Lord Romer.[51] There were plenty *causae sine qua non* or "but for" causes. The rain, the decision to drink tea, the decision not to use the tea rooms for making the tea, the presence of the Rutherglen party, the decision of Mrs Alexander to break the rules and allow the use of the tea rooms in the circumstances, and so on. But the dominant or legally effective causes are more limited. It seems clear, as already indicated, that the causes of the accident were (1) the decision to carry the urn through the narrow passage crowded with excited children; and (2) the failure of Mr McDonald to keep hold of the urn. On both issues Mr McDonald would have had questions to answer. On all accounts responsibility rested with the Milton Free Church party not with Glasgow Corporation.

Could the Free Church have been vicariously liable for the actions of its members? We do not know the details of the relationship with the church,[52] and this hampers a full discussion. It is unlikely that Mr McDonald was an employee. Modern cases arising from sexual abuse have tended to suggest that a relationship akin to employment may suffice for vicarious liability.[53] It may be that the church officer was an agent of the church. But as the law was probably understood in 1940 it is understandable that there would have been a reluctance to sue the church. Also, presumably, there was no practical point in suing Mr McDonald. The difficulties for the pursuers are obvious. Similar difficulties can arise today and can make advising clients an anxious business.

Nevertheless one lesson of the case is the crucial need to sue the correct defender. It would be better for individuals not to sue at all than

---

[51] 1943 SC (HL) 3 at 19.

[52] Detailed records of the church for this period, apart from the Kirk Session Minute Book, are missing. The church united with the St Vincent Free Church in 1994: Act of the General Assembly of the Free Church of Scotland anent Consolidation of Milton and St Vincent Street Free Church, Glasgow 1994, No 19 of Class II. I am grateful to the Rev Dr Colin Dow and Evan G Macdonald, Session Clerk, for trying to trace information.

[53] Eg *E v English Province of Our Lady of Charity* [2011] EWHC 2871 (QB), [2012] 2 WLR 709; also an unincorporated association can be liable for the acts of one or more of its members; *Catholic Child Welfare Soc v Various Claimants* [2012] UKSC 56 esp the speech of Lord Phillips.

risk the consequences of an unsuccessful action. Should all the pursuers have sued? Eleanor Muir's injuries were clearly worse than others and seem to have justified a claim in the Court of Session. But the risks of litigation are shared jointly and severally. In this case the reasoning might have been that young children and their parents from a council housing estate would never have been able anyway to pay expenses so the practical exposure to them of risk was minimised. Did each parent receive separate legal advice? Probably not. Their interests were all similar but they were not the same. For example, the parent of May Yardley from Cambuslang with her "wee burn" was embarking on litigation where the risks were very much greater than the potential benefit. In modern practice there might be an agreement on the share of liability for any award of expenses against the pursuers. There would be issues about separate legal advice for each claimant. There may be questions about raising some actions in the sheriff court and trying to have them sisted pending the outcome of a Court of Session action. The procedure adopted by the pursuers' solicitor in 1940 (and prior to the existence of legal aid) should not be unfairly compared to modern practices. In any event even now however the problem is viewed there is a conundrum.

CONCLUSION

For the Muir family there was some happiness a few years later. On 16 September 1949 Agnes or "Nan" Muir, then aged twenty-one, and a shop assistant, married Archibald McInnes, a thirty-year-old van driver. She had a subsequent marriage to Alexander Menzies. She died, a widow, in the Western Infirmary, Glasgow, on 10 July 2011, aged eighty-three years.[54]

Eleanor Muir at age twenty married George Lloyd on 30 December 1955 in Rutherglen after banns according to the forms of the Church of Scotland. She was a clerkess and, at the time, he was a postman.[55] The marriage ended in divorce twenty-four years later. There is no good reason to give further publicity to the details of this sad part of Eleanor's life but there were averments about domestic abuse, alcohol and a criminal conviction. Part of the evidence was an affidavit by one of her sons David, then aged nineteen. He followed his grandfather's interests and became a professional footballer.[56] Lord Stott awarded divorce on 20 December 1979.[57] On 30 May 1980, Eleanor, described as a "clerkess typist", married Douglas Trevor

---

[54]   Entry in the Register of Deaths in the District of Glasgow 2011/492.
[55]   Entry in the Register of Marriages in the District of Rutherglen in the County of Lanark.
[56]   Playing for Clyde, Raith Rovers and East Fife (according to Douglas Graham). He is now working for Sheffield Wednesday FC. Eleanor Lloyd had another son, Brian.
[57]   NAS, CS 258/1979/11131.

Graham, a maintenance engineer in Glasgow.[58] Eleanor now lives with her husband Douglas in a modern retirement complex in Millbrae Gardens about 600 yards from Victoria Hospital where she was treated all these years ago and not far from King's Park.

Eleanor remembers only a little about the accident which was seventy-three years ago. She recollects standing in the shop beside her sister Agnes, the floor being wet and shouting at visitors in the hospital for dry clothes. But she is reminded of the event every day. There are scars on her left ankle and thigh and on intimate parts of her body. Over the years she has had serious psychological problems from which she continues to suffer. She is convinced that they were triggered or caused by the accident. She looks at her body every day and the scars which she will take to her grave. The thought that for this no one was held accountable brings her to tears. Anyone who thinks that the law of negligence is about dry opinions of judges or theoretical analysis should spend some time with Eleanor. The law is about people.

Eleanor's mother told her that the family had been let down by the doctor and the lawyer. It is difficult at this distance to discern what their problem was with Dr Carnduff. But reading his evidence in the Court of Session he appears to have discounted present and future emotional problems.[59] In any event the family were so upset that they changed GP. The reasons for their distress with their lawyer are obvious. Both children were injured and no one had to pay compensation. Eleanor did not know about the award of expenses against the pursuers but she thinks that the old-fashioned honesty and morality of her parents meant that they would have tried to pay the sums due.

Sitting in her neat living room, drinking mugs of tea, it is impossible to avoid the carefully framed photographs of the family on a table by the window. The pride of a grandmother reflects the successes in her life. A photograph of her taken by the writer shows a fine attractive face but with, perhaps, a slight tinge of sadness in the eyes. Thankfully warmth and a ready smile are not far away.

It remains possible to follow much of the route of the urn in King's Park. From the swing park down the long slope to Aikenhead House and the steps which led to the fateful corridor. Under one of the large trees beside the swings is a discarded galvanised industrial sink which possibly could have been part of the original water supply. The occupant of the flat which occupies the site of the shop and tearoom may be unaware of the importance of the place in Scottish legal history. There

---

[58] Entry in the Register of Marriages in the District of Glasgow 1980/174.
[59] There was no record for this so he could not have given evidence on it, but this is a technicality that lay persons find difficult to understand.

is no plaque. No indication of a wartime drama involving a dropped urn. No celebration of a famous Glasgow case decided seventy years ago by the House of Lords.

Language and Law:
The Protection of Minority Languages

S H Naismith *

CONVENTION PROVISIONS ON LANGUAGE

The European Convention on Human Rights has few provisions which relate directly to the use of language.[1] Article 5(2) provides that "everyone who is arrested shall be informed promptly, in a language which he understands, of the reasons for his arrest and of any charge against him", while article 6(3)(a) similarly provides that everyone charged with a criminal offence has, among his minimum rights, the right "to be informed, in a language which he understands ..., of the nature and cause of the accusation against him". However, these are rather specific rights relating to the provision of information in the context of criminal charges. The only other provision which mentions language is article 14, which prohibits discrimination in the enjoyment of the rights and freedoms protected by the Convention "on any grounds such as sex, race, colour, language, religion, political or other opinion, national or social origin, association with a national minority, property, birth of other status".

THE COURT'S JURISPRUDENCE

Under article 6

Alleged breaches of the Convention in relation to the use of language have consequently been infrequent. Until recently neither the European Court of Human Rights nor the former Commission was particularly favourable to interpreting Convention rights in a manner that would create any specific

---

* The views expressed in this essay are personal to the author and not those of the Court or the Council of Europe.

[1] The International Covenant on Civil and Political Rights, conversely, provides in article 27: "In those States in which ethnic ... or linguistic minorities exist, persons belonging to such minorities shall not be denied the right, in community with the other members of their group ... to use their language." Similarly, the UN Declaration on the Rights of Persons Belonging to National or Ethnic, Religious and Linguistic Minorities states in article 2(1): "Persons belonging to national or ethnic and linguistic minorities ... have the right to ... use their own language, in private and in public, freely and without interference or any form of discrimination."

protection for minority languages. The Commission's approach was that states did not have to allow for the use of minority languages in dealings with its authorities,[2] including in court proceedings, at least where the person concerned had no particular difficulty communicating in the official language.[3] In criminal proceedings, an accused who does not understand the language of the proceedings is, in any event, entitled to have the services of an interpreter, by virtue of article 6(3)(e) of the Convention. Although no such guarantee exists for civil proceedings, few cases seem to have arisen in which an applicant complained that he or she did not understand the language of the proceedings.[4]

Family names

The Court has been similarly restrictive with regard to family names, essentially confirming the Commission's approach to the use of official languages in relations with state authorities. Thus, it declared inadmissible the case of *Birk-Levy v France*,[5] which concerned the obligation to use French in the Assembly of French Polynesia. It also rejected as inadmissible a complaint under article 8 of the Convention (right to respect for private and family life) relating to the issuing by the Latvian authorities of a passport in which the holder's name, "Mentzen", acquired after her marriage to a German national, was "Latvianised" to "Mencena", although a note in the section of the passport for special remarks certified that the original form was "Mentzen".[6] A similar issue concerning different Russian and Ukrainian forms arose in *Bulgakov v Ukraine*,[7] where the Court held that there had been no violation of article 8 or article 14. In *Baylac-Ferrer and Suarez v France*,[8] in which the French authorities refused to register the applicant's son's name with the Catalan spelling of Martí, on the ground

---

[2] See eg *Un groupe d'habitants de Leeuw-Saint-Pierre v Belgium*, 2333/64, decision of 16 December 1968.

[3] See eg *Isop v Austria*, 808/60, decision of 8 March 1962, in which the applicant wished to use Slovene in civil proceedings although he had sufficient knowledge of German to lodge his complaint with the assistance of a lawyer; *Bideault v France*, 11261/84, in which a court had refused to allow witnesses to give evidence in Breton; *Lagerblom v Sweden*, 26891/95, decision of 14 January 2003, in which a Finnish speaker living in Sweden wished to have a Finnish-speaking lawyer although he spoke Swedish (interpretation was in fact provided); and *Zana v Turkey*, 18954/91, decision of 21 October 1993, in which the accused had wished to speak Kurdish although he did not claim that he did not understand Turkish.

[4] In the recent case of *Dachnevič v Lithuania* (41338/06, judgment of 20 November 2012), the Russian-speaking applicant did not understand Lithuanian but had, in fact, had an interpreter for the court hearings, and the Court dismissed her complaint on that basis.

[5] 39426/06, decision of 21 September 2010.

[6] *Juta Mentzen, also known as Mencena v Latvia*, 71074/01, decision of 7 December 2004.

[7] 59894/00, decision of 11 September 2007.

[8] 27977/04, decision of 25 September 2008.

that the letter í does not exist in the French language, the Court declared the applicants' complaints under both article 8 and article 14 inadmissible.

Education in Flanders

As early as 1968 the Court did find a limited breach of article 14 in conjunction with article 2 of Protocol No 1 to the Convention (which *inter alia* protects the right of parents to ensure the education of their children in conformity with their own religious and philosophical convictions) in the *Belgian Linguistics* case.[9] In that case, French-speaking parents complained primarily that French-language education was not provided in the districts in which they lived, as these districts were in a region considered by law as Dutch speaking. Indeed, the state did not allow the applicants' children to attend French classes which existed in certain places.

The Court affirmed that the right to education "would be meaningless if it did not imply in favour of its beneficiaries, the right to be educated in the national language or in one of the national languages". But the Court also made it clear that article 14, even when read in conjunction with article 2 of Protocol No 1, did not have the effect "of guaranteeing to a child or to his parent the right to obtain instruction in a language of his choice". It took the view that if the intention had been to create a specific right with respect to language of instruction, this would have been done in express terms in article 2 of Protocol No 1. Moreover, it considered that in the second paragraph of that provision the terms "religious and philosophical convictions" did not cover linguistic preferences, a proposal relating to the right of parents to have education conducted in a language other than that of the country in question having been rejected during the preparatory works. While also finding that article 8 in no way guaranteed either a right to education or a personal right of parents relating to the education of their children, the Court nonetheless did not exclude that "measures taken in the field of education may affect the right to respect for private and family life or derogate from it". It consequently decided to examine the applicants' various complaints under both article 2 of Protocol No 1 and article 8 of the Convention, both separately and taken in conjunction with article 14.

The principal complaint of the applicants related to the legislation which prevented the state from establishing or subsidising, in a region deemed by law to be unilingual, education in another language.[10] The result of this policy was that parents who wished their children to be taught in

---

[9] *Case relating to certain aspects of the laws on the use of languages in education in Belgium* 23 July 1968, Series A, no 6 (merits). The vote was eight to seven.

[10] The same policy applied to Dutch speakers in Wallonia as to French speakers in Flanders.

French had to send them either to a private French-language school or to a school in a French-speaking region or abroad.

The Court found that the law was not incompatible with the requirements of the first paragraph of article 2 of Protocol No 1. That conclusion was reached in reference to the Court's interpretation of the provision which excluded any right to the establishment of schools in which instruction is provided in any given language. Similarly, the Court found no breach of article 8, which does not guarantee either the right to be educated, by the public authorities or with their aid, in one's mother tongue. Finally, the Court found that there was no violation of article 14 in conjunction with these provisions:[11]

> [T]he Court finds that [the contested legal provisions'] purpose is to achieve linguistic unity within the two large regions of Belgium in which a large majority of the population speaks only one of the two national languages. This legislation makes scarcely viable schools in which teaching is conducted solely in the national language that is not that of the majority of the inhabitants of the region. In other words, it tends to prevent, in the Dutch-unilingual region, the establishment or maintenance of schools which teach only in French. Such a measure cannot be considered arbitrary. To begin with, it is based on the objective element which the region constitutes. Furthermore it is based on a public interest, namely, to ensure that all schools dependent on the state and existing in a unilingual region conduct their teaching in the language which is essentially that of the region.

The Court reached the same conclusion with regard to the somewhat more draconian provision which denied subsidies to private schools which, while conducting education in the majority language, also provided some classes in the other language. States, the Court observed, have no obligation to subsidise private schools. Moreover, nothing actually prevented the private schools from providing education in the minority language. No violation was found with regard to certain other aspects of the law. For instance, in one of the Dutch-speaking areas, demographic changes had resulted in a large French-speaking population. A limited degree of nursery and primary education in French was provided for by the legislation on account of the "special status" of the area (composed of six districts). Conversely, the Court did find that there had been a violation of article 2 of Protocol No 1, in conjunction with article 14 of the Convention, in so far as francophone education was not available to children whose parents lived outside the special status area, while no such limitation applied to Dutch classes, accessible to all children, including Dutch-speaking children living in the nearby French-speaking region. For the Court, this difference in treatment,

---

[11] *Belgian Linguistics* (n 9) section II, para 7 of judgment.

based on language considerations, was not justified. Nevertheless, the general tenor of the judgment is unfavourable to the protection of minority languages, which is understandable in the light of the wording of the relevant Convention provisions.

Furthermore, the Court confirmed this approach in *Skender v "the former Yugoslav Republic of Macedonia"*,[12] which related to the lack of Turkish education in the district where the applicant lived. It is only in more recent years that the Court's evolving interpretation has begun to show signs of recognition of linguistic rights as potentially implicit in certain provisions of the Convention and its Protocols.

The Cyrillic script in Transdniestria

An important development in respect of linguistic rights was the judgment of a Grand Chamber of seventeen judges in the case of *Catan v Moldova and Russia*.[13] This case is complicated by the fact that it relates to Transdniestria, with all the complexities of state responsibility which that background involves. The Court had previously dealt with the situation there in the cases of *Ilaşcu*,[14] and *Ivanţoc*,[15] although in a rather different context. Nevertheless, much of the *Catan* judgment is given over to issues relating to the respective responsibilities of Moldova – of which Transdniestria technically forms part – and Russia, which provides support for the breakaway "Moldavian Republic of Transdniestria" ("MRT"). This is, in fact, one of those political impasses where no real solution has been found but where the Court is nevertheless required to take a position with regard to who is responsible for the protection of Convention rights.

The problem at the root of the case was a provision of the MRT Law on Languages of 1992 which required that, for all purposes, "Moldavian" (which is essentially Romanian) must be written in Cyrillic. Use of the Latin script was therefore prohibited in schools, including in Moldovan-speaking schools administered by the Moldovan Ministry of Education and following the Moldovan curriculum. From 2004, the MRT authorities started to close down all schools using Latin script, including those attended by the applicants or their children. These were able to reopen, but in other, unsuitable premises, some of which were attacked by vandals, and the pupils were in general subjected to harassment.

Although earlier cases concerning Transdniestria had concerned issues such as detention, the Court essentially applied the approach it had

---

[12] 62059/00, decision of 22 November 2001.
[13] 43370/04, 8252/05 and 18454/06, judgment of 19 October 2012.
[14] *Ilaşcu v Maldova and Russia*, 48787/99 ECHR 2004-VII (Grand Chamber).
[15] *Ivanţoc v Moldova and Russia*, 23687/05, judgment of 15 November 2011.

taken in those cases. The Court found that, first, while Moldova did not have effective control over that territory or the acts of the MRT, it had an obligation to use all legal and diplomatic means available to guarantee the enjoyment of Convention rights to those living there; and, secondly, that, at the relevant time, as established in *Ilaşcu*, the MRT survived by virtue of the military, economic and political support of Russia and was under the effective authority, or at least the decisive influence of, Russia. The Court maintained those findings in *Catan*, concluding that the applicants fell within the jurisdiction of Russia by virtue of that overall control, while recognising that there was no evidence of any direct involvement of Russian agents.

On the merits of the application, the Court considered that it was difficult to establish in detail the facts relating to the applicants' experiences following the reopening of the schools in question. The Court nonetheless noted three elements: (1) the prohibition on use of the Latin script under the Law on Languages, (2) the fact that it was clear the schools had had to move to new premises, and (3) the large drop in the number of pupils attending Moldovan/Romanian schools in Transdniestria, which corroborated the general thrust of the allegations of harassment. In that light, the forced closures and subsequent harassment constituted interferences with the pupils' rights of access to existing educational institutions and to be educated in their national language. Moreover, the forced closures and harassment amounted to an interference with the parents' rights under article 2 of Protocol No 1:[16]

> [the parents] were placed in the invidious position of having to choose, on the one hand, between sending their children to schools where they would face the disadvantage of pursuing their entire secondary education in a combination of language and alphabet which they consider artificial and which is unrecognised anywhere else in the world, using teaching materials produced in Soviet times or, alternatively, subjecting their children to long journeys and/or substandard facilities, harassment and intimidation.

The Court was presented with no evidence that the measures pursued any legitimate aim, appearing rather to enforce the Russification of the language and culture of the Moldovan community. In its view, "[g]iven the fundamental importance of primary and secondary education for each child's personal development and future success, it was impermissible to interrupt these children's schooling and force them and their parents to make such difficult choices with the sole purpose of entrenching the separatist ideology".[17]

---

[16] *Catan* (n 13) para 143.
[17] *Catan* (n 13) para 144.

As to the respective responsibilities of the two defendant states, the Court found that, in contrast to the situation in *Ilaşcu*, the Moldovan Government had made considerable efforts to support the applicants, in particular in providing funding for the schools in their new premises, so that there had been no violation of article 2 of Protocol No 1 by Moldova. Conversely, in the light of Russia's exercise of effective control over the MRT during the period in question, Russia therefore incurred responsibility for the violation of the applicants' rights. The Court found it necessary to determine whether Russia exercised detailed control over policies and actions in Transdniestria. The Court also found it unnecessary to examine the complaints under articles 8 and 14, although several judges expressed a separate opinion on that respect.

Discussion

Both the *Transdniestria* case and *Belgian Linguistics* are language rights cases. But each case concerned languages that were not, in the round, "minority languages" in the sense of languages spoken exclusively in a small geographical area, as is the case with, say, Scots Gaelic. Both French and Dutch are widely spoken outside Belgium; and Moldovan is not only spoken in the rest of Moldova but is essentially a form of Romanian, spoken by an estimated 24 million people. In neither case, however, was the language a minority language in the narrow sense, namely that it is a language threatened with extinction.

Interference "in accordance with law"

Mention may also be made of a series of cases against Turkey relating to the refusal of the authorities to transmit prisoners' letters written in Kurdish. In the case of *Mehmet Nuri Özen v Turkey*,[18] the Court found a violation of article 8 of the Convention on the ground that the interference was not "in accordance with the law", as the reason for refusing to transmit the applicants' correspondence (lack of resources to translate them, rendering it impossible to verify that the content was "inoffensive") was not among those set out in the law.

The issue has primarily arisen in the context of elections. The starting point is the decision of the Commission in *Association "Andecha Astur" v Spain*.[19] The applicant association's list of candidates was presented in Asturian rather than Spanish and the authorities refused to register it. The Commission held the applicant association's claim to be inadmissible. The

---

[18] 15672/08, 24462/08, 27559/08, 28302/08, 28312/08, 34823/08, 40738/08, 41124/08, 43197/08, 51938/08 and 58170/08, judgment of 11 January 2011.

[19] 34184/96, decision of 7 July 1997.

public authority's decision did not hinder the free expression of the opinion of the people in the choice of the legislature (article 3 of Protocol No 1 to the Convention), as Asturian was neither the official language of the state nor a "co-official" language in the Autonomous Community of Asturias, despite enjoying a degree of recognition. The exclusion of Asturian, the Commission held, was not discriminatory for the purposes of article 14 of the Convention. A similar complaint concerning the use of Frisian in Dutch elections was declared inadmissible.[20]

Against that background, the recent case of *Şükran Aydın v Turkey*[21] falls to be considered. The case concerned the criminal conviction of the applicants for speaking Kurdish during an election campaign, in breach of a domestic law containing the fundamental provisions governing elections and voter registration. At the material time that law prohibited the use of any language or script other than Turkish in election campaigning on radio or television or by other means.[22]

In *Şükran Aydın*, the first two applicants, each standing for election as a candidate of the People's Democratic Party, had addressed crowds in Kurdish because the population was Kurdish and many of the elderly people and women did not understand Turkish. The applicants were sentenced to six months' imprisonment and a heavy fine. The prison sentences were commuted to a fine and ultimately a stay of execution was granted. The third applicant was also convicted for having similarly addressed a crowd in Kurdish in support of an independent candidate. He was sentenced to six months' imprisonment (later reduced to five) and it was finally decided to defer delivery of the judgment for five years. The fourth applicant was also convicted, on the basis of video evidence, although he maintained that he had spoken Turkish while acknowledging that he had perhaps greeted people in Kurdish. He was sentenced to six months' imprisonment but the delivery of the judgment was deferred for five years. The fifth applicant was also sentenced to six months' imprisonment, later commuted to a fine. This decision was quashed by the Court of Cassation and subsequently the trial court deferred delivery of its judgment for five years.

The Court considered it appropriate to examine the applicants' complaints in this respect under article 10 of the Convention, which protects the right to freedom of expression, including freedom to receive

---

[20] *Fryske Nasjonale Partij v The Netherlands*, 11100/84, decision of 12 December 1985.

[21] 49197/06, 23196/07, 50242/08, 60912/08 and 14871/09.

[22] Mention should also be made of the case of *Podkolzina v Latvia*, 46726/99, judgment of 9 April 2002, in which the Court found a violation of article 3 of Protocol No 1, on the ground that the striking of the applicant out of the list of candidates in a general election on account of her insufficient knowledge of the national language could not be regarded as proportionate.

and impart information and ideas without interference by public authority. The applicants' criminal convictions constituted such an "interference" and the central issue in the case was whether that interference was "necessary in a democratic society", as required by the second paragraph of article 10.

In that respect, the Court distinguished the case from those relating to the use of an unofficial language in the context of communications with public authorities or before official institutions. The Court observed that the case concerned rather a restriction on the use of language by persons in their relations with other private individuals, albeit in the context of public meetings during election campaigns. The Court recalled that article 10 of the Convention,[23]

> encompasses the freedom to receive and impart information and ideas *in any language that allows persons to participate in the public exchange of all varieties of cultural, political and social information and ideas ... and in such contexts, language as a medium of expression undoubtedly deserves protection under Article 10.*

It referred in that respect to another recent judgment, *Eğitim ve Bilim Emekçileri sendikası v Turkey*,[24] which concerned the threatened dissolution of a trade union on the ground that its statute defended the right to receive education in one's mother tongue. The Court did not consider that the issue before it was whether states should in general allow the use of non-official languages during election campaigns but whether the scope and manner of application of an existing prohibition were compatible with article 10.

The prohibition applicable in Turkey at the material time was a blanket one accompanied by criminal sanctions ranging from imprisonment of from six months to one year and payment of a fine. In the Court's view, the prohibition had been interpreted and applied "very extensively and inflexibly" in the applicants' cases. The courts had thus failed to conduct any meaningful judicial scrutiny. No consideration had been given to the status of the applicants (one of whom had not been a candidate), or to the content or duration of the speeches at issue (for example, by differentiating between a full speech and the uttering of a few words of greeting), or to the motivation of the applicants (namely that their audiences may have largely been unable to understand Turkish). The courts' examination had essentially been limited to verifying from video recordings that the applicants had spoken some Kurdish. Furthermore, the Court took account of the serious criminal sanctions, noting that out of twenty-two states' parties surveyed, Turkey was the only one to subject the use of a non-official language during election campaigning to criminal penalties. The Court

---

[23] *Şükran Aydın* (n 21) para 52, emphasis added.
[24] 20641/05, judgment of 25 September 2012.

concluded unanimously that the prohibition was not proportionate to the legitimate aim and consequently could not be regarded as "necessary in a democratic society".

THE EUROPEAN CHARTER FOR REGIONAL AND MINORITY LANGUAGES

Overview

The Council of Europe, under the auspices of which the European Convention on Human Rights was adopted, fulfils a valuable function in developing European standards and establishing monitoring activities in a wide range of matters. One of these is the protection of minority languages, which it has addressed primarily through the European Charter for Regional or Minority Languages.[25] The Charter entered into force in 1998 and has been ratified by twenty-five states, including the United Kingdom (although, interestingly, not by Ireland). It entered into force in respect of Scottish Gaelic – which is considered a "territorial language", although the declaration did not specify the territorial scope – on 1 July 2001. The other languages protected in the United Kingdom, although not all to the same degree, are Cornish, Irish, Manx Gaelic, Scots, Ulster-Scots and Welsh. There are various other international texts relating to the rights of minorities and the prohibition of discrimination, *inter alia*, on the ground of language, in particular the Framework Convention for the Protection of National Minorities of 1994 and the (UN) Universal Declaration on Linguistic Rights of 1996, but the Charter is the instrument which sets out binding obligations in the field of minority language protection.

The Preamble to the Charter affirms, *inter alia*, that:

> [T]he protection of the historical regional or minority languages of Europe, some of which are in danger of extinction, contributes to the maintenance and development of Europe's cultural wealth and traditions

and that:

> [T]he right to use a regional or minority language in private and public life is an inalienable right conforming to the principles embodied in the United Nations International Covenant on Civil and Political Rights, and according to the spirit of the Council of Europe Convention for the Protection of Human Rights and Fundamental Freedoms.

---

[25] See further P Thornberry and M A Martin Esbebanez, *Minority Rights in Europe* (2004) chapter 3, and *Minority Language Protection in Europe: into a New Decade* (2010) chapters 2, 3 and 5.

Regional or minority languages are defined in article 1 of the Charter as languages that are "traditionally used within a given territory of a state by nationals of that state who form a group numerically smaller than the rest of the state's population". The Charter aims to support such languages by requiring states parties to implement a panoply of measures, including a minimum of thirty-five paragraphs or sub-paragraphs in Part III ("Measures to promote the use of regional or minority languages in public life ..."). At least three must be chosen from article 8 (Education) and three from article 12 (Cultural activities and facilities), with at least one being chosen from each of articles 9 (Judicial authorities), 10 (administrative authorities and public services), 11 (Media) and 13 (Economic and social life). These are the five main axes on which the Charter is based. It should be noted, however, that a number of the provisions relate to alternative levels of protection, and the choice of the state thus relates to different degrees of undertaking. In other words, it is not envisaged that a state should accept the requirements of the Charter in their entirety. Rather, it is a "menu system" or "*à la carte*" choice which "makes it possible for a state to tailor a set of obligations in accordance with the situation of each regional or minority language".[26] It also permits the state to modulate the extent of its commitment to the protection of a particular language.

The Charter established a monitoring mechanism in the form of a Committee of Experts which examines periodic reports (every three years after an initial one-year period) and then submits its own report to the Committee of Ministers of the Council of Europe. The Committee of Experts may make proposals for the preparation of recommendations to be adopted by the Committee of Ministers. To date, the United Kingdom has submitted four reports (in 2002, 2005, 2009) and 2012 (not yet having been presented at the time of writing (April 2013)).

Scottish Gaelic

The Scottish Parliament has been responsible for Gaelic since it was (re-)established in 1999. Its adoption of the Gaelic Language (Scotland) Act 2005, the cornerstone of legal measures to strengthen the position of Gaelic, was the most significant consequence of ratification of the Charter.[27] Prior to that, only a few arcane statutory provisions dealt with Gaelic: notably the Small Landholders (Scotland) Act 1911, which requires that at least one member of the Scottish Land Court be a Gaelic speaker (although apparently there have never been any written

---

[26] S Gramstad, "The Charter's monitoring mechanism: a practical perspective" in *Minority Language Protection* (n 25) p 31.

[27] See R Dunbar, "The Gaelic Language (Scotland) Act 2005" (2005) 9 Edin LR 466.

proceedings in Gaelic before it); and the Crofters (Scotland) Act 1993, which has a similar requirement for the Crofters Commission. The Local Government (Gaelic Names) (Scotland) Act 1997 allowed a local authority to adopt a Gaelic name, resulting in the Western Isles Council re-styling itself *Comhairle nan Eilean Siar*.

The aim of the 2005 Act was to secure the status of Gaelic, promote its use and increase the number of Gaelic speakers. The 2005 Act set up *Bòrd na Gàidhlig*, the development agency whose role is to secure the status of Gaelic as "an official language of Scotland commanding equal respect to the English language". The Act also required the elaboration of a National Gaelic Language Plan. This was approved by the Scottish Parliament in March 2007 and identified four key themes: language acquisition, usage, status and corpus planning. A revised plan was subsequently adopted for 2012–17. The fact that the term "national" is used for the plan is a recognition that Gaelic is spoken throughout Scotland, though of course to widely varying degrees, and that it is "a language of all of Scotland". *Bòrd na Gàidhlig* can also require public bodies to prepare statutory Gaelic Language Plans setting out how they intend to promote the use of Gaelic. According to the United Kingdom's 2009 report submitted under the Charter, four bodies – three local authorities (*Comhairle nan Eilean Siar*, Highland Council and Argyll and Bute Council) and the Scottish Parliamentary Corporate Body – were already implementing such plans, while several other bodies were due to submit their plans or had been issued with statutory notices.[28]

Furthermore, as part of the National Plan, a comprehensive National Gaelic Education Strategy was established and in October 2007 *Bòrd na Gàidhlig* set up a National Gaelic Education Steering Group to oversee implementation of that strategy.[29]

The United Kingdom's specific undertakings with regard to Gaelic place emphasis on education, the administration, media and cultural activities. As far as economic and social life is concerned, while it is recognised that "the fact that English is usually either *de facto* or *de jure* the language of law and administration in Scotland does inevitably mean that Gaelic remains excluded from many areas of public life", it is considered that implementation of the Act and in particular the development of Gaelic language plans by public bodies will help to address this issue.[30] With regard to the functioning of the courts, the sole provision in respect of which an undertaking has been

---

[28]   *Third Periodical Report presented to the Secretary General of the Council of Europe under Article 15 of the Charter by the United Kingdom* (2009) p 25.

[29]   2009 report (n 28) p 123.

[30]   2009 report (n 28) p 163.

given relates to allowing documents and evidence to be produced in Gaelic, if necessary with the use of interpreters and translators, in civil proceedings in "those judicial districts in which the number of residents using [Gaelic] justifies [it], ... and on condition that the use of the facilities ... is not considered by the judge to hamper the proper administration of justice". Such provision has been made at Portmaddy, Portree and Stornoway.[31] The undertaking does not extend to criminal proceedings. The Scottish Courts Service was, however, one of the bodies which *Bòrd na Gàidhlig* was due to require to develop a language plan.[32]

EDUCATION

In the field of education, which is undoubtedly one of the key areas in supporting any threatened language, the United Kingdom has undertaken to make available pre-school, primary and secondary education in Gaelic (but not to make available "a substantial part" of such education in Gaelic). A limited undertaking has been given in respect of technical and vocational education, namely to make provision where pupils or their families desire such education in sufficiently high numbers; such education is in fact available at the Gaelic College on Skye, *Sabhal Mòr Ostaig*, and at Lews Castle College in Stornoway. There is no concrete undertaking with regard to university and other higher education, but the reason for this exclusion is the nature of the state's role in tertiary education in the United Kingdom, which required a less concrete obligation "to encourage and/or allow the provision of university or other forms of higher education in [Gaelic] or of facilities for the study of these languages as university or higher education subjects".[33] In the same vein, encouragement will be given to offering Gaelic as a subject of adult or continuing education.

The Education (Scotland) Act 1980 imposed on local authorities a duty to provide teaching in Gaelic in "Gaelic-speaking areas". But a number of concrete measures which have been taken in implementing the Charter have created additional opportunities for Gaelic education and in particular Gaelic-medium education. Indeed, education is one of the six key development areas identified in the 2012–17 National Plan.[34] The first Gaelic-medium primary classes had opened in 1985[35] and in recent years there has been an increase in financial support as well as in the number of

---

[31] 2009 report (n 28) pp 140–41.
[32] 2009 report (n 28) 141.
[33] European Charter for Regional or Minority Languages, art 8(1)(e)(iii).
[34] The others are Home and Early Years; Communities; Workplace; Arts & Media, Heritage and Tourism; and Corpus.
[35] 2009 report (n 28) p 85.

local authorities providing Gaelic education. The 2009 report described the developments in Gaelic education as a "success story" while recognising the need for a co-ordinated approach.

According to that report,[36] in 2007–08 pre-school education in Gaelic was provided by twelve local authorities and there were 718 pupils in fifty-five pre-school centres; in addition, the Gaelic Pre-School Council, *Comhairle nan Sgoiltean Araich*, had 108 playgroups and parent and toddler groups for 0–3 year olds. However, according to the evaluation report of the Committee of Experts (hereafter "the 2009 evaluation report"), the Committee was informed during its on-the-spot visit that this was insufficient to meet parents' demands, a major difficulty being the lack of qualified staff.[37] Primary education was provided by fifteen local authorities, with 2,164 pupils in sixty-one centres throughout Scotland; moreover, an estimated 6,000 pupils were getting some basic Gaelic language instruction through the "Gaelic Language in the Primary School" programme.[38] Two primary schools had been opened since the previous report, one in Glasgow in 2006 and one in Inverness in 2007. Moreover, *Bòrd na Gàidhlig* was liaising with parent groups in Portree, Lochaber and Barra and there was pressure for a second Gaelic school in Glasgow;[39] there was one Gaelic school in the Western Isles, with Gaelic-medium streams in twenty-three.[40] Furthermore, numerous initiatives were being pursued in other cities and towns, even in areas outwith the traditional Gaelic-speaking areas.[41]

As far as secondary education is concerned, in 2007–08 there were 2,733 learners (an increase from 2,583 in 2004–05) and 968 pupils taking courses for fluent speakers (up from 307 in 2004–05), with thirty-nine secondary schools offering Gaelic for the latter,[42] of which twenty offered a range of subjects taught in Gaelic. However, it was acknowledged in the 2009 report that this represented a "significant dip" which was attributed to the inability of individual schools to guarantee a range of subjects due to dependency on teacher availability for the subjects concerned. The Glasgow Gaelic School opened in 2006 as the only dedicated secondary school in Scotland. In the Western Isles, where all first and second year pupils study Gaelic as a second language, it is interesting to note that from third year it was more popular as a modern language than all others combined.[43]

---

[36] 2009 report (n 28) p 128.
[37] European Charter for Regional or Minority Languages, *Report of the Committee of Experts on the Charter* ECRML (2010) p 4, para 221.
[38] 2009 report (n 28) p 130.
[39] 2009 report (n 28) pp 130–31.
[40] 2009 report (n 28) p 131.
[41] 2009 report (n 28) pp 131–32.
[42] 2009 report (n 28) p 132.
[43] 2009 report (n 28) pp 133–34.

The Committee of Experts, in its 2009 evaluation report, recognised that there had been positive initiatives, plans and strategies in relation to education but considered that they needed time to produce concrete results. During its on-the-spot visit, the Committee was informed that there were some systematic deficiencies throughout the field of education, such as too few teachers, inadequate teaching materials and lack of appropriate buildings.[44] The lack of teachers is a recurrent concern which was identified by the Committee as one of the reasons underlying the "comparatively little progress made on the ground" since the previous report.[45] The Scottish Executive is committed to tackling this shortage as a priority and Bòrd na Gàidhlig has a dedicated teacher recruitment officer, as well as a national recruitment working group. The Committee of Experts considered that the undertakings with regard to pre-school, primary, secondary and technical/vocational education had only been partly fulfilled,[46] while it had insufficient information to reach a conclusion on the obligation to ensure the teaching of Gaelic history and culture.[47]

With regard to tertiary education, three universities – Edinburgh, Glasgow and Aberdeen – have a Department for Celtic Studies where undergraduate and postgraduate students may study Gaelic and conduct research into it.[48] The partner institutes of the University of the Highlands and Islands (UHI) also promote the study of and research into Gaelic.[49] Finally, adult education is provided in numerous local authority areas.[50]

ADMINISTRATIVE AUTHORITIES AND PUBLIC SERVICES

The United Kingdom's principal obligation under this heading is to allow administrative authorities, within areas where the number of users justifies it, to draft documents in Gaelic. The Committee of Experts noted in its 2010 evaluation report that, during its on-the-spot visit, representatives of Gaelic speakers had pointed out that since there was no obligation on authorities to use Gaelic, few people expected them to do so. The Committee considered that the term "allowing" in this context obliged the responsible authorities to expressly inform the relevant bodies that they were allowed to use Gaelic and, if necessary, create the conditions

---

44 2010 evaluation report (n 37) para 218.
45 On teacher shortage, see 2010 evaluation report (n 37) paras 238–39.
46 2010 evaluation report (n 37) paras 222, 226, 230 and 233.
47 2010 evaluation report (n 37) para 236.
48 2009 report (n 28) p 135.
49 2009 report (n 28) pp 92 and 135.
50 2009 report (n 28) p 136.
51 2010 evaluation report (n 37) para 254.

to make it possible.[51] The Committee had not been informed of any concrete measures in that respect and considered that the obligation was only partly fulfilled. A further undertaking relates to allowing and/or encouraging the use of Gaelic by local and regional authorities, for example in permitting the submission of oral or written applications in Gaelic (considered fulfilled by the Scottish Executive and those authorities which had adopted a language plan),[52] the publication of official documents in Gaelic (considered partly fulfilled despite a lack of detailed information[53]) and the use of Gaelic in meetings (considered fulfilled by *Comhairle nan Eilean Siar* and partly fulfilled by Highland Council, where this is limited to the Gaelic Committee; otherwise, the undertaking was not considered to be fulfilled).[54]

According to the United Kingdom's 2002 report, the Scottish Executive produces Gaelic versions of important national documents where appropriate.[55] Moreover, Standing Orders for the Scottish Parliament provide that while it shall normally conduct its business in English, its members may use Gaelic (or, indeed Scots or any other language) with the agreement of the Presiding Officer.[56] The United Kingdom's 2005 report specifies further that the Scottish Parliament encourages the use of Gaelic in debate and in committee meetings, "without excluding the use of the predominant language of the state".[57] Simultaneous interpretation is provided. Members may submit written questions in Gaelic and the public may also correspond in Gaelic with the Parliament,[58] which has a dedicated Gaelic Service.[59] *Comhairle nan Eilean Siar* and Highland Council both operate a bilingual policy in contacts with the public and each has a Gaelic development officer.[60] In addition, the 2005 report highlights various measures taken by a number of governmental and public bodies to promote the use of Gaelic, including the establishment of a Gaelic Unit by the

---

[52] 2010 evaluation report (n 37) paras 261 and 262.

[53] 2010 evaluation report (n 37) paras 264–65.

[54] 2010 evaluation report (n 37) paras 267–68

[55] European Charter for Regional or Minority Languages, *Initial Periodical Report presented to the Secretary General of the Council of Europe in accordance with Article 15 of the Charter* MIN-LANG/PR (2002) pp 5, 40.

[56] 2002 report (n 55) p 41. Christian Allard MSP, who was born in France, took the solemn affirmation of allegiance to Her Majesty Queen Elizabeth II in both English and French when he was admitted as a member of the Scottish Parliament on 15 May 2013: *http://www.bbc.co.uk/news/uk-scotland-scotland-politics-22538511*.

[57] European Charter for Regional or Minority Languages, *Second Periodical Report presented to the Secretary General of the Council of Europe in accordance with Article 15 of the Charter* MIN-LANG/PR (2005) pp 5, 55.

[58] 2009 report (n 28) p 145.

[59] See *http://www.scottish.parliament.uk/PublicInformationdocuments/GaelicServiceLeafletEnglish.pdf*.

[60] 2002 report (n 55) p 41.

Scottish Executive and the employment of two Gaelic officers by the Scottish Parliament,[61] as well as specific initiatives by three local councils (*Comhairle nan Eilean Siar*, Highland, Argyll and Bute) with regard to communication in Gaelic.[62] *Comhairle nan Eilean Siar* and Highland Council were the only ones which the Committee of Experts considered in the 2009 evaluation report to have fulfilled (and the latter only partly) the undertaking as to bilingual place names: *Comhairle nan Eilean Siar* had decided that all council signs, directional signs and street names would be bilingual, with the Gaelic name first, and that place names would mostly appear in Gaelic only.[63] The Scottish Government's policy in this respect is to replace signs on trunk roads passing through Gaelic-speaking communities and directly linking with ferry services to the Western Isles.[64]

MEDIA

With regard to the media, the United Kingdom has undertaken "to encourage and/or facilitate the creation of at least one radio station and one television channel" in Gaelic and to encourage and/or facilitate the broadcasting of radio and television programmes in Gaelic on a regular basis. A similar undertaking has been given in respect of newspaper articles, but not in respect of encouraging and/or facilitating the "creation and/or maintenance of at least one newspaper". Until 2008, the level of television and radio production remained rather low: the 2002 report indicated that Scottish Television was required to transmit not less than ninety minutes per week in Gaelic (including thirty minutes of repeats), while Grampian Television was required to transmit at least seventy-two hours per year. It was only in September 2008 that a dedicated Gaelic-language television channel, BBC Alba, was launched. It has proved highly successful, with a wide variety of high-quality programmes such as *Eòrpa*, and even non-Gaelic speakers are attracted by certain programmes such as live rugby. It was reported in 2009, when it was not yet available on Freeview, that around 220,000 viewers – two and a half times the number of those who understand Gaelic – watched the channel every week.[65] *Radio nan Gàidheal*, the BBC's Gaelic radio channel, was at that time broadcasting for fourteen hours on weekdays (with limited programmes at the weekend).[66]

---

[61] 2005 report (n 57) p 53.
[62] 2005 report (n 57) pp 54–55.
[63] 2009 report (n 28) p 146.
[64] 2010 evaluation report (n 37) para 270, and 2009 report (n 28) p 146.
[65] 2010 evaluation report (n 37) para 273.
[66] 2010 evaluation report (n 37) para 275.

While newspaper articles do appear in the national and local press, they are rather scarce and the absence of a quality Gaelic-language newspaper or even periodical is perhaps one of the most significant lacunae in the Gaelic revival: it was noted in the 2009 report that "[t]here also remains a lack of a regular newspaper directed specifically towards a Gaelic audience". According to the report, the Scottish Government does not make specific interventions to encourage and/or facilitate the publication of newspaper articles but there are regular columns in *The Scotsman*, *The Press and Journal*, *The Inverness Courier*, *The West Highland Free Press*, *The Oban Times* and *The Stornoway Gazette*, each of which is also available online.[67] There was at that time a monthly newspaper, *An Gàidheal Ùr*, but it was closed shortly afterwards due to funding issues.[68] There was also a bilingual quarterly, *Cothrom*, as well as regular Gaelic features in Free Church and Church of Scotland monthly magazines.[69] The Committee of Experts nevertheless observed that it seemed that Gaelic articles were "few and far between", and in the absence of information as to the extent to which the authorities encouraged and/or facilitated the publication of newspaper articles in Gaelic, it could not reach a conclusion on this undertaking.[70]

There is also a shortage of contemporary literature, with a relatively strong continuation of the long tradition of poetry not being replicated in prose. Mention should be made of poetry collections such as those of Sorley Maclean (for example, *Dàin do Eimhir*, edited by Christoper Whyte), "Modern Scottish Gaelic Poems" (*Nua-Bhàrdachd Ghàidhlig*), a bilingual anthology introduced by Donald MacAulay, and *Aibisidh*, by Angus Peter Campbell, as well as the "The Harp's Cry" (*Gàir nan Clàrsach*, edited by Colm Ó Baoill), a collection of much older poetry and songs.

CULTURAL ACTIVITIES AND FACILITIES

The undertakings under this heading are essentially to encourage the use of Gaelic in these particular spheres. The Scottish Government provides funding for a number of associations which promote cultural activities, the principal one being the Gaelic Arts Agency, *Pròiseact nan Ealan*, which promotes music, dance, visual arts, etc, and in 2007 produced the St Kilda Opera, a theatre and multi-media event performed simultaneously in five countries as well as on the internet.[71] A number of bodies collaborate in the

---

67 2009 report (n 28) p 150.
68 See 2010 evaluation report (n 37) para 288; *Stornoway Gazette*, 19 March 2009.
69 2009 report (n 28) p 150.
70 2010 evaluation report (n 37) para 288.
71 2009 report (n 28) p 148.

Gaelic Arts Strategic Development Group, which has contributed to the development of a National Gaelic Arts Strategy.[72] In addition, the National Mòd, organised by *An Comunn Gàidhealach*, perpetuates Gaelic poetry and song,[73] while the more recent revival in popular music has been built on the lead taken by groups such as Runrig and Capercaillie. Numerous other initiatives have also been taken and cultural activities can be found throughout Scotland, including in areas where Gaelic has not been spoken for centuries, such as Ayrshire and the Borders.[74]

Comhairle nan Leabhraichean, the Gaelic Books Council, has all Gaelic and Gaelic-related books in print,[75] and runs a bookshop (with a website and online order service) in Partick. Special mention should also be made in this context of the unique and laudable Gaelic-language feature film, *Seachd* (or *The Inaccessible Pinnacle*). Contacts are maintained between Gaelic authorities/bodies and their equivalents in Ireland and Nova Scotia, as well as with minority language groups elsewhere, including Wales,[76] while *Bòrd na Gàidhlig* has joined the Network to Promote Linguistic Diversity, established at the end of 2007 "to facilitate the sharing of existing best practice and the development of new and innovative ideas across the field of language planning".[77]

CONCLUSION

The protection offered to minority languages by the European Convention on Human Rights is limited in scope and to a large extent incidental. The European Charter for Regional or Minority Languages is the instrument which provides a framework within which national authorities can protect and promote the use of minority languages. There are those who argue, especially in times of economic austerity,[78] that investment in supporting a language which is spoken by little more than 1 per cent of the Scottish population is disproportionate or even entirely unjustified.[79] However, the

---

[72] 2009 report (n 28) p 157.

[73] 2009 report (n 28) p 152.

[74] 2009 report (n 28) p 161.

[75] 2009 report (n 28) p 158.

[76] 2009 report (n 28) pp 162 and 164.

[77] 2009 report (n 28) p 162.

[78] R Dunbar, "The Charter as a living instrument: legal challenges and perspectives", in *Minority Language Protection* (n 25) p 182.

[79] According to the 2001 census (see 2009 report (n 28) p 14) there were 58,652 Gaelic speakers; 65,674 people over the age of three were able to speak, read or write the language (compared to 69,510 in 1991), while altogether 92,396 could speak, read, write or understand it. While speakers are to be found in every council area (see 2005 report (n 57)), numbers are largely confined to specific geographical areas, in particular the somewhat diminished *Gàidhealtachd*.

same might be said of all endeavours to conserve cultural, architectural and artistic heritage, not to mention threatened flora and fauna. Indeed, the protection of living languages is not merely a question of preserving them for academic interest or aesthetic appreciation; it is rather a matter of perpetuating a vibrant vehicle of interpersonal communication and individual expression which moreover represents an entire cultural heritage. Fortunately, there has now been express recognition of the value of preserving minority languages, at the supranational level by the Charter itself (see the citation from the Preamble above) and at the national level in the Gaelic Language (Scotland) Act 2005 and the National Plan, in which it is affirmed: "Gaelic is important, as it provides Scotland with an active bilingual community. There is growing consensus regarding the benefits of bilingualism in education, culture and in personal life."

For centuries, Gaelic was suppressed and ridiculed as barbaric by English speakers who aspired to a centralised cultural hegemony (and many other languages have suffered and continue to suffer a similar fate, exacerbated by modern means of communication). This attitude was epitomised by the not-so-enlightened Samuel Johnson in his *Journey to the Western Islands of Scotland* in the late eighteenth century: "It is the rude speech of a barbarous people, who had few thoughts to express."[80] Such perceptions were the precursor of a wider suppression of minority languages as part of a misguided attempt to ensure political unity within the emerging nation-states:

> At a time when the emphasis was on strengthening the nation-state, linguistic diversity was sometimes perceived as a problem or even a threat. This negative perception was the result of the role played by language in defining and constructing national identities; also, minority languages are seen as a barrier to communication to the detriment of the consolidation of a single national identity. Linguistic diversity within the modern nation-state is therefore seen as an element that undermines the establishment and stability of a single,

---

[80] To be fair to Johnson, he also wrote to the Society for the Propagation of Christian Knowledge criticising its opposition to the use of Gaelic. The Society was at one time not at all pro-Gaelic but its attitude changed and it actually became one of the main motors in strengthening the use of Gaelic in the nineteenth century, as illustrated by this extract from William Mackay, *History of Glenurquhart and Glenmoriston* (The Northern Counties Newspaper and Printing and Publishing Company Ltd, 1893): "For many years the progress of education in the Highlands was greatly impeded by the absurd manner in which the language of the people was treated. The excellent Lowlanders who directed the affairs of the Society ... bound their schoolmasters ... to 'discharge [prohibit] their scholars to speak Earse [Irish or Gaelic]'. ... The directors of the Society at last realized the error of their ways; and in 1767 they printed a Gaelic translation of the New Testament, which was used in their schools. Translations of other works followed ... After this the teachers worked on a more rational system, and the ancient tongue was treated with some degree of respect."

unified political community, one that sows the seeds of division and instability. It may even be considered to pose a threat to the political unity of the state.[81]

This is, in fact, an attitude which pervades the thinking of numerous political authorities even today, and it can only be hoped that an increasing number of states will recognise the value of minority languages and, in Europe at least, ratify and implement the Charter.

Centuries of decline – encouraged by such attitudes – has resulted in Gaelic being largely exiled to the northern and western fringes of Scotland, and there are now no monoglot Gaelic speakers. Yet, while difficult for the non-native speaker to master, Gaelic is a language of beauty and richness, lending itself to poetry and song, and inextricably linked to a tradition and culture which, if not as romantic as Walter Scott's portrayals, nevertheless has many qualities worth maintaining in its contribution to the rich tapestry of "Europe's cultural wealth and traditions", as the Charter puts it. The financial cost may be out of proportion to the number of speakers, but seen as an investment in the conservation of cultural heritage and linguistic diversity, no price can be put on the value of preserving Gaelic as a living language.

Legal instruments, both international and national, can create favourable conditions for a minority language to flourish. But the real key to language revival and health lies with those who speak it and their determination to keep it alive as a means of every-day communication. The National Plan recognises this:

> It is Gaelic speakers who will determine whether or not the language has a future and we have to restore their confidence and their pride in the language by offering more opportunities for Gaelic to be used and valued, and for greater involvement in revitalisation initiatives.

A strong cultural identification with language and culture can indeed foment interest in preserving them, as can be seen for example in Ireland and Wales, as well as the Basque country.[82] One of the crucial factors is the

---

[81] M Lezertúa Rodríguez, "The European Convention on Human Rights and minority languages" in *Minority Language Protection* (n 25) p 19; see also M Kontra, "'Don't Speak Hungarian in Public!' – a documentation and analysis of folk linguistic rights", in M Kontra et al (eds) *Language: A Right and a Resource: Approaching Linguistic Human Rights* (1999).

[82] P Baztarrika, "The evolution of the Basque revival", in *Minority Language Protection* (n 25) p 141: "The recent history of Basque is, without question, a success story. Since the 1980s, Basque has grown and gathered strength, because that is the wish of a majority of the people, because we have used self-government in favour of Basque, because it has enabled a fundamental political consensus between the different political parties, because we have nurtured an effective public linguistic policy, with laws and regulations to normalise Basque, and because it has received the encouragement of many citizens and several organisations

transmission of the language within the family. In a study of Basque, the following observation was made:[83]

> It goes without saying that family language transmission is not enough in the language-revival process, but it also goes without saying that a language which is not transmitted in the family is a language condemned to disappear sooner or later. Family language transmission is the most certain route by which we acquire a language in any kind of natural way, and it also goes without saying that a language acquired naturally tends to be used with greater frequency in day-to-day life.

Transmission within the family is not necessarily a straightforward issue, especially once the number of native speakers has declined to a critical level: for one thing, it is not obvious for those who marry non-speakers to use with their children a language which the other parent does not understand, while both emigration of the young to non-Gaelic-speaking areas and the immigration of non-Gaels to the *Gàidhealtachd* militate against use of the language in every-day situations. Even if incomers are motivated to learn what is, after all, a difficult language with a structure very different from that of English (or, indeed, other Germanic and Romance languages, with which English speakers tend to be more familiar), it is unusual for a learner to acquire fluency or, if such a level can be attained, to have a broad enough knowledge as to emulate the usage of a native speaker as far as vocabulary and syntax are concerned (especially as there are numerous dialects and no real standard form), thus introducing an element of artificiality into the development of the language.

Nevertheless, the extensive learning of a minority language by non-speakers is the other main way of supporting it and a strong programme which promotes this can make a real contribution to the survival of the language. The stated aim of the National Plan 2012–17 is "to secure an increase in the number of people learning, speaking and using Gaelic in Scotland". Learning of Gaelic by non-native speakers is being achieved through Gaelic-medium education as well as in the provision of courses and lessons for adults. The Scottish Government has set a target of the proportion of Gaelic speakers being by 2021 at the very least at 2001 levels, and this is not an unrealistic aspiration: of the 800,000 Basque speakers, 300,000 have learned Basque at school or as adults[84] and similar successes

---

of civic society. Basque has never had so many speakers in its history, and it is used in more contexts than ever before." It should be noted, however, that, despite its suppression under Franco, Basque, with 800,000 speakers, never reached the depths of weakness that Gaelic has.

[83] Baztarrika (n 82) p 144.

[84] Baztarrika (n 82) p 146: "It is the education system that has contributed most to spreading the Basque language."

have been achieved both in Israel and closer to home in Wales, in both of which places the Ulpan immersion system has been used to great effect.[85] Even the number of people who speak, read or write Manx, the last native speaker of which died in 1974, is now approaching 2,000.[86]

These encouraging statistics give reason to be optimistic for the future of Gaelic, but there is no room for complacency. The legislative framework and supranational monitoring have been put in place but the real litmus test will be the concrete implementation of the various national plans, and this will be dependent on the strength of commitment of all actors, but in particular Gaelic speakers and the public authorities. As the chairperson of *Bòrd na Gàidhlig* observed in her introduction to the National Plan: "the National Gaelic Language Plan will require a concerted effort on the part of public authorities in Scotland, as well as Gaelic speakers themselves, if we are to make the progress required to ensure the Gaelic language has a viable future".[87]

---

[85] 2009 report (n 28) p 136.

[86] 2005 report (n 57) p 6.

[87] Baztarrika (n 76) pp 147–48: "As with any language revival anywhere in the world, three factors have helped Basque: 1. legislation to support and promote the language, 2. an effective linguistic policy promoted and financially backed by the authorities, and 3. public commitment. The first two are very important: it is no coincidence that these explain to a great extent why Basque has evolved very differently in the Basque Autonomous Community, Navarre and the Northern Basque Country, and why the most positive development of Basque has taken place in the community that has promoted the most effective public authority linguistic policy and has approved the most supportive legal framework for the Basque language – in the Basque Autonomous Community, in other words. However, the most decisive of the three factors is public commitment, because the first two would be pointless without that. In the absence of the first two factors one may struggle to make any progress; but without public commitment it is utterly impossible, even if the first two factors exist. Even mere survival is impossible without public commitment."

Human Rights and
Domestic Legal Traditions

Robert Reed*

I am grateful to have been invited to give this lecture in honour of Sir Gerald Gordon, as he approaches his eighty-fourth birthday, and in the year when the School of Law of this university celebrates an even older anniversary. The tercentenary of its foundation in its modern form makes it the first university in the UK at which a modern legal system was taught, forty years before the teaching of English law began at Oxford. Glasgow is a university which I only came to know after my own student days were past, but it is one for which I have come to feel admiration and affection. Two important influences on me, the late Neil MacCormick and Alan Rodger, were Glasgow graduates; and Alan appeared to regard it as a misfortune for his pupils to have been educated anywhere else. But I have attempted to overcome my early disadvantages, as an honorary professor here; and in my daily work at the Supreme Court I am surrounded by Glasgow graduates, who form almost half of our current judicial assistants.

But it was at a university at the other end of the M8 that I first encountered Sir Gerald. In October 1974 I was in my first week as an undergraduate when I attended my first lecture in criminal law. Sir Gerald had been appointed Professor of Scots Law two years earlier, and was already one of Scotland's leading academic lawyers, having published *The Criminal Law of Scotland* in 1967. The lecture theatre was packed with eager students: it was the first week of term. As the clock turned to the hour, in briskly strode the professor. Virginia Woolf describes a lecturer from whose face, she said, "the depressing and impossible nature of his task had removed all traces of ordinary humanity".[1] Sir Gerald's task of leading us to understand the principles of criminal law was perhaps impossible, but

---

* This is the text of a lecture delivered on 7 June 2013 at the Gerald Gordon Seminar on Criminal Law at the University of Glasgow. Since the lecture was delivered, some of the ideas in it have been reflected in my observations about proportionality in *Bank Mellat v HM Treasury (No 2)* [2013] UKSC 39, [2013] 3 WLR 179. Some of the ideas discussed in the lecture are also relevant to the case of *R (Osborn) v Parole Board*, in which the judgments of the Supreme Court were awaited at the time of writing. See now [2013] UKSC 61, [2013] 3 WLR 1020.

[1] "Why?" in *Selected Essays* (OUP edn by D Bradshaw, 2008) p 160 at 161.

he gave no sign of finding it depressing. He rightly treated lecturing as one of the performing arts; an art in which I should at once confess I am by comparison inexperienced and unskilled.

It was only many years later that I encountered Sir Gerald again, when I was a judge sitting on circuit in Glasgow, where he also sat in the High Court. I found him to be the most genial of colleagues, always ready to discuss the problems which all too frequently arose. I was relieved to discover that he shared my own pragmatic approach to criminal law as a trial judge, giving juries directions which gave priority to clarity over pedantic accuracy, and, where there was room for doubt, erring on the side of the defence so as to minimise the risk of a successful appeal. Sir Gerald was also by then the editor of the *Scottish Criminal Case Reports*, where his commentaries were treated as being at least as valuable and authoritative as most of the judgments on which he was commenting. Not a few judges anxiously awaited Sir Gerald's commentaries like prima donnas awaiting the reviews in the morning papers.

When I was invited to give this lecture, the invitation said that it was appreciated that I had not worked primarily in the field of criminal law, but that my expertise in human rights and European law would make me an appropriate person to weigh up the future challenges to Scots law. Taking that as my cue, I have decided to speak about the manner in which international human rights law has in recent years been received into our law, and how it might be approached in the future. I should make it clear that my remarks reflect a purely personal view.

I have had the privilege of sitting on the European Court of Human Rights as an *ad hoc* judge, and I am currently a member of the court's panel of *ad hoc* judges. There is no doubt in my mind as to the importance of the European Convention on Human Rights and of the role of the European court in promoting human rights protection across Europe. Its body of case law is a substantial achievement. When it comes to applying the Convention and the case law of the European court in our own courts, however, there are distinctions between an international instrument and national law, and between an international court and domestic courts, which have to be borne in mind. The issue I want to discuss is how those distinctions affect the way in which the Convention and the case law is, or ought to be, applied in our own courts.

I would like to begin with an anecdote. I spent a few weeks some years ago at the Criminal Chamber of the Cour de Cassation in Paris, the highest criminal court in France. The President of the court made the sign of the cross when he first met me, jocularly warding off the influence of the European court, on which I had recently been sitting. The French courts were at that time implementing reforms which had been made to the Code of Criminal Procedure to introduce more adversarial elements, following a judgment against France in the European court. The President and other members of the court were courteously critical of Strasbourg as a body which appeared to them to have diluted French traditions in the field of criminal law by introducing ideas about evidence and procedure derived from what they called the Anglo-Saxon tradition. It became evident to me how different our ways of thinking were. Although French procedure was designed to meet the same fundamental objectives as our own, it did so by very different means.

I sat for example on a hearing before the *Commission de Révision des Condamnations Pénales*, a body which determines whether convicted persons should be granted permission to appeal to the Cour de Cassation on the ground of fresh evidence, and whether they should be granted interim liberation. It comprises five judges of the Cour de Cassation, who have the power to carry out investigations, but must hold a hearing in court, with an adversarial procedure, before reaching their decision. The case was based on an affidavit by a newly discovered witness to the effect that he had seen the applicant painting the outside of his house at the time when the robbery of which he had been convicted was being committed many miles away. Shortly after the applicant's counsel had begun his submissions, the President of the Commission interrupted him and said that she had telephoned the witness and had been told by him that he had no real recollection of the matter and had been pressurised by lawyers into signing the affidavit. The application was dismissed on that basis. My sense of shock reflected assumptions about the role of the judiciary which are not shared on the other side of the Channel.

During my time with the French court, the Convention was rarely referred to, and I cannot recollect any occasion on which reference was made to a judgment of the Strasbourg court. French lawyers rarely referred to the Convention in the pleadings that I saw, and it appeared that the French judges did not regard it as their function to attempt to anticipate how the Strasbourg court might view French law or practice. Nevertheless, the French are not often found to have contravened the Convention.

I had a less dramatic but not altogether different experience during a visit by Supreme Court Justices in 2012 to the German Federal Constitutional Court. Our German colleagues were keen to discuss relations with the European Court of Justice, but the Strasbourg court appeared to be of less interest to them. Issues of human rights were discussed by them under reference to the guarantees of fundamental rights in the Federal Constitution, which has a higher standing than the Convention in their legal system. Their approach to these issues was again based on different assumptions from our own. For example, when we discussed the use in legal proceedings of material which could not be made public or disclosed to one of the parties for reasons of national security, we explained how some recent UK statutes seek to secure participation on behalf of the party who cannot see the material through the appointment of a security-cleared special advocate. The procedure thus enables an adversarial hearing to take place without national security being compromised. We learned that under the German system that is considered unnecessary: the court examines the material itself, without its being discussed at the hearing of the case.[2] As we discussed this, it became clear that it is regarded as the function of the German court to arrive at the truth, not to adjudicate between competing versions of the truth; and the participation of lawyers in a hearing of the case is therefore not regarded as absolutely essential to the court's performance of its function. As in the example I gave of the French criminal appeal, the German procedure for protecting national security in legal proceedings thus approaches differently from ours the claims of establishing the truth, on the one hand, and respecting the rights of the parties, on the other. I find it difficult to imagine the German approach being any more acceptable in this country than the Lord Justice-General's telephoning a witness, but it illustrates how the same fundamental objective – ensuring a just outcome without jeopardising national security – can be achieved in the context of a different legal tradition.

I have narrated these anecdotes to illustrate two related points. First, some at least of the other contracting states do not construct a domestic jurisprudence on the articles of the Convention, based on an examination of the case law of the Strasbourg court. Secondly, the way in which the different contracting states comply with the Convention may legitimately vary from one system to another. This is entirely consistent with the case law of the Strasbourg court, which has often referred to "the fundamentally subsidiary role of the Convention".[3]

There is a fairly striking contrast between the approach taken to human rights law in France and Germany and the approach often taken in this country. If you watch a hearing in the Supreme Court on the internet, or if you go and listen to a case being argued in the Criminal Appeal Court in Edinburgh, you are likely to be struck by the amount of time counsel spend citing judgments of the European court. The judgments are discussed and analysed in much the same way as if they were judgments of our own courts.

This might be thought to be slightly odd. The UK adopts a dualist approach to international law, so there is a distinction of principle between

---

[2] See eg BVerfG, Judgment of 27 October 1999 – 1 BvR 385/90, BVerfGE 101; 106, NJW 2000, 1175 on §99 Verwaltungsgerichtsordnung; BGH Judgment of 4 March 2004 – 3 StR 218/03, BGHSt 49, 112.

[3] See eg *Hatton v United Kingdom* (2003) 37 EHRR 611 at para 97.

domestic law and the state's obligations under public international law. Given that we differ in this respect from monist legal systems such as those of France and Germany, it would seem somewhat paradoxical if we were to attach greater significance than them, in our domestic law, to the judgments of an international court.

A second reason why this situation might be thought to be odd arises from the nature of the Strasbourg case law. In the first place, it always has to be remembered that it is the case law of an international court, which inevitably approaches many issues in a different way from a national court. One reason is that the court applies the principle of subsidiarity which I have already mentioned. Another important factor is that, when the court applies the principle of proportionality, which is central to the application of the Convention, it recognises that it may be less well placed than a national court to decide whether an appropriate balance has been struck in the particular national context. For that reason, in the Convention case law the principle of proportionality is indissolubly linked to the concept of the margin of appreciation. That concept does not apply in the same way at the national level, where the national court is of course in a better position to form a judgment in the particular national context, and where the degree of restraint practised by courts in applying the principle of proportionality, and the extent to which they will respect the judgment of the primary decision-maker, will depend upon the context and will in part reflect national traditions and institutional culture. For example, the German Federal Constitutional Court may, for historical and constitutional reasons, tend to adopt a more assertive role in relation to legislation than a British court would do.

The nature of the Strasbourg case law also reflects the nature of international guarantees of human rights. Different societies may be able to agree on what rights should be recognised, but they are unlikely to agree on how those rights should be applied in detail; and differences between societies may require differences in application. As I have explained, that is recognised by the Strasbourg court. It follows that international guarantees of human rights, such as the Convention, are expressed at a high level of generality, and function as broad standards rather than specific rights. The international guarantees have to be implemented in detail at a national level through much more specific laws, which vary from one jurisdiction to another, reflecting differences between their culture and traditions. An international court monitoring the compliance of states with the obligations they have undertaken then has to apply these broad standards to particular factual situations, and will understandably tend to be slower than a national court to articulate specific statements of general principle.

The Strasbourg court is well aware of these factors. It recognises that the Convention cannot be applied in a uniform manner throughout the forty-seven states which subscribe to it. It recognises that many of the issues which come before it turn on an assessment of the social conditions, culture and values of a particular society, the balancing of competing rights or interests, or an assessment of proportionality, which is in principle best carried out by institutions operating within the context of the society in question. As the court said in one of its earlier judgment:[4]

> [I]t cannot assume the role of the competent national authorities, for it would thereby lose sight of the subsidiary nature of the international machinery of collective enforcement established by the Convention. The national authorities remain free to choose the measures which they consider appropriate in those matters which are governed by the Convention. Review by the court concerns only the conformity of these measures with the requirements of the Convention.

There are other respects in which the Strasbourg case law differs from our own. One difference concerns the way in which judgments are written, and the form of reasoning employed. Judgments of the higher courts in the common law tradition analyse issues in detail and at length, and are designed to articulate binding statements of legal principle in the context of a system based on precedent. That method of reasoning is not of course common to all the forty-seven contracting states, and one could hardly expect it to be adopted by an international court. In practice, although the style in which Strasbourg judgments are drafted is not as foreign to us as that of the Luxembourg court, it is nevertheless noticeably different from our tradition. The discussion of the law is in most cases comparatively short, with a tendency to repeat well-worn formulae, and it is relatively unusual to find authoritative statements of general principle other than in judgments of the Grand Chamber.

As someone who has sat on the Strasbourg court and seen how its judgments are prepared, I also formed the impression that they are not generally designed to be subjected to the degree of detailed textual analysis which is customary in a common law system, but which one does not find in some other major European systems. Differences of detail between the drafting of a passage in one Strasbourg judgment and the slightly different wording of a corresponding passage in another do not in general bear the same weight as they might, for example, in judgments of the Supreme Court. The Supreme Court commented on this in S v L,[5] a recent Scottish appeal concerned with adoption law in which we were referred to numerous

---

[4] *Belgian Linguistic Case* (1968) 1 EHRR 241 at para 10.
[5] [2012] UKSC 30, 2013 SC (UKSC) 20.

Strasbourg cases. They offered slightly different formulations and different shades of emphasis, with different ways of summarising the previous case law, but little help was to be gained by detailed comparative or historical analysis. Such variations are unsurprising given the enormous workload of the court and the varied composition of the chambers to which cases are allocated. The judges no doubt attempt to maintain internal consistency, but their primary task is to outline the main principles and apply them to the facts of the case before them, not to establish any new proposition of law, or even to offer authoritative restatements of existing law.[6]

This of course has implications for the value of extensive citation of Strasbourg authorities, if indeed "authorities" is an entirely apt description. Since the judgments are in general heavily fact dependent, to understand them properly requires an understanding of the facts. Since few of us are familiar with, say, the arrangements for pre-trial detention in Bulgaria, this can present a serious challenge; but it is a challenge which is not necessarily worth taking up, if the arrangements bear little resemblance to our own, and the discussion of the law does no more than repeat familiar formulae and apply them to the facts. Added to this, it is necessary to remember that the Strasbourg court's approach is constantly developing, in accordance with the doctrine of evolutive interpretation. So, for the most part, the judgments give a UK court at best a broad indication of the approach which Strasbourg is likely to take to problems in a particular area of the law.

Despite this, we often receive an extensive citation of Strasbourg cases, as I have mentioned; and that sometimes goes hand in hand with a relative lack of attention to our domestic legal tradition, or to the judgments of foreign courts belonging to the same tradition. This has particularly struck me in the field of public law, where there appears at times to be a deliberate disregard of our own administrative law; and one sometimes sees a similar approach adopted in the field of criminal law.

Counsel's focus upon the Convention and the case law of the Strasbourg court reflects a particular understanding of how the Human Rights Act 1998 should be applied. Convention rights have I think been thought of as being of a similar nature to rights in the domestic law of obligations, such as the right in tort or delict to the performance of a statutory duty owed to the individual in question, and to damages in the event of default. If that is the correct approach, then it is understandable that these rights should be regarded as constituting a discrete area of the law, derived from an international convention of which an international court is the authoritative interpreter. But I am not sure that that is the correct approach. The Convention guarantees, in international law, impose obligations upon

---

[6] At paras 67 and 76.

states. Individuals are not vested in corresponding rights which they are entitled to enforce against the state, but they can make complaints that the guarantees have not been met, provided they meet a fairly broad test of being victims of the alleged infringement. The guarantees are therefore perhaps best understood as setting enforceable standards, or even (given the heavily qualified nature of a right such as the right to freedom of expression) as expressing principles or values. They are also general in nature: so general that, if they were given the status in domestic law of rights of a conventional nature, they would subsume much of our law. For example, article 6 of the Convention, if it confers an enforceable right to a fair trial, extends over most of the territory covered by our law of evidence and procedure, civil and criminal, plus a large part of our administrative law. That being so, why bother citing domestic authorities to the court? Why not cut straight to article 6, and cite judgments of the Strasbourg court concerned with, say, the Ukrainian criminal code?

In case you think that is far-fetched, I remember hearing an appeal in the Criminal Appeal Court concerned with the admissibility of evidence which the police had obtained by carrying out a search without a warrant. The issue was presented as a breach of article 8. So counsel had a sheaf of Strasbourg judgments on article 8 issues that had arisen in relation to a variety of foreign jurisdictions. When counsel was reminded that this was a familiar issue in our own law, on which we had developed a substantial body of case law before the Convention was signed, she appeared to be rather taken aback, but responded that it was quicker just to look at the Strasbourg cases: either the domestic law was in conformity with the Convention, in which case it added nothing to the Strasbourg cases, or it was not, in which case it was equally pointless to examine it. One also sometimes sees the same approach in civil cases. I remember for example a case in the Inner House of the Court of Session concerned with the suspension of an office-holder without his being given any form of hearing. Bundles of Strasbourg judgments on article 6 were put up. When I mentioned *Ridge v Baldwin*,[7] one of the most important cases in the history of public law in the UK, which was concerned with that very issue, counsel was nonplussed.

The central error in the approach I have described, as it seems to me, is thinking that because an issue falls within the ambit of a Convention guarantee, it follows that the legal analysis of the problem has to begin and end with the Strasbourg case law. But the Convention guarantees are primarily protected by our own domestic law. As the Supreme Court stated recently in the case of *R (Sturnham) v Parole Board*,[8] the ordinary approach

---

[7] [1964] AC 40.
[8] [2013] UKSC 23, [2013] 2 AC 254 at para 29.

to the relationship between domestic law and the Convention is that the courts endeavour to apply, and if need be develop, the common law, and interpret and apply statutory provisions, so as to arrive at a result which is in compliance with the UK's international obligations, the starting point being our own legal principles rather than the judgments of an international court. It is of course possible that our common law or statute law may fail to meet the requirements of the Convention. In that event, the correct response will often be for the courts to develop our domestic law in the light of our international obligations, in accordance with long-established principles of the common law; or, if more heroic surgery is required, by using the additional tools provided by the Human Rights Act; or, if the change required is too great to be carried out by the courts, the matter will have to be left to Parliament, or to the Government, exercising the power conferred by section 10 of the Human Rights Act.

How then are the Convention rights set out in the Human Rights Act to be conceptualised? Section 1 states that the expression "the Convention rights" means the rights and fundamental freedoms set out in certain articles of the Convention and its protocols, and provides that "those articles are to have effect for the purposes of this Act".[9] That provision gives domestic legal effect to the standards or principles set out in the articles of the international convention. As I have explained, the guarantees set out in the relevant articles of the Convention are not, as it seems to me, rights in a private law sense, but express standards or principles of human rights protection with which the contracting states must comply, and which can be invoked by persons who are affected by infringements in a way which satisfies the victim test.

Sections 2, 3 and 4 of the Act, concerned respectively with the interpretation of Convention rights, the interpretation of legislation, and declarations of incompatibility, are consistent with that understanding. So is section 6(1), which states that "it is unlawful for a public authority to act in a way which is incompatible with a Convention right": not that a person has a right not to be treated in a manner which is incompatible with a Convention right. The difference is subtle, but the focus is on the legality of the act of the public authority rather than on an entitlement of the individual. Section 7(1) enables a person who claims that a public authority has acted in a way which is made unlawful by section 6(1) to bring proceedings against the authority under the Act or to rely on the Convention right or rights concerned in any legal proceedings, but only if he is a victim of the unlawful act. That provision does not say that the person *has* a Convention right, but that he can *rely on* the Convention

---

[9]   Section 1(2).

right: that is to say, he can rely on the article of the Convention that sets a standard which, the person claims, the public authority has failed to meet. And he can only rely on the Convention right if he meets the victim test, which is defined by section 7(7) as meaning that he would be a victim for the purposes of the international Convention if proceedings were brought in Strasbourg. Similarly section 11 refers to a person's "reliance" on a Convention right, rather than to his possessing such a right. All of this is consistent with an understanding of the Act as establishing public law principles which reflect at a domestic level the standards set by the international convention.

That reading of the Act makes sense of section 8, which is concerned with remedies. Those remedies are discretionary: under section 8(1), the court "may grant such relief or remedy, or make such order, within its powers as it considers just and appropriate". The award of damages, in particular, is discretionary, and under section 8(3) is to be made only if "the court is satisfied that the award is necessary to afford just satisfaction to the person in whose favour it is made"; applying, in other words, the same test as is applied by the international court.[10] As the Supreme Court explained in the recent case of *R (Sturnham) v Parole Board*,[11] this discretionary remedy is of a different nature from those provided by our domestic law of obligations. Section 8 introduced into our domestic law an entirely novel remedy, the grant of which is discretionary, and which, although it is described as damages, is not tortious or delictual in nature, but is inspired by article 41 of the Convention. Naturally enough, given the international origins of the remedy and its lack of any native roots, the statute requires the courts to take into account the principles applied by the international court which is its native habitat. Even so, the Supreme Court observed that over time, and as the practice of the European court in relation to such awards comes to be absorbed into our own case law, the remedy should become naturalised. While it will remain necessary to ensure that our law does not fall short of Convention standards, we should, the Supreme Court said, have confidence in our own case law and not be perpetually looking to the case law of an international court as our primary source.

The approach to remedies adopted in section 8 would be surprising if the Act vested rights in individuals of the kind one finds in private law; but it is not in the least surprising if the Act is a public law measure setting standards to be met by public authorities which the courts can enforce at the instance of individuals possessing the necessary *locus standi*.

---

[10] Section 8(4) in terms requires the court to "take into account the principles applied by the European Court of Human Rights in relation to the award of compensation under article 41 of the Convention".

[11] [2013] UKSC 23, [2013] 2 AC 254 at para 29.

Understanding Convention rights as standards to be complied with by public authorities, including courts, rather than as rights vested in individuals in the sense in which "rights" exist in private law may perhaps seem a rather narrow and theoretical distinction, but may I think be of some assistance in resolving a number of problems. One which I have already mentioned is the treatment of Convention rights as a discrete body of domestic law derived from the judgments of the European court, rather than as a basis for the development of our domestic law when it fails to meet the standards required. I would like to say something more about that.

There are many reasons why it is important that we should not neglect the development of our own legal tradition of human rights protection. I say that not primarily because the coverage of the Convention is in some respects narrower than our domestic law, although that is a relevant consideration. Article 6, for example, does not apply in a number of contexts, such as immigration and deportation, where common law concepts of procedural fairness undoubtedly apply; and article 5 applies to the Parole Board when it is deciding whether a prisoner should be released, but not when it is deciding whether to recommend a prisoner's transfer from closed to open conditions. But there are other reasons for our courts to take our domestic law as their starting point and to check compliance with Convention rights at a later stage in the analysis.

One factor is the reputation of the common law. The domestic law of the United Kingdom has protected human rights more consistently, and over a longer period of time, than any other legal system I know of. For example, the independence of the judiciary has been protected by statute since the end of the seventeenth century and the beginning of the eighteenth. The 110-day rule in Scotland, designed to ensure that persons held in custody are tried within a reasonable time, dates from the same era. Habeas corpus in England is of course much older. Much of our law of criminal evidence and procedure has its roots far in the past, and has been designed to ensure a fair trial. Our law of tort and delict is designed to protect people's bodily integrity, their reputation, and their freedom to live free of unlawful interference of all kinds. Our law of property protects their possessions. Freedom from illegal searches of premises or correspondence has been protected under the common law since the eighteenth-century case of *Entick v Carrington*.[12] Slavery was held to be unlawful at common law at about the same time, in the case of *Somersett*[13] in England, and in the clearer ruling of the Court of Session in the case of *Knight*.[14] When

---

[12] (1765) 2 Wils KB 275, 95 ER 807.
[13] *R v Knowles, ex p Somersett* (1772) 20 State Tr 1.
[14] *Knight v Wedderburn* (1778) Mor 14545.

the House of Lords recently rejected the admission of evidence obtained by torture, they did so on the basis of the English common law and on the basis of one of the earliest statutes passed by Parliament after the Union, which prohibited the use of torture in Scotland and brought to an end the practice of extraordinary rendition of English prisoners for interrogation in Scotland.[15] A number of recent cases, such as *Pierson*,[16] *Simms*[17] and *AXA*,[18] have established the special status of common law fundamental rights.

If one works abroad in the field of human rights, as I have done in the past, one soon becomes aware of this country's reputation as an upholder of the rule of law, human rights and democratic values. To give one illustration, when I acted for the EU Commission and the Council of Europe some years ago, along with a French judge, on a project to assist Turkey in meeting requirements for accession to the EU, I was told that Turkey had insisted that the external advisers should come from the UK or France, as it had a longer history of continuous democracy than any of the other EU member states of comparable size. Our domestic tradition is something we should value and endeavour to maintain.

A second factor is the influence of the judgments of our highest courts, in particular the Supreme Court, in other common law jurisdictions around the world. This point was emphasised in the case of *Daly*,[19] concerned with a requirement that prisoners should be absent from their cells while they were being searched for contraband. The claimant challenged this practice on the ground that he had privileged correspondence with his solicitor in his cell. The House of Lords upheld his challenge on the basis of the common law principle of legal professional privilege. Lord Cooke, who had been the President of the Court of Appeal of New Zealand, said:[20]

> ... it is of great importance, in my opinion, that the common law by itself is being recognised as a sufficient source of the fundamental right to confidential communication with a legal adviser for the purpose of obtaining legal advice. Thus the decision may prove to be in point in common law jurisdictions not affected by the Convention.

It is also important that we should actively engage with the judgments of the highest courts in other common law jurisdictions. That point was reinforced recently by the Court of Appeal in a case concerned with access by the press to documents referred to in court, which was decided on the basis of

---

[15] *A v Secretary of State for the Home Department (No 2)* [2005] UKHL 71, [2006] 2 AC 221.

[16] *R v Secretary of State for the Home Department, ex p Pierson* [1998] AC 539.

[17] *R v Secretary of State for the Home Department, ex p Simms* [2000] 2 AC 115.

[18] *AXA General Insurance Ltd v Lord Advocate* [2011] UKSC 46, 2012 SC (UKSC) 122, [2012] 1 AC 868.

[19] *R v Secretary of State for the Home Department, ex p Daly* [2001] UKHL 26, [2001] 2 AC 532.

[20] At para 30.

the common law, including authorities from Canada, New Zealand, South Africa and the USA, rather than on the basis of article 10. Toulson LJ, with whose reasoning the other members of the court agreed, observed that the development of the common law did not come to an end on the passing of the Human Rights Act, but was in vigorous health and flourishing in many parts of the world which share a common legal tradition: a category in which I would include Scotland in relation to that area of the law. Toulson LJ commented that the case provided a good example of the benefit which could be gained from knowledge of the development of the common law elsewhere.[21]

One would expect that the requirements of the Convention can usually be met by our domestic law, developed by the courts if need be, without having to rely specifically on the Human Rights Act. There are, however, situations where our ordinary domestic law does not meet Convention requirements, and where the deficiency cannot be made good by the courts without recourse to the Human Rights Act. These are often situations governed by legislation, where section 3 of the Act is important. But, as the Supreme Court explained in the recent adoption case of *S v L* which I mentioned earlier,[22] it is necessary to remember that the special interpretative duty imposed by section 3 arises only where the legislation, if read and given effect according to ordinary principles, would result in a breach of the Convention rights. It is therefore necessary to decide in the first place what the legislation means, applying ordinary principles of statutory interpretation. Those principles themselves protect human rights, by presuming that retroactivity is not intended, that penal statutes are to be narrowly construed, and so on. More fundamentally, the Supreme Court explained in the *AXA* case[23] that legislation has to be construed bearing in mind the societal values which Parliament can be taken to have intended it to embody. As Lord Hoffmann stated in the case of *Simms*,[24] the courts presume that even the most general words were intended to be subject to the basic rights of the individual. The court will also incline towards an interpretation of legislation which does not place the United Kingdom in breach of its international obligations, including the obligations arising under the Convention.

There are two other points which may be worth mentioning. The first is that if a Strasbourg judgment appears to conflict with our domestic law,

---

[21] *R (Guardian News & Media Ltd) v Westminster Magistrates' Court (Article 19 intervening)* [2012] EWCA Civ 420, [2013] QB 618 at para 88.

[22] [2012] UKSC 30, 2013 SC (UKSC) 20 at paras 15–17 and 33.

[23] *AXA General Insurance Ltd v Lord Advocate* [2011] UKSC 46, 2012 SC (UKSC) 122, [2012] 1 AC 868 at para 153.

[24] *R v Secretary of State for the Home Department, ex p Simms* [2000] 2 AC 115 at 131.

it does not automatically follow that the court will adjust our domestic law to bring it into line. For example, Lord Hoffmann said in the *Alconbury* case that, if he thought that decisions of the European court compelled a conclusion fundamentally at odds with the distribution of powers under the British constitution, he would have considerable doubt as to whether they should be followed.[25] In the *Pinnock* case, Lord Neuberger made a similar remark about the position where application of a Strasbourg decision would produce a result which was inconsistent with a fundamental feature of our law. If our courts decide, after careful consideration, that they should not follow a judgment of the European court, that is lawful under the Human Rights Act: section 2 requires only that judgments of the European court should be taken into account. Respectful disagreement is unusual but not unknown, and may give rise to adjustment on one side or the other. That has been demonstrated on several occasions, for example when the Strasbourg court had not properly understood aspects of our law of negligence[26] or courts martial.[27] A recent example is the *Animal Defenders* case,[28] in which the House of Lords declined to follow a judgment of the Strasbourg court which was said to require the abandonment of the UK's ban on political advertising, and the Grand Chamber subsequently accepted the House of Lords' assessment of what was appropriate in the circumstances of the UK. Another recent example is the *Horncastle* case,[29] in which the Supreme Court declined to follow a Strasbourg judgment concerned with hearsay evidence, and the Strasbourg court was persuaded by the Supreme Court's reasoning to modify the approach it had previously adopted. There are other cases where the House of Lords and the Supreme Court have decided to alter their previous position in the light of Strasbourg judgments.[30] Whether our courts should follow a Strasbourg decision is always a matter of judgment, exercised in the light of Parliament's intention in enacting the Human Rights Act.

It also has to be borne in mind that to give effect to a Strasbourg judgment may in some circumstances take the courts beyond their proper function under our constitution. The courts can develop the common law, but only incrementally. Section 3 of the Human Rights Act permits the

---

[25] *R (Alconbury) Ltd v Secretary of State for the Environment* [2001] UKHL 23, [2003] 2 AC 295 at para 76.

[26] See *Osman v United Kingdom* (1998) 29 EHRR 245; *Z v United Kingdom* (2001) 34 EHRR 97.

[27] See *Cooper v United Kingdom* (2004) 39 EHRR 171; *R v Spear* [2002] UKHL 31, [2003] 1 AC 734; *Morris v United Kingdom* (2002) 34 EHRR 1253.

[28] *R (Animal Defenders International) v Secretary of State for Culture, Media and Sport* [2008] UKHL 15, [2008] 1 AC 1312.

[29] *R v Horncastle* [2009] UKHL 14, [2010] 2 AC 373.

[30] See *Manchester City Council v Pinnock* [2011] UKSC 6, [2011] 2 AC 104.

courts to adopt a robust approach to the interpretation of legislation, but not to amend it, so major changes in our law remain the constitutional responsibility of the legislature.

The second point I would mention is that there appears to me to be a question as to whether our courts are limited by the terms of the Human Rights Act to giving effect to Convention rights only to the extent that they have already been clearly established by judgments of the European court. This question arose before the Supreme Court in the Scottish criminal case of *Ambrose v Harris*.[31] The issue in that case was whether the requirement that a criminal suspect must have access to legal advice before being interviewed at a police station, which the Strasbourg court had held to be required by article 6 of the Convention, also applied where the suspect was questioned before being taken to a police station. The majority held that it did not. Part of their reasoning was to the effect that, since Strasbourg had not yet considered such a situation, therefore the claim could not succeed. There is, however, an argument, powerfully expressed in that case by Lord Kerr, that the Human Rights Act does not permit, let alone require, our courts to sit on their hands until Strasbourg has pointed the way.

There have indeed been a number of cases in which the House of Lords and the Privy Council have not waited for a lead from Strasbourg before making their own assessment: for example, the case of *Ullah*,[32] ironically often cited as authority for an approach to Convention rights according to which domestic courts merely reflect the decisions of the Strasbourg court on similar facts, but actually a case in which the House of Lords went further than Strasbourg in accepting that article 9 of the Convention might be violated by the removal of a person from the UK to a country where he would suffer religious discrimination; *Limbuela*,[33] where the House held that article 3 prohibited the Government from deliberately reducing asylum seekers to destitution; *Holland v HM Advocate*,[34] concerned with dock identification; *EM (Lebanon)*,[35] where the House held that a mother and child should not be deported because they would then be separated, contrary to article 8; the Northern Ireland case of *Re G*,[36] where the House held that a blanket ban on unmarried couples adopting was incompatible with article 8 read with article 14; and the

---

[31]   [2011] UKSC 43, 2012 SC (UKSC) 53, [2011] 1 WLR 2435. The same approach was followed in *HM Advocate v Jude* [2011] UKSC 55, 2012 SC (UKSC) 222, and in *McGowan v B* [2011] UKSC 54, 2012 SC (UKSC) 182, [2011] 1 WLR 3121.
[32]   *R (Ullah) v Special Adjudicator* [2004] UKHL 26, [2004] 2 AC 323.
[33]   *R (Limbuela) v Secretary of State for the Home Department* [2005] UKHL 66, [2006] 1 AC 396.
[34]   [2005] UKPC D 1, 2005 SC (PC) 3.
[35]   *EM (Lebanon) v Secretary of State for the Home Department* [2008] UKHL 64, [2009] 1 AC 1198.
[36]   *Re G (Adoption: Unmarried Couple)* [2008] UKHL 8, [2009] 1 AC 173.

recent case of *Rabone*,[37] where the Supreme Court equated the position of voluntary patients in mental hospitals with that of detained patients for the purposes of the operational duties arising under article 2 in relation to the risk of suicide.

Drawing together the various threads of these remarks, the European court's aim is not to construct a code to be adopted by the forty-seven contracting states. It knows very well that there are important differences between the various societies and their legal systems. But the court is developing a body of high level principles which can be taken to be applicable across the different legal traditions. We for our part should read the European cases with that in mind, not attempting to mimic the Strasbourg court, but standing back from the cases to identify the broader principles with which our law should comply, rather than casting around for decisions on the same facts as those before the national court. This should be a familiar technique. In our own system, as Sir Frederick Pollock once said: "judicial authority belongs not to the exact words used in this or that judgment, nor even to all the reasons given, but only to the principles accepted and applied as necessary grounds of the decision".[38] In the Strasbourg law, as in our own, we need to identify the principles underlying the development of a line of authorities on a particular topic. We should then find the best way, faithful to our own legal tradition, of giving expression to those principles. If we do, our domestic legal tradition can continue to develop.

Viewed in this way, the Human Rights Act, and the Convention to which it gives effect, should not be regarded as exotic interlopers sitting apart from the common law, but rather as guaranteeing standards which have deep roots in the common law and in our parliamentary tradition. The protection of human rights is not alien to us: it is deeply embedded in our legal and political culture. The Convention system is a particular way of institutionalising respect for human rights at the international level; and, properly understood, the effect given to it by the Human Rights Act should in my view support the continuing development of our domestic law, in step with this country's international obligations.

---

[37] *Rabone v Pennine Care NHS Trust* [2012] UKSC 2, [2012] 2 AC 72. The Strasbourg court subsequently reached the same conclusion, expressly relying upon the approach taken in *Rabone: Reynolds v United Kingdom* (2012) 55 EHRR 1040.

[38] F Pollock, "Introduction", in J H Drake and others (eds), *The Progress of Continental Law in the Nineteenth Century* (1918) p xli at xliv.

A Note on the Doctors of the Law and their Books

O F Robinson

The Regius Chair of Civil Law in the University of Glasgow was founded in 1713 by Queen Anne. William Forbes was appointed to the chair early in 1714; he had been an advocate since 1696.[1] It is not clear how much he knew about the library in Glasgow, since almost certainly he had taken his MA at St Andrews. However, since he had been joint Keeper of the Faculty of Advocates' Library since 1705, when he had been appointed by the Faculty to collect Court of Session decisions for the benefit of its members, he must have been aware of its existence. The first catalogue of Glasgow University Library dates from 1691,[2] two years after the formal opening of the Advocates' Library. There were clearly also many other books elsewhere in Scotland, particularly in Aberdeen University Library, that reflected Scotland's place in European legal history. Glasgow's library, however, does not seem to have specialised in law books at this period, but rather in theological works – Andrew Melville, fresh from Geneva, had become Principal of the University in 1574. The legal collection was later; perhaps Forbes had some influence here. He bought many books for the Advocates' Library in the 1730s, especially Dutch and English texts. While Sir George Mackenzie is hardly relevant to Glasgow's tercentenary celebrations, it was my work on his *Matters Criminal* that drew my attention to the use of the doctors made by Scots lawyers.

What use did Forbes make of the resources available to him, whether in Edinburgh or Glasgow, or indeed in private collections? To judge what awareness there was in Scotland of the legal thinking in the rest of Europe, let us look at our institutional writers, Stair (1619-95), Mackenzie (1636-91), Forbes (1668x71-1745), and Erskine (1695-1768). We shall look first at their description of their sources, then at their treatment of *negotiorum gestio* as being a very Civilian concept, and finally a glance at criminal law in Mackenzie, Forbes and Erskine.

---

[1] For Forbes's life, see M P Clancy, "Forbes, William (1668x71-1745)", *Oxford Dictionary of National Biography* (2004).

[2] Dr Stephen Rawles has kindly made available to me the disc of his transcription of this first catalogue.

STAIR

Stair's *Institutions*[3] are not modelled on Justinian's *Institutes*, but rather follow "the institutional writings" of continental scholars such as Coquille or Loisel in France, Stryk or Carpzov in the German lands, Grotius in the Netherlands, scholars who were seeking to establish their own municipal law. His scale is therefore much, much larger than the Justinianic model, but what it drew from that was the concept of municipal law as private law, based on persons, things – a comprehensive view of private assets, including inheritance as well as both property and obligations – and actions, largely ignoring commercial, public and criminal law. As an example of the sources Stair chose to cite, his introductory title on the Common Principles of Law refers nineteen times to the Bible, four times to ancient literary sources, five times to Justinian's codification, ie the *Corpus Iuris Civilis*, ten times to Scots statutes and ten times to Scottish cases; there is also one reference to Craig. Stair was dismissive of the doctors as lacking a principled system, simply piling up opinions:[4] "Yet there are not wanting of late of the learnedest lawyers who have thought it both feasible and fit that the law should be formed into a rational discipline", as Duarenus' *de ratione discendi docendique juris*, and Grotius, especially in the Prolegomena to *de jure belli ac pacis*.

In *Institutions* Book I, title 8, dealing with quasi-contract (which Stair held to be based on obedience rather than a kinship to contract,[5] we find the following references: twenty-nine to the *Corpus*, one to Cicero, fourteen cases, and one reference (I.viii.3) to Grotius. In the following title on reparation, based on the Roman quasi-delict, there is one reference to Cujas.[6] Stair, however, seems elsewhere, when he did find a convenient exposition, to have followed one primary source among the doctors and used its citations rather than reading more widely.[7] This is in marked contrast to Mackenzie.

MACKENZIE

In his *Institutions*, Mackenzie deliberately followed the model of Justinian's *Institutes* "to the end there may be as little difference found betwixt the civil law and ours as is possible, and that the reader may not be distracted by different methods".[8] In the opening title on Laws in General, Mackenzie

---

[3] I have used the edition of D M Walker (1981), which is of Stair's second edition.

[4] Stair, *Inst* I.i.17.

[5] Stair, *Inst* I.viii.1

[6] Stair, *Inst* I.ix.4.

[7] W M Gordon, "Stair, Grotius and the sources of Stair's *Institutions*" in *Roman Law, Scots Law, and Legal History: Selected Essays* (2007) p 255.

[8] G Mackenzie *The Institutions of the Law of Scotland* in *The Works of the Eminent and Learned Lawyer, Sir George Mackenzie of Rosehaugh*, Vol II (1722) 278, I.ii.1

did describe the division into the Law of Nature, the Law of Nations, Civil law (known as the common law), canon law, and the municipal law of Scotland, partly written – Acts of the Parliament of Scotland, Acts of Sederunt, the Auld Lawes – and partly unwritten, including judicial decisions as well as custom. In these elementary books the authority of the lecturer is deemed sufficient for the student, for there are no citations.

Mackenzie's *Institutions* explained quasi-contracts as having "the resemblance and are of the nature of contracts".[9] He devoted a paragraph to *negotiorum gestio* and then listed – but not explicitly as such – the heads of Justinian's other paragraphs in *Institutes* 3.27,[10] but he then went on to say that he had treated of tutory, etc, elsewhere, as also of the obligations from quasi-delict.

Mackenzie devoted one title, and like his model the last, to crimes. Again there are no citations. The title is curious as covering so many crimes so briefly; further, it is laid out illogically.[11] The contrast with *Matters Criminal* is marked, but there he was breaking new ground.

FORBES

Forbes generally, in his *Institutes*,[12] cited very little other than statute. After all, Scots law was nearly half a century further developed from Stair and Mackenzie, and particularly there was the effect of the Act of Union. It is worth noting that Forbes's *Institutes* are on a scale somewhere between Stair and Mackenzie. In the Preface to his *Institutes*, Forbes – explaining that the *Institutes* were drawn from his *Great Body of the law of Scotland* "for the use of such as shall study law under my care and direction in the University of Glasgow",[13] said that he was copying John Voet of Leiden, whose *Compendium* was published before his *Commentary*, as well as following Justinian's example.[14] He felt the need to produce his own work because Mackenzie's *Institutes*, though excellent, were out of date in many matters, and whole areas of law were there omitted or barely mentioned; Forbes wanted a work adapted to his style of teaching.[15] In the first chapter, he quoted the definition of justice as "a constant and perpetual desire of giving

---

[9] Mackenzie, *Institutions* III.iii.23.

[10] Mackenzie, *Institutions* III.iii.24.

[11] See my Stair Lecture, "Law, Morality and Sir George Mackenzie", in H L MacQueen (ed), *Miscellany VI* (Stair Society vol 54, 2009) p 11.

[12] I have used the facsimile reprint (2012) with Introduction by H L MacQueen of *The Institutes of the Law of Scotland* (1722 and 1730).

[13] Forbes, *Institutes* (n 12) p 10.

[14] Forbes, *Institutes* (n 12) p 11.

[15] Forbes, *Institutes* (n 12) p 12.

to every one his due", but without giving the source.[16] In describing the canon law (p 28) as a source of Scots law, he referred not only to the constituent parts of the *Corpus Iuris Canonici* – which is all that Stair mentioned in this context – but also to the seventh book of decretals collected in 1590 by Peter Matthaeus of Lyons and to Giovanni Paolo Lancelotti's *Institutes of Canon Law* of 1563.[17] Forbes also explained the role of Girardus Niger and Obertus de Orto in the collection of the *Libri Feudorum*, which Hugolinus inserted in the *Corpus Iuris Civilis* after Justinian's *Novels*. He also referred to editions of the *Libri Feudorum* by Alvarotti and by Cujas, also Julius Pacius and Dionysius Gothofredus.[18] These comments on the sources are not profound, but they were not lifted from Stair or Mackenzie; clearly Forbes did do some reading from the sources available to him.

Forbes's *Institutes* has three and a half pages on obligations arising from quasi-contract. The paragraph on *negotiorum gestio* simply reads: "He whose affairs are carried on prudently, tho' by some accident unsuccessfully, in his absence, without his knowledge or authority from him, is liable to the manager for his necessary expenses; and the latter is answerable to the former if he fail in the exactest diligence."[19] There is no source given for any of the remarks in the title. In contrast, the discussion in Forbes's *Great Body*[20] on *negotiorum gestio* does give authority. He cited the Digest some dozen times, the Institutes once and the Code two or three times. He cited Stair's opinion on a mother's claim for expenses, but there is otherwise no citation of the doctors, even in this most Civilian of contexts. Unsurprisingly, there is no citation of statute here, and only four cases. It seems to me a little strange that the *Body* is content to give the literal sources, the Roman texts, but not any learned expatiation upon them. This section of the major work seemed to me sound but hardly original.

Criminal law and procedure takes up almost half of Forbes's *Institutes* – quite extraordinary for an institutional work, but presumably this was for the sake of his teaching. The Preface to this part mentions Mackenzie,[21] but explains that there was need not only to bring up to date the exposition of the criminal law but to provide the decisions of the Justiciary Court which nobody had yet set forth. But the whole treatment in fact simply echoes Mackenzie. There was nothing new in the general part, the discussion of the principles of liability, etc except the occasional statute. Forbes's treatment was of course useful for the new kinds of offence. However, remarkably,

[16] Forbes, *Institutes* (n 12) p 22.
[17] Forbes, *Institutes* (n 12) pp 27–28.
[18] Forbes, *Institutes* (n 12) pp 29–31.
[19] Forbes, *Institutes* (n 12) p 212.
[20] GU MS Gen. 1246-52, available at *http://www.forbes.gla.ac.uk/*, 908–12.
[21] Forbes, *Institutes* (n 12) p 511.

in an appendix to the title on witchcraft, "Nothing seems plainer to me than that there may be and have been witches, and that perhaps such are now actually existing."[22] In the actual title dealing with witchcraft,[23] not abolished as a specific crime until 1735, five years after the publication of this second part of his *Institutes*, Forbes talks of compacts with the Devil, the distinction between good and bad witches – "but this term of a good witch is very improper for all who have commerce with Satan are certainly bad".[24] Really, he has if anything receded from Mackenzie's scepticism. Hume's *Commentaries on the Law of Scotland respecting Crimes* (1797) reflected the new world.

ERSKINE

In his introductory title to *The Institute of the Law of Scotland*,[25] "Of laws in general", Erskine did refer to Pufendorf and Hobbes, also several times to Bacon, and once to Grotius (incorrectly cited). Erskine, a younger contemporary of Forbes, still saw it as necessary to cite a dozen texts from the *Corpus* in his discussion of *negotiorum gestio*, but nothing from elsewhere.

In the title on Crimes with which Erskine ends his *Institute*, specifically on the model of Mackenzie's *Institutes* but at greater length, he did refer to "the doctors" a couple of times. On fatal wounding he referred specifically, but only through Mackenzie, to Gomez and Zacchiaeus; he also cited Coke.[26] Then, on assassination, there were citations from the Decretals, and Caballus, but these are just copied from Mackenzie.[27] Perhaps he looked up the *Corpus* texts for himself, perhaps not. The reference to Pufendorf as well as to Grotius in the justification of theft in case of necesssity, as for example to preserve one's life, are not texts used by Mackenzie.[28] (Incidentally the Pufendorf citation should be 1.5.23, not 2.6.5, though the Grotius citation is correct.)

Matters Criminal[29] was, of course, an entirely different work, a major statement, innovatory, thorough. But it is interesting that Mackenzie's citations in *Matters Criminal* were not mechanical and repetitive. I found almost no "copying" from his sources. Indeed far otherwise; mostly he seems to have relied on his memory, or perhaps on notes made during his

---

22 Forbes, *Institutes* (n 12) p 891.
23 Forbes, *Institutes* (n 12) pp 552–61.
24 Forbes, *Institutes* (n 12) p 554.
25 I have used the third edition (Edinburgh, 1793).
26 Erskine, *Institute* IV.iv.44.
27 Erskine, *Institute* IV.iv.45.
28 Erskine, *Institute* IV.iv.60.
29 G Mackenzie, *The Laws and Customs of Scotland in Matters Criminal* (1678) (ed O F Robinson, Stair Society vol 59, 2012); see especially the Index of Sources.

reading. In Mackenzie's introductory title to *Matters Criminal*, "Of crimes in general", there are thirty citations from the *Corpus Iuris Civilis* (including one mention of the *Basilika* and one of the *Libri Feudorum*), twenty-two from Scots statutes (including the Auld Lawes), fourteen cases, five citations from older Scots jurists, and twenty-five from the doctors (including the English Fortescue and Duck). None of these turns out to be a string of citations from some later doctor, which is why I have not included Gomez, cited – as Mackenzie pointed out – by Clarus, in my count. In the introductory title to criminal procedure, "Of jurisdiction in general", there are three citations from the *Corpus*, four from older Scots jurists and two from the continental doctors.

The Library of the Faculty of Advocates, inaugurated by Mackenzie on 15 March 1689 but already in existence as a functioning entity, was unsurprisingly the most important legal library of the day.[30] Some forty-seven out of the 118 doctors cited by Mackenzie appear in the first catalogue, whereas only twenty or so of his sources were certainly in the Glasgow University library in 1691. But the Glasgow catalogue is much less accurate; it was, after all, recording books given or collected over a considerable time, whereas the Faculty Library was in its infancy, and had only 433 entries, less than a tenth of Glasgow's contemporary collection, which may well have been larger than we can prove. Apart from Mackenzie's own library, which has vanished without trace, there were many other important collections in private hands, particularly among the legal profession, for example the library of Charles Areskine.[31]

What conclusions can one draw? One of the effects of the Act of Union may well have been that Scots lawyers felt less intellectual need to consult the continental doctors. After all, one reason for such consultation had been due to the very small size of the Scots jurisdiction. Another effect – obviously – was that English law had become more relevant. Once English statutes, and even to some extent English cases, could be incorporated into the discussion of Scots law, the base of legal knowledge was enlarged in a different direction.

But, quite simply, there is the point that doctrine, the learning of the Civilian academics and their copious writings, had been incorporated into Scots law by Stair (even if in a somewhat slapdash manner) and Mackenzie, and so, like the Roman civil law itself, it had become only an indirect source.

---

[30] M Townley, *The Best and Fynest Lawers and Other Raire Bookes* (1990), gives a list of the books in the Library in 1683.

[31] See the abstract of Dr Karen Baston's paper given at the Scottish Legal History Group 2011 in (2012) 33 JLH 103.

The Trial of Captain Green

J Irvine Smith *

INTRODUCTION

Piracy, one of the oldest and apparently still ineradicable of crimes, has always intrigued the minds of humanity, and its details corrupted their imagination. It does not, however, occupy a significant place in the calendar of Scottish crimes. Here was a country which for centuries had an unenviable reputation for violence in most of its many forms, but the criminal records of Scotland contain few cases of piracy. Scotland had neither the coast, the climate nor the commerce found in the traditional pirate areas of the world in the seventeenth and eighteenth centuries – the Mediterranean, the Caribbean, the Indian Ocean ("most strange, sequestered and beautiful of Seas") and the South China Seas – on profitable trade routes and comparatively calm seas. Baron Hume's classic *Commentaries* on Scots criminal law refer only to some eight Scottish cases of piracy in the period 1535 to 1781.[1] In 1705, however, the trial of Captain Green, and his crew in Edinburgh, gave Scotland the most noted trial for piracy in the modern era. Hume describes this case as "one of some interest and curiosity in itself, but which attracted still more attention, owing to the prevailing discontents and political complexion of the times".[2] Most trials of importance, and this is certainly one, concern and interest only the parties, their relatives and friends. There are, however, a few cases which involve, acutely and immediately, the issues which at their date are the concern of their societies. The trial of Captain Green and his crew in 1705 by the Scottish Admiralty Court was one such case which had many claims on the interest of Scotland and of England and of their lawyers. It provoked violent passions in both countries and was the last public demonstration, before the Union of Parliaments, of Scotland's ancient hatred for her Auld Enemy – England. In England it was regarded as proof positive of the corruption, inefficiency and rottenness of the

---

* The text represents a revised version of a lecture given to the Annual General Meeting of the Stair Society in Edinburgh in 1998.

[1] D Hume, *Commentaries on the Law of Scotland, Respecting Crimes* (4th edn, 1844) vol I, p 480.
[2] Hume, *Commentaries* (n 1) vol I, p 484.

then Scottish system of criminal justice and of the violence and instability of her people. It was a case which proved to both countries that the two could no longer be separately governed, and it precipitated the Union of their Parliaments. Most histories of England and of Scotland refer to the trial of Captain Thomas Green. In England the general view has been that the captain's conviction was one of the great miscarriages of justice in the history of the two countries. In Scotland, Anglophobia was endemic from the early Middle Ages but not until this case – and, as yet, never since – has the loathing of each country for the other reached the intensity it did over the prosecution, conviction and execution of Green, Madder (his mate) and Simpson (his gunner), and the conviction for piracy of eleven of the crew. Daniel Defoe's contemporary comment on the subject, on which, as an eyewitness, he took much interest, was: "Never two nations that had so much affinity in circumstances have such inveteracy and aversion to one another in their blood."[3]

HISTORICAL BACKGROUND

Politics

The antecedents of the trial lay in the disastrous history of Scotland from the end of the Cromwellian Union in 1660. In that period Scotland experienced one misfortune after another, for most of which she blamed England and King William III, and all of which eventually drove the old ancestral hatred of England into frenzy. The closing of the English colonial markets, which, during the Cromwellian Union, had been open to them, was a blow to Scottish traders. The Massacre of Glencoe in 1692 shocked even the Lowlanders and was execrated as an act of English tyranny. The harvests of the late 1690s were disastrous. There was famine in which one in five of the population in Scotland died – "The hungry years of King William". It was the period of the war between the two Parliaments which, in the early eighteenth century, produced an impossible situation. The English Act of Settlement 1701 adopted the Hanoverian and Protestant succession. In 1703 the Scots Parliament refused to follow. At one point the English Government considered the possibility of an Anglo-Scottish War. In March 1705 the English Alien Act provided that until Scotland adopted the Hanoverian Succession, Scottish imports to England of linen, coal and cattle were forbidden. Defoe commented that, at one point, England had twenty-four warships fitted to prevent the Scots trading with France.

---

[3] D Defoe, *The History of the Union of Great Britain* (1709) p 1.

The Company of Scotland

In Scotland, in the 1690s, there was the unprecedented enthusiasm for, followed by the tragedy of, the Darien Scheme. This was the age when chartered companies, like the East India Company in England, were granted exclusive monopolies and their trading was regarded as the state's proper commercial activity. Scotland watched with envy the wealth that flowed to England from its trade and, by an Act of 1695, the Scots Parliament provided for the setting up of a Company of Scotland, with extensive powers to found colonies and to trade with Asia, Africa and America.[4] When English investors in the new company withdrew, leaving the necessary capital short, the Scottish capital share was increased to half the total capital available in Scotland. It became the particular and accepted duty of Scots to subscribe. Not since the Reformation had there been a national movement like it. Great and small subscribed[5] and all Scotland followed the fortunes of the company as these ranged from unbridled optimism to unmitigated disaster. By 1697 the Company of Scotland was committed to a settlement of Darien on the Isthmus Panama – "The door of the seas and the key of the Universe", which geographically it was, but the land in question belonged to Spain and its climate was fatal to Europeans. Scotland sent two expeditions to Darien both of which were disastrous. Of the first (1698), fewer than one in four of the immigrants survived hostile natives and fever-ridden swamps. Only one of the five ships sent out survived the horrendous voyage returning to Scotland. It was accepted in Scotland that that ship made its return because of the determination and efforts of her captain, Robert Drummond. Another relief expedition sailed under an order from William III but English colonies in the area refused any help and eventually this relief expedition surrendered to Spanish troops. The Company of Scotland had collapsed with a loss of two thousand lives, untold misery for those who survived and the loss of £250,000 sterling.

The Company then planned a trading venture to the East. They secured the use of a ship, *The Annandale*, then moored in the Thames, where they started to fit her out for the India trade and to recruit English sailors. To the English East India Company these were breaches of the English company's charter. They had *The Annandale* seized; an expensive

---

[4] Act for a Company Tradeing to Affrica and the Indies 1695 (APS IX, 377, c 10; RPS 1695/5/104). This implemented the undertaking given in the Act for Encouraging of Foreign Trade 1693 (APS IX, 314, c 50; RPS 1693/4/107).

[5] The Faculty of Advocates, for instance, invested £1,000 sterling in the venture: J M Pinkerton (ed), *Minute Book of the Faculty of Advocates 1661–1750* (Stair Society vol 29, 1976) pp 167–69, entries for 24 March, 3 June and 13 June 1696, directing the Faculty Treasurer, Mr John Fairholm, to subscribe.

litigation followed with seventeen counsel engaged and, in the end, the ship was forfeited to the English Company. The Scottish reaction was that here was another example of England's determination to thwart Scottish commercial ambitions.

The last venture of the Darien Company was to be as ill-fated as its predecessors. It sent two ships, *The Speedy Return*, captained by the formidable Robert Drummond, and a smaller vessel – a brigantine – *The Content*, under Captain Stewart, and with Robert's brother, Thomas Drummond, as supercargo. Their destination was to be The Indies and their professed object trade. They sailed from the Clyde on 25 May 1701 with crews of twenty-four and twenty respectively. Not one of these men would ever return to Scotland. In 1705, shortly after Green's trial, two men, who claimed they had been two of the crew of *The Speedy Return*, appeared in Portsmouth and swore affidavits that *The Speedy Return* and *The Content* had been pirated. Having so sworn these two men then disappeared. They are referred to later in this account. The result, however, was that both these ships and the crews had disappeared without trace. Captain Green's trial, which absorbed the attention and passions of both countries, concerned the fate of these two vessels and the alleged doings of an English ship, *The Worcester*, which had also been in Indian waters for some two years.

ENTER *THE WORCESTER*

Background

The Worcester – between 130 and 160 tons (the figures at this time were always vague) – was what was called a "separate stock ship", that is to say, separate from the East India Company. She had a crew of about thirty-two and was armed. Her owners were a group of London merchants headed by Thomas Bowrey and, in 1701, they appointed Thomas Green, then aged twenty-one, as master, with a view to trading to the East. Green seems a rather colourless, unassertive figure with a weakness for alcohol and some indifference to his instructions. He was forbidden to carry drugs or deal in slaves but, when he returned, he had on board two black slaves and some opium. On 8 March 1702, *The Worcester*, with a crew, most of whom were under twenty-one, sailed from England and, for some two years, was in Indian waters: according to her owner, trading; according to the Scots, turning pirate. Returning home in 1704, to avoid French privateers in the Channel, she took the route round the west of Ireland and the north of Scotland, eventually putting into Fraserburgh; from there she sailed south and, waiting for an escort, on 3 July 1704, dropped anchor in Leith, in a Scotland seething with anti-English feeling.

Boarding of *The Worcester*

To the disillusioned directors of the Company of Scotland, the arrival of this English ship appeared a godsend which gave them the opportunity to avenge the loss of *The Annandale* and recoup some of their consequent losses. The Act founding the Darien Company gave it a right to make reprisals and seek reparation for damage done by sea or land. Founding on this the Company issued a warrant to the Company's secretary, Roderick MacKenzie, for the seizure of *The Worcester*. The phraseology of the warrant was interesting: MacKenzie and "such others as he should think fit to call to his assistance" to "go on board in a prudent and a discreet manner to make seizure of the ship". This was, even for those days, an unusual order for a company secretary. It was in fact an order to seize an armed merchantman with a crew of thirty-two in a "prudent and discreet manner". The warrant, it will be noted, says nothing about legal manner. MacKenzie, in a long report, which he obviously enjoyed writing,[6] described how these instructions were obtempered. He described how he collected eleven "good gentlemen and (I must own) much prettier fellows than I pretend to be".[7] Their numbers were later increased. They proposed to go on *The Worcester* on 12 August in three different parties, each party equipped with brandy, limes, sugar and the prerequisites of an acceptable and hopefully powerful punch. These three parties of pretty fellows, who purported not to recognise one another, boarded *The Worcester*. The visitors, in MacKenzie's words, were soon "lulling all the crew into a full security with drinking, singing &c".[8] At the "passing of a watchword", however, the pretty fellows took up various positions and produced their weapons. The few of the crew who offered resistance were overcome; some of them, according to Mackenzie, attempted to give the visitors "a pretty rugged chorus by laying hands on some brass blunderbushes that hung ready charged in the cabin, but they were quickly made to lose their holds". By 9 pm MacKenzie had seized the vessel or, as he put it, "The ship was at last taken with a Scots song".[9] It was undoubtedly an unorthodox and remarkable bag for 12 August. The next day, with a prize crew on board, the ship was laid up at Burntisland.

Unfortunately the Company had confused nationality with ownership. They had a case against the East India Company, to which company they believed *The Worcester* belonged. *The Worcester*, however, did not belong to the East India Company but to a group of English merchants, headed by

---

[6] A copy of his report is reproduced in J Hill Burton, *Narratives from Criminal Trials in Scotland* (1852) vol I, pp 159 ff.

[7] Hill Burton, *Narratives from Criminal Trials* (n 6) vol I, pp 160–61.

[8] Hill Burton, *Narratives from Criminal Trials* (n 6) vol I, p 163.

[9] Hill Burton, *Narratives from Criminal Trials* (n 6) vol I, p 164.

Thomas Bowrey, against whom the Scots had no civil claims, and who set about attempting to recover his ship. In short, the Scots now had on their hands not a "prize" but a liability.

In his report, MacKenzie states that when the ship was taken, he sealed the hatches, chests etc on *The Worcester* with the Company of Scotland's seal, and "by the transient view which I have already had of the captain's books and papers, and by some very odd expressions dropt now and then from some of the ship's crew, I have reason to suspect him as guilty of some very unwarrantable practices".[10] These "odd expressions" were the subject of evidence at the trial; but, long before the trial, expressions dropped by the ship's crew demonstrated that, whatever *The Worcester* had been up to, she had a crew, which to use a description of a certain Glasgow murderer "talked too much". To Hill Burton, a mid-nineteenth-century historian and advocate, "the crew of the *Worcester* were of a suspicious aspect – profligate in their lives and conversation".[11] Daniel Defoe, who was in Edinburgh at the time, blamed such indiscretions of the crew for their ultimate conviction. They not only talked too much, they talked too much in a community avid for anything they said. Their expressions became the talk of Edinburgh and the Firth towns.

The Privy Council's investigation

The conclusion Scotland drew from all this was that Green had pirated *The Speedy Return* and *The Content* and murdered Drummond and the crews. Eventually the talk reached such a pitch that the Scottish Privy Council decided they had no alternative but to investigate the whole matter. As the Chancellor put it, "the matter was in everybody's talk" and he was "under some obligation to call the Council and acquaint them of the business".[12] In the result the Privy Council appointed a committee of twelve to investigate the whole matter. Such investigation by a committee of the Scottish Privy Council was neither unusual nor sinister nor arbitrary. It was standard practice in Scotland at that time for the Privy Council, or a committee of the Privy Council, to judicially investigate allegations of serious crime and, in particular, crimes which endangered the public peace.

They were no "tyros" (beginners in learning) as some of their critics have suggested. The personnel of the committee of twelve here was distinguished. It included the Lord Chancellor and two judges. They were thorough as well as experienced. This was no rushed job: their enquiries took four months and they judicially examined the whole crew, some of

[10] Hill Burton, *Narratives from Criminal Trials* (n 6) vol I, pp 166–67.
[11] Hill Burton, *Narratives from Criminal Trials* (n 6) vol I, p 170.
[12] Hill Burton, *Narratives from Criminal Trials* (n 6) vol I, p 175.

them several times. One sailor, Alexander Taylor, claimed to have appeared about twenty times before several committees of the Lords and the Queen's Advocate. The committee had witnesses confront one another – then a well-known practice and not just in Scotland. They examined the ship and its contents. By December, the committee had "declarations from some of the crew and verbal acknowledgement from others" concerning piracy and murder committed at sea by Captain Green and his crew. This Privy Council committee, well aware of the implications, national and international, of their investigation and conclusions, on 13 February 1705, ordered that Captain Thomas Green, John Madder, chief mate, John Reynolds, second mate, and fifteen of the crew should be tried by the High Court of Admiralty of Scotland for the crimes of piracy, robbery and murder. Six other members of the crew, upon recommendation of the Council, were admitted as Queen's evidence. To describe the Council's decision, as it has been described in some English texts, as a "trumped up" case ignores the personnel, experience, duration and character of the Council's investigation, and the detail of the charges framed from their deliberations. Their conclusion was that "having taken precognition of the grounds of the information against Thomas Green and others of his crew, they ordered the said captain and crew to be put on trial upon the crimes informed, before the judges of the High Court of Admiralty".

In addition they appointed five members of the examining committee to be assessors to the Admiralty Court, that is, to sit as additional judges with the Judge Admiral during the trial – again in Scotland a common practice. The five assessors included two High Court judges. The court that tried the accused was unquestionably a strong and a distinguished one. One comment was that "there can be no doubt that the case was tried by some of the most approved of the Judicial Authorities in Scotland – as befitted its importance".[13] Having reached the conclusions they did, holding there was a case against Green and his crew, for the Privy Council not to have ordered prosecution here would have been perverse. *The Worcester's* owners at first could not believe that the Scots were serious; but, when they realised they were, they instructed seven respected and established counsel for the defence – respected, but whose forensic efforts, I fear in this particular case, were wholly uninspiring and ineffective.

The indictments

Two indictments in identical terms charged Green and his crew with piracy of an unnamed ship, robbery and murder. Piracy, it will be noted, of an unnamed ship, not *The Speedy Return*; robbery from the ship, and the

---

[13]   Sir Richard Temple, *The Tragedy of the Worcester* (1930) p 222.

murder of persons unknown, upon days in February to May 1703 on the coast of Malabar near Calicut, said vessels having English or Scots aboard. The indictments then set forth in detail, and – as was then the practice in Scottish criminal trials – the facts and testimonies which the prosecution claimed it would prove, and which, if proved, were held to be cumulative probation against all the accused.

THE TRIAL COMMENCES

Counsel

The trial started on 5 March 1705 with a formidable representation of counsel on both sides. For the pursuers: the procurator fiscal of the Admiralty Court (Mr Alexander Higgins), Her Majesty's Advocate (Sir James Stuart), Her Majesty's Solicitor General (Sir David Dalrymple, Bt), Sir Patrick Horne, Sir George Elliot, Sir Francis Grant and Mr Alexander Macleod – a collection of surnames which, generation after generation, appeared as advocates in Scotland. Seven advocates appeared for the accused headed by Sir David Cunningham, Sir David Thoirs, Sir Walter Pringle, Mr David Forbes, Mr George Alexander, Mr John Elphinston and Mr John Spottiswood. They represented the accused as a group and I am unable to find any evidence that any particular accused had a particular counsel.

Initial arguments

The prosecutor deserted the case against three of the accused whom he accepted had joined the ship after the alleged piracy.[14] The defence then challenged the relevancy of the indictments with their detailed specification – a practice then inevitable in Scottish criminal trials and, in particular, where the charges and the facts were as unusual, and detailed, as those here. One of the earliest defence submissions was that the libel was too general and undefined as it did not specify the name of the ship alleged to have been pirated; the names of the pirates said to have been murdered; nor any circumstances by which the ship in question might be specially distinguished. There was no *corpus delicti*. The court rejected this submission: a course which Hume, in his *Commentaries*, considered in the circumstances narrated in the libel, to be acceptable.[15]

These defence submissions on relevancy, their length, their ingenuity, their display of Civilian and other legal authorities make far from easy or even interesting reading. The *State Trials* report devotes seventeen pages to the debate on the relevancy as against some five and a half pages for

---

[14] See n 22 below.
[15] Hume, *Commentaries* (n 1) vol I, p 484.

the whole evidence heard in the trial.[16] Such elaborate defence pleas to
the relevancy, as those tabled here, resulted from the statute of 1695, c 4,
which ordered relevancy to be pleaded first viva voce, and afterwards in
written informations. "Under this ordinance," Hume reflected, "a double
debate on the relevancy, first viva voce and then in writing, became an
ordinary, or rather a necessary part of every criminal process."[17] But it
was a procedure which resulted in a "great load of frivolous objection and
sophistical argument".[18] The court here rejected what they considered, with
much justification, to be "a great load of frivolous objection and sophistical
argument" of the defence. The exact terms of the court's interlocutor were,
"having advised both the indictment and the foregoing debate [they] repelled
all of the defence submissions, and, find the crimes of piracy, or robbery,
or murder, as libelled, being proven by clear and plain evidence relevant to
infer the pains of death".[19] This was, at the time, a conventional interlocutor
where pleas to the relevancy were rejected. The conclusion English opinion
drew from these words was that it was in fact a direction to the future jury to
convict: that was neither the function nor the intention of the interlocutor
nor the understanding of it by the jurors here.

Early in the debate the defence moved for separate trials for certain of
the accused, in order that they might have defence evidence from some of
the co-accused. At that time an accused could not give evidence on his own
behalf. This was strenuously resisted by the prosecution who pointed out that
the defence must name those whom they intended to use as witnesses from
among the other accused and at the same time obtain, for the individual
selected, a precept of exculpation – ie evidence that the proposed witness
had a defence. "Why the trial of one [accused] should proceed before the
trial of another", the prosecutor claimed, "it never was, nor could be left
to the arbitriment [sic] of the panels."[20] This defence motion, according to
the prosecutor, was "never allowed unless some ground of exculpation was
positively alleged for clearing of their innocence".[21] None of the accused
attempted to take that course and the motion was refused. By dropping the
charges against three of the crew[22] the prosecution made three witnesses
available to the defence and it did not come too late for them to appear at

---

[16] There are numerous collections of State Trials. See eg *A Complete Collection of State-Trials,
    and proceedings for high treason, and other crimes and misdemeanours; from the reign of King
    Richard II to the end of the reign of King George I* (2nd edn, 1730) vol 5, pp 576 ff; and T B
    Howell (ed), *A Complete Collection of State Trials* (1816) vol 14, pp 1199 ff. Citations are given
    to each report.
[17] Hume, *Commentaries* (n 1) vol II, p 284.
[18] Hume, *Commentaries* (n 1) vol II, p 284.
[19] 5 *State Trials* (n 16) pp 598–99; 14 *Howell's State Trials* (n 16) p 1259.
[20] 5 *State Trials* (n 16) p 584; 14 *Howell's State Trials* (n 16) p 1226.
[21] 5 *State Trials* (n 16) p 584; 14 *Howell's State Trials* (n 16) p 1226.

later stages of the trial. The three were all members of the crew of *The Speedy Return* after she left the Malabar coast.

THE CONDUCT OF THE TRIAL

Empanelling

On 14 March 1705 the jury of fifteen men were empanelled. They were chosen by the court and consisted of five local ship's captains, eight Edinburgh merchants and two lairds, only one of whom was a shareholder in the Darien Company. The Scottish procedures for empanelling of jurors and the swearing of witnesses were of particular significance in the present case and are described later. Two of the witnesses were Indians and required an interpreter, and Captain Yeaman, a Dundee merchant, was appointed.

Evidence of the prosecution witnesses

The first witness, Antonio Ferdinando, was an Indian. The defence objected to him on the ground that he was not worth "the King's unlaw", namely ten pound Scots (16s 8d),[23] and was a heathen whose evidence was inadmissible. The witness swore that he believed in God and was born of Christian parents. The court repelled the objections. Ferdinando then testified that some two and a half years earlier he had joined *The Worcester* at Callicoiloan on the Malabar coast.[24] *The Worcester* then had a sloop with her. There *The Worcester* and her sloop attacked another ship, bearing English colours, sailed by white men speaking English. (This last fact was obtained in answer to a question the defence asked of the witness.) The engagement, which was a running fight, lasted two days. On the third day the unknown ship was boarded, her crew were killed with hatchets and thrown overboard and her cargo was transhipped to *The Worcester*. The unknown ship was then manned by some of *The Worcester* crew who sailed her to Callicoiloan and there sold her to one Coge Commodo acting on behalf of a local king. In the engagement Ferdinando received an arm wound which he exhibited to the court. He also showed to the court the coat he then wore which was, he declared, his share of the spoils.[25] Ferdinando recounted that he was

---

[22] 5 *State Trials* (n 16) p 581; 14 *Howell's State Trials* (n 16) p 1219: ie against Samuel Urlines, carpenter's mate; Henry Barnes, seaman; and Daniel Stringman, cook.

[23] The defence team was chancing its luck. Hume, *Commentaries* (n 1) vol II, p 368 doubts whether there was ever any settled rule of witness disqualification on this ground.

[24] Presumably a reference to the historic port town known today as Kollam or Quilon, on the south-west Indian coast, near the Asthamudi Lake.

[25] Sir David Dalrymple, in addressing the jury, gave it as his judgement that this coat "was of Scots Rugg" (5 *State Trials* (n 16) p 605; 14 *Howell's State Trials* (n 16) p 1272), which might suggest Sir David considered the pirated ship to have been *The Speedy Return*.

told by Madder, the mate, that he would kill him and heave him overboard if he mentioned the affair to any person either white or black. During the engagement, eight of the accused were aboard *The Worcester* and the others, including the witness, were on the sloop, except Reynolds who was ashore. Captain Green's ship carried about twenty guns.

Here, then, was one eyewitness to the whole charge: a witness, the prosecuting Solicitor General commended to the jury as reliable for his "stayedness, simplicity and constancy, ... who, in many examinations before the Council, and Committee of the Council, has uniformly given the same account which he has now deponed before this Honourable Court" and "it adds to the weight of his testimony", he submitted, "[that] it was emitted while he was under heavy sickness and forced to lie down at the End of the Table".[26] The Scots have always had a high opinion of dying confessions and the jury could be relied on to place much weight on the testimony of a witness who looked, and indeed was, a dying man. Ferdinando died on 22 March 1705 – a death for which rumour and gossip claimed Roderick MacKenzie to be responsible. No one appeared to consider that, for a man from a warm climate, the experience of living through a Scottish winter might prove fatal.

The next witness, Charles May, surgeon of *The Worcester*, testified that he went ashore at Callicoiloan apparently to attend certain patients. He remained there for two weeks during which time he heard the firing of guns at sea and met Coge Commodo and Francisco de Olivera, the ship's linguister (interpreter) who told him that *The Worcester* had gone out and was fighting another ship. Next morning May saw from the shore *The Worcester* in her former berth some four miles out with a strange vessel riding at her stern. The ship's longboat presently came ashore in haste and her crew told him the captain had sent them for water because they had "spilt and staved" all their water aboard and they had been "busking" all night, which word, May understood, meant they had been at heavy labour and fatigued. May returned to Callicoiloan a few days later; on going aboard to get some medicines he required, he found *The Worcester's* deck lumbered with goods and casks and said to Madder, "What have you got there? You are full of business", whereupon the mate did curse him and bid him "go mind his plaister-box".[27] He afterwards learned the prize was sold to Coge Commodo who, as the linguister informed him, complained he had bought the ship too dear. May dressed Ferdinando's wound which, in May's view, was occasioned by a gunshot. Two of the other sailors also required surgical aid but, when he asked how they came by their wounds, the mate told him

---

[26] 5 *State Trials* (n 16) p 605; 14 *Howell's State Trials* (n 16) p 1274.
[27] 5 *State Trials* (n 16) pp 600–01; 14 *Howell's State Trials* (n 16) p 1263–64.

to ask no questions and forbade the men to answer upon their peril. On May persisting in his enquiries, an altercation arose and Madder ordered him to be put ashore. It was discovered *The Worcester* had sprung a leak but, instead of having her repaired at any port on that coast, Captain Green sailed her to Bengal – a five-week voyage – preferring, it appears, to risk the loss of his ship than face a local court of enquiry. The surgeon, May, dated all this as having occurred in January or February 1703.

Antonio Francisco, Captain Green's black servant, was next called. The objections taken to him that he was worth nothing, was a slave to Captain Green and had no religion, were repelled. The witness swore that he was a Christian. He joined the ship at Delagoa off the Malabar coast and he heard firing from *The Worcester* but saw nothing of the engagement being at that time chained and nailed to the floor of the forecastle. Two days afterwards he saw goods brought aboard which Ferdinando told him were from a captured ship whose men had been killed after she was taken. Ferdinando exhibited his wound received in the fight. He told Francisco to say nothing about the engagement. The witness Francisco remained chained in the forecastle for two months.[28]

James Wilkie, tailor, burgess of Edinburgh, stated that, in the October after *The Worcester* was taken, he accompanied his mother to Burntisland with a design to learn some news of his brother, Andrew, who had sailed as a surgeon on *The Speedy Return*. At the house of Mrs Seaton they fell in company with the prisoner Haines who in answer to his enquiries replied, "Damn me – what have I to do with Captain Drummond" but, "after that they had taken some cups about", Haines became more communicative and said that, when upon the Malabar coast he heard from a Dutch vessel that Drummond had turned pirate. Haines added that he "had in his custody, at the time the ship the *Worcester* was seized in the road of Leith, that which he would not have fall into the seizer's hands for twice the value of the ship, [and] threw it overboard ... saying, '*Let them seek it now in the bottom of the sea*'".[29] What was thrown overboard, we learn later, was his diary.

Kenneth MacKenzie, inhabitant of the Canongate, said that he was present on the occasion referred to by Wilkie and heard Mrs Wilkie entreat Anne Seaton to obtain from *The Worcester* crew some news of her son. The next day Anne Seaton told him that Haines fell in a passion when she questioned him, swearing (not indeed without reason), "that they had a design to pump him", but he would tell nothing.[30]

---

[28] 5 *State Trials* (n 16) p 601; 14 *Howell's State Trials* (n 16) p 1266.
[29] 5 *State Trials* (n 16) p 602; 14 *Howell's State Trials* (n 16) p 1267.
[30] 5 *State Trials* (n 16) p 602; 14 *Howell's State Trials* (n 16) p 1267.

William Wood, gunner, described his meeting at Burntisland with Haines, who having "drunk pretty warmly", fell into a melancholy fit for which he accounted as follows: "It is a wonder that, since we did not sink at sea, that God does not make the ground open and swallow us up when we are come ashore, for the wickedness that has been committed during this last voyage on board of that old bitch Bess."[31] He said this pointing to the dismantled ship. Thereafter, as they walked upon the Links, Wood observed that Madder's uncle had been boiled in oil at Amsterdam for piracy, whereupon Haines rejoined that, if what Madder had done during the voyage were known, he deserved as much as his uncle. (It is extraordinary but there was no cross-examination by the defence of this evidence.) John Henderson, writer in Edinburgh, who was present, corroborated, as did Anne Seaton. She also had heard his reference to the item he committed to the deep. Haines told her he knew more of Captain Drummond than what he would express at that time.[32]

John Brown and Archibald Hodge, both skippers in Leith, said they assisted at the discharge of *The Worcester's* cargo when she was rummaged by order of the Privy Council. They found upon the goods no such marks or numbers as was customary for identifying the owners to whom they were consigned. The goods were, however, regularly enough stowed.[33]

John Glen, goldsmith in Leith, stated that the second day after *The Worcester* arrived in the roads he visited the ship. In the cabin, Madder took a seal out of his pocket and asked Glen what he thought of the Scots African Company's arms. Glen examined the seal and found thereon the St Andrew's Cross, a dromedary or camel with a castle on the back of it, a ship with a rising sun above the helmet and two wild men as supporters. "In a word," Glen deponed, "the official blazon of The Darien Company". But the seal produced in court was not, he said, the same as the seal Madder had shown him.

Productions

The prosecution proof was closed by the prosecutors lodging in court, and therefore accessible to the jury, instructions and letters found among Captain Green's papers. From these it appeared that his owners had given him unusual, and to the Scots suspicious, orders regarding the conduct of the voyage. He was to write to them in cypher only, without title, date or signature, and under cover to a third party, "the names of any dead" to be appended at the end of his letters without comment. He was to allow no

---

[31] 5 *State Trials* (n 16) pp 602–03; 14 *Howell's State Trials* (n 16) p 1268.
[32] 5 *State Trials* (n 16) pp 602–03; 14 *Howell's State Trials* (n 16) p 1269.
[33] 5 *State Trials* (n 16) p 603; 14 *Howell's State Trials* (n 16) pp 1268–70.

letters whatever to be sent to England by any other of the ship's company and, when *The Worcester's* cargo for England was provided, he was to sell the sloop for what she would fetch. The care and secrecy of the crew would be rewarded at the voyage's end by a month's pay and a share in the benefits accruing from "the whale fishing" – this strange addition referring to an idea of Thomas Bowrey's, *The Worcester's* owner, but which had not been pursued by the crew on their voyage.

The Solicitor General's speech

In these days, when a trial started it continued, uninterrupted, until it was concluded. The leading of evidence took some twelve hours. It must have been late in the evening when Sir David Dalrymple, son of James Dalrymple, 1st Viscount Stair, rose to address the jury. His speech is comprehensive and balanced.[34]

The prosecution's view was that such sailing orders were inconsistent with the pursuit of peaceful trading. But "Why all this mystery?" the Solicitor General inquired, "... Fair trading requires no such affectation".[35] He then added: "[b]ut further you will be pleased to take notice, that the outward cargo for a ship of 200 tons and 20 guns mounted, sailed with 36 men, was in value but £999. 17s and 2d sterling, which appears by the document produced by themselves, for instructing their entry at the Custom-house; and that too, for the most part, arms".[36] Here, I suggest, is subtle and perceptive pleading. He added, "to me it seems very strange, that a voyage so exceedingly hazardous and expensive, should have been undertaken with so small means".[37]

The defence case

What appears to be remarkable about the conduct of this trial is the passive and disinterested part played by the accused's seven "respected" defence counsel. They called no witnesses. After the prosecution speech, the defence advocates, or some of them, did "speech the assize, by resuming the defences for the pannels, and for taking off the weight of the probation led against them, and by alledging what could be further said for their exculpation and defence".[38] These are words of style and all too generous to the pleaders here. The report records only that the defence speeches were made "extempore and viva voce" which presumably meant that they lacked

---

[34] 5 *State Trials* (n 16) pp 604–08; 14 *Howell's State Trials* (n 16) pp 1271–80.
[35] 5 *State Trials* (n 16) p 606; 14 *Howell's State Trials* (n 16) pp 1275–76.
[36] 5 *State Trials* (n 16) p 606; 14 *Howell's State Trials* (n 16) pp 1275–76.
[37] 5 *State Trials* (n 16) p 606; 14 *Howell's State Trials* (n 16) pp 1275–76.
[38] 5 *State Trials* (n 16) p 608; 14 *Howell's State Trials* (n 16) p 1280.

coherence and were undocumented. Later, however, when the report of the trial was being printed and they were desired "to give in to be printed, a full copy of what they had said in defence to the assize, they declined to do the same". In the report, the refusal of the defence to submit any of their remarks ensured that the public of the day, in Scotland and England, and in particular Bowrey and his colleagues, would never know what was the substance of the accused's defence. In short, these counsel were instructed and paid for conducting a defence without apparently ever saying formally to the court and the jury what the defence was. The failure of the defence here to make what, even then, was the conventional jury speech, in the absence of other explanation, could be taken as a sign of desperation in a profession whose very life blood is speech.

The jury retires

This was a case in which there was a strong bench and an intelligent jury. There was no formal charge by the judge – such charges to juries came much later – but, after the evidence here closed, the jury sought the guidance of the court on the words: "Being proven by clear and plain evidence" in the judge's interlocutor. They asked:[39]

> [I]f the same did require, that the said crimes of piracy, or robbery, or murder should be proven by two or three witnesses, directly proving the foresaid crimes: or, if it were only required, that the crimes of piracy, or robbery, or murder, as libelled, being proven by a clear and plain evidence, as to the cumulative and concurring presumptions, whereby the same were alledged to be inferred, although two concurring witnesses should not be found as to every several presumption, were sufficient?

This was clearly a jury that knew they had duties to perform and meant to perform them. They wanted direction on whether corroborated evidence was required for every circumstance and modification. The court's answer was:[40]

> [I]f the crimes did appear by the qualifications and circumstances, as they were libelled, to be made out *per indicia ad probationem indubitata et luce clariora*, by undoubted presumptions as clear as sun-shine, albeit every circumstance and qualification were not proven by two direct witnesses, the same should be held for a clear and plain evidence.

One senior High Court judge, after I quoted this passage in the lecture I gave on this trial, described it as "a model formula".

---

[39] 5 *State Trials* (n 16) p 604; 14 *Howell's State Trials* (n 16) p 1271.
[40] 5 *State Trials* (n 16) p 604; 14 *Howell's State Trials* (n 16) p 1271.

The verdict

Thereafter the jury were enclosed, it must have been in the early morning of 15 March, and directed to return their verdict at 10 am. This was the verdict:[41]

> They by plurality of votes, find that there is one clear witness as to the piracy, robbery, and murder libelled; and that there are accumulative and concurring presumptions proven, for the piracy and robbery so libelled: But find, that John Reynolds, second mate of the said ship, was ashore at the time of the action libelled.

It bespoke their understanding and approval of the directions they had been given. It was, in addition, a special verdict and a highly illuminating and perceptive one. It was not one of the now standard verdicts guilty, not guilty or not proven. It was a special verdict much used in Scots criminal law from the seventeenth until the nineteenth centuries. The majority verdict was that "there was one clear witness as to the piracy, robbery and murder libelled" (ie Ferdinando), and that there are accumulative and concurring presumptions proven for the piracy and robbery so libelled (ie not for murder). They found, in effect, the charge of murder *not proven*. In addition, they acquitted John Reynolds, the second mate of the ship, who was ashore at the time of the action libelled. In short, then, they had accepted Ferdinando as a clear, reliable witness but did not consider that his evidence of the killings was corroborated; a view which was entirely in accord with the evidence. This was certainly no rubber-stamp verdict. It was technically an impeccable one.

Sentence

Sentences were passed on 21 March on fourteen of the accused. They were to be hanged in batches on the Sands of Leith within the flood mark – the traditional place in Scotland for the execution of its rare pirates.

THE REACTION

The confessions

The Edinburgh mob, now much reinforced from the surrounding country-side, reached fever pitch, demanding the blood of those convicted and, as the time passed between the sentence and the execution date, their determination to have blood became ever more passionate, particularly when the post-trial confessions were known, and even more when news of the Queen's attempt to prevent or delay the executions became known. In

---

[41] 5 *State Trials* (n 16) p 608; 14 *Howell's State Trials* (n 16) p 1281.

England, infuriated public opinion claimed that the witnesses had been suborned; that the confessions had been induced by threats of torture; and that the whole affair was a Jacobite plot. However, hot on the conviction, came confessions from three of the accused. Thomas Linstead and George Haines gave long and circumstantially detailed confessions in which they alleged that the ship pirated was, in fact, Captain Drummond's *The Speedy Return*. These confessions were later retracted by them. John Bruckley, *The Worcester's* cooper, made two confessions and retracted neither.

English opinion was shocked both by the verdicts and by sentence; it was even more shocked by what followed – the conduct of the Scots Privy Council and the circumstances in which the three were executed.

Affidavits from England

The first move from England was the transmission to Scotland of affidavits taken from two alleged Scottish sailors, calling themselves Freeland and Phippany. Having given affidavits, these two sailors disappeared and Scotland neither saw nor heard of them again. The Scots Privy Council did not accept the terms of their affidavits, which are referred to later.

Her Majesty, the Scots Privy Council and the mob

The Queen wished the execution to be delayed but it was the opinion of her Chancellor that such a move would so exasperate Scotland that it might endanger the entire project for the Union of the Parliaments. On 25 March, the Scots Privy Council received intimation from the Queen wishing the executions to be delayed until Her Pleasure was known. The Scots Privy Council protested that the trial had been regular. They sent the Queen the new confessions claiming that they, the Privy Council, had no doubts about the verdicts or about the sentences. They begged her to make no attempt to interfere with the sentences: "If the Queen will grant them remissions it will spoil the business in Parliament [ie the Union] and I am afraid will so exasperate the nation as may render it difficult to make them join with England upon any terms whatever."[42]

The day before the first execution was due to take place the Queen ordered a reprieve until further enquiry and the Scots Privy Council postponed the execution for one week until 11 April. On 10 April the Scots Privy Council, or as many of them as the Chancellor could persuade to attend, met together. The majority had excuses for their absence, some of these of the most specious nature; one, for example, because his son had gone to the West Country and had taken all the horses. The Chancellor was in despair. The issue of postponement was on the agenda and it was that

---

[42] Quoted without attribution by W Roughead, *The Riddle of the Ruthvens* (1936) p 276.

issue which brought tens of thousands to Edinburgh from all parts of the country determined to see what they considered to be justice done. They were excited, incensed, and passionate. Many were armed and ready for any violence. The reason, put by Seafield, was that "[t]he English they see will now be protected though they murder, rob and pillage Scots by sea or land". The choice before the Privy Council was an unenviable one: to obey the Royal Pleasure would let loose on the city the rage of the mob. Three of the Council voted for further reprieve; three voted against it. The others who were present would not vote. The Chancellor who had the casting vote declined to exercise it. He said he was in favour of the reprieve and would sign it if those who had not voted would join him. They refused. Accordingly the last decision of the Scots Privy Council on the matter was that the first batch of prisoners would be hanged.

On 11 April, the mob, estimated at eighty thousand, was menacing, bloodletting. The Privy Council was in a situation where they must either have the men executed, or themselves be assaulted and possibly murdered. A flying post from London excited the mob who thought it was a reprieve; instead it left matters in the hands of the Council. They reached a compromise of sorts: Green, Madder and Simpson would be executed, the rest reprieved.

THE EXECUTIONS

The three men died reluctantly, Green in particular. To the end he expected a reprieve. Madder accepted his fate, and once the mob had seen the three hanged, their mood changed. According to the ecclesiastical historian, Robert Wodrow, who was present, "[t]here was at the scene of the execution the greatest confluence of people there that ever I saw in my life for they cared not how far they were off so be it they saw". Green was first executed; then Simpson; and, last of all, Madder. "Every one of them when the rope was about their necks," Wodrow recorded, "denied they were guilty of that for which they were to die. This indeed put all people to a strange demur", and with the death of each of these accused the rage of the crowd appeared to abate. The bloodletting had had dramatic effect. Rage appeared to give way to remorse.[43]

AFTERMATH

Reaction at the time, and since, to the trial and its results has largely divided on national lines. Scots opinion, immortalised in contemporary ballad, was clear:

---

[43] M Fry, *The Union: England, Scotland and the Treaty of 1707* (2006) pp 168-70.

"Of all the pirates I have heard or seen
The basest and bloodiest is Captain Green"

In the nineteenth and early twentieth centuries three Scots historians – Hill Burton, Andrew Lang and William Roughead – conceded Captain Green to have been guilty of some acts of violence at sea but stopped short of blaming him for the fate of *The Speedy Return*. English opinion, with one notable exception, has made Green a martyr to Scottish Anglophobia. That one exception, however, was significant. It was Daniel Defoe, the greatest and most prolific journalist of his time who was in Scotland, at the time of the trial, to report on the Union negotiations. The principal, and much quoted, support for the English view, was Lt Col Sir Richard Temple's book *The Tragedy of The Worcester*, published in 1930, whose thesis is that Green and his crew were innocent of any illegal practices, and the Scottish trial a travesty of justice. For Temple, and his followers, the conception of "a fair trial" was that which prevailed from the nineteenth century: the presumption of innocence, strict rules of evidence, and a procedure fair to both sides. But the criminal procedure of 1705 was very different from what it was to become.

In considering the entire case, Sir Richard offers complaints and a catalogue of the classic constituents of miscarriages of justice, and claims they all appeared in Green's trial. His complaints and allegations of miscarriages of justice catalogued can be listed as follows:

(1) A harsh and unscrupulous prosecution instigated by the Scots Privy Council.

(2) New and exonerating witnesses found after the trial, ie Phippany and Freeland.

(3) Fresh evidence, which was said to confirm Green's innocence, in documents found in Bowrey's papers, that is the owner's papers, correspondence and a memorandum which it is claimed was made from Green's journal. All these papers had been impounded and were put to the jury at the trial.

(4) Affidavits taken in England after the trial from members of the crew who returned there, particularly Haines and Bruckley, containing allegations of pressure, bribery, inducements to confess, at the instigation of the prosecutors. Perhaps the only thing these post-trial affidavits do not allege is threat of torture, which would have been competent, but which the Privy Council did not utilise. The number of conflicting statements which members of this crew signed does not encourage belief in either their honesty or consistency.

(5) A packed jury incapable of giving the accused a fair trial because of the prevailing Scots hostility to England. Having five Scottish ships' captains as jurors is regarded as part of the alleged unfairness.

(6) It was claimed prosecution witnesses were said to be not just lying, but lying from "a wicked spirit of revenge" against Green.

THE SCOTS PRIVY COUNCIL

The prosecution was at the instance and order of the Scots Privy Council. That Council, as described earlier, investigated the whole evidence and ordered the prosecution after these investigations. In doing so they were conducting an inquisitorial investigation, a process in which they were experienced, and which was then customary in Scotland. This process, lasting four months, examined all the various accused and witnesses, some several times, and some in confrontational situations. None of the defence counsel at the trial, experienced in Scottish practice, suggested that the Privy Council were not entitled to examine in the way they did, or that that process was harsh and oppressive. The Council examined certain witnesses frequently but no allegation was made at the trial, where it should have been made if it was to be made, that their examination had been harsh or pressurised, or that they had been offered inducements.

NEW WITNESSES

The "evidence of new witnesses" was the last-ditch attempt to have the execution of Green and his two companions postponed. The incident concerns two men and four names. In March 1705, two men, calling themselves Israel Phippany and Peter Freeland, arrived in Portsmouth, England, on an English ship, *The Rapier*, from Mauritius. They claimed that they had escaped from pirates. The timing of their arrival was impeccable – post-trial and pre-Green's execution. They were to be the only two men claiming to have been members of the original crew of *The Speedy Return* who ever appeared in either England or Scotland after the trial. In London they were initially interrogated by an unidentified Scottish official who found that they were "not very distinct in answering some of the questions askt concerning the trafique Captain Drummond had made, and what sort of goods he had at the time his ship was taken".[44] How their arrival came to be known to John Green of Green & Thornhill, Attorneys in London, the

---

[44] P Insh, *The Company of Scotland* (1932) p 301

elder brother of Captain Green, is not known, but he went to Portsmouth, contacted the two men and, doubtless in the hope of helping his brother to "cheat the wuddie", had the two men swear affidavits before the mayor of Portsmouth.

This I take to mean that the formalities of preparing and swearing an affidavit were seen to by the lawyer and, in particular, that the statements to be sworn were compiled by him or approved by him or both. The affidavits sworn[45] are comprehensive and ordered documents. They are the products of a literate and articulate man of business who knew the matters which had to be covered. John Green was already familiar with the case. Not only was he brother to Captain Green, he was in constant touch with him from the beginning of this case and, at one early stage, was in Edinburgh in consultation with his brother. He was also a close friend of Bowrey and became his solicitor, and as all the London world of shipping and trade knew, Bowrey was seeking compensation for the loss of The Worcester held by the Scots.

The terms of both affidavits purport to give a history of their ship The Speedy Return in Indian waters. Each of them admitted being members of the crew when the ship sailed from Port Glasgow under Captain Drummond, and afterwards they arrived at Bengal at Guinea and from thence sailed to Madagascar where both The Speedy Return and brigantine (ie The Content) took on board slaves.

> From thence they sailed to the port of Maritan [Saint Mary's Island] in Madagascar aforesaid, where the said Captain Drummond went on shoar, and about 9 or 10 hours after his going on shoar, five several persons, who afterwards appeared to be pirates, armed with pistols, swords and other weapons, came on board the said Speedy Return, with a pretence to buy something, and taking the advantage of the said Captain Drummond, Andrew Wilky, his surgeon, and several of the said ship's company being on shoar, and others working in the hold, the said five persons by force of arms took possession of the said ship and immediately made a signal, upon which about 40 or 50 other pirates came on board, ... and then took the said briganteen (which was afterwards burnt), and the said pirates forced these appearers and the other persons on board the said ship the Speedy Return to sail in her till such time as she arrived at Rajapore, a place so called, where the said Speedy Return was also burnt, and then these appearers, and the other men that did belong to the said Speedy Return went on board a Moca [Mocha] ship called the Deffiance, which some time after touched at the island Mauritius, where the appearers made their escape; and the said Raper galley soon after arriving there, the said appearers went on board her, and are since arrived at the port of Portsmouth. And the said appearers did farther declare that, at or, after the time of taking the said ship the Speedy Return, neither the said Captain Drummond, nor [any] other persons

---

[45] Temple, Tragedy (n 13) pp 266–67.

belonging to her were killed or wounded, neither was she ever attacked by a ship called the *Worcester*, Captain Green commander, or any other ship, sloop or vessel whatever.[46]

These affidavits were immediately sent to London, then sent express to Scotland and arrived there before Green and his companions were executed. The content of these documents did not impress the Scottish Privy Council whose response was to send to England the recent confessions of Haines and Bruckley.

The other two names involved here were Israel Fisonne, a native of New England who had been apprenticed to a Glasgow merchant, and Peter Parlane, born at Milton of Slains. Both had been to Darien and figure in the Company's papers. Both signed their names when the crew signed on at the departure of *The Speedy Return* from Scotland, their signatures being witnessed by Captain Drummond. There is no name on the original crew list which is, or resembles, the surnames of Phippany and Freeland.[47] It was, however, men calling themselves Phippany and Freeland who swore and signed the affidavits at Portsmouth. Their use of these names was repetitive. On the voyage to England on *The Rapier*, they used the names Phippany and Freeland. The affidavit they signed at Portsmouth relates that "there personally came and appeared before the Mayor of Portsmouth Israel Phippany and Peter Freeland now belonging to the *Rapier* galley ... and did solemnly declare upon the holy evangel that they did belong to a ship called the *Speedy Return*". Affidavits were then unknown in Scotland but English practice required a written statement and the name of the person (deponar) who makes and signs it, and swears to its truth before an official, in this case the mayor of Portsmouth, authorised to deal with such matters. It would certainly involve, as it still does, the oath taker, ie the mayor, asking the applicants their names to confirm the names they used in the application. There is then no question of anyone having any doubts of the applicant's claims to be known as Israel Phippany and Peter Freeland. According to the crew list neither of these names belonged to the crew of *The Speedy Return*. There was nothing to stop the two from adopting new names but the matter is not so simple or innocent when they take to using false names in making, signing and swearing an affidavit. After swearing the affidavits nothing more is heard of, or from, them again. Their alleged history leaves a multitude of questions unanswered, not least: When did they change their names? And why?

---

[46] 14 *Howell's State Trials* (n 16) p 1299; and reproduced in Temple, *The Tragedy of the Worcester* (1930) pp 267–68. Spellings as in original.

[47] Insh, *The Company of Scotland* (n 44) p 301 takes Freeland to be Fisonne and Phippany to be Parlane, although suggests too that he mistranscribed Parlane for Phippany.

The critical question is why the two men abandoned the names they used as their name when they signed on the crew list of *The Speedy Return*. I have no doubt John Green would be consulted on this before he drafted the affidavit. One obvious answer, where an individual changes his name, is to deceive as to his true identity, which raises the questions of if, and why, these two men were trying to deceive as to their true identity. Today, it is still a familiar tactic where fraud is contemplated.

Temple and Insh accept that the evidence establishes that it was Israel Fissone and Peter Parlane who unquestionably were on the crew of *The Speedy Return* who appeared in London and before the mayor of Portsmouth, calling themselves and swearing they were Israel Phippany and Peter Freeland.[48] Here, then, we start with a fraud – false names – and in the result what we have are false, perjured and worthless affidavits, which at least throws some doubt on the reliability of their evidence thus far never questioned.[49]

BOWREY'S PAPERS

Bowrey, the principal owner of *The Worcester*, was a meticulous collector and keeper of all documents concerning his many business enterprises and ships which he owned or in which he had an interest. His collected papers were discovered in 1913. They record Bowrey's trading activities and, in particular, the voyage of *The Worcester*. It was the contention of Sir Richard Temple that these papers showed Captain Green to have been involved in a normal, law-abiding, trading voyage. The relevant papers from *The Worcester* had all been put to the jury who tried Green. How they came into the possession of Bowrey is not explained but he unquestionably obtained and kept them. The Scots' reply to the peaceful commercial entries in these

---

[48] G Pratt Insh (ed) *Papers relating to the Ships and Voyages of the Company of Scotland trading to Africa and the Indies 1696–1707* (1924) p 248. It is strange if they knew then what they published in their affidavits – no one belonging to *The Speedy Return* killed or wounded; never attacked by *The Worcester* or any other ship – that they did not give the glad news to the Scottish official they met in London.

[49] The terms of the affidavits have rarely been questioned: either from indifference or innocence neither Temple nor his supporters make anything of the change of names; and the two deponents have invariably been treated by all who supported Temple's view as honest, reliable witnesses and as unchallengeable testimony of the innocence of Captain Green. One distinguished example is G M Trevelyan, *Ramilles and the Union with Scotland* (1932) p 254. He accepts the affidavits of Phippany and Freeland "to the effect that their ship had been seized by the pirate Bowen ... on a date when the *Worcester* was far distant". His comment is that their new evidence "read by the Scottish Privy Council must have further shaken the faith of several present on the guilt of Green". Another factor relating to these two men is that the only evidence that they were members of the crew of *The Speedy Return* comes from themselves. As with all affidavits, however, there was no cross-examination of their content.

papers was that it was highly unlikely that Green would refer to any piracies he had undertaken in such papers or indeed on any paper.

THE CREW'S STATEMENTS AFTER THE TRIAL

Under sentence of death three of the accused confessed to the charges against them: Linstead, Haines and Bruckley. In Scotland, Haines made a confession and a declaration;[50] the latter does more than confess the crime. It does so in astonishing, incriminating and lurid detail which could be expected to come only from an eyewitness describing what he had seen and certainly not just what he had heard or imagined. He declared that, after the ship was seized he saw men which were therein "all white and sickly, killed and murdered with pole axes and cutlasses and saw these dead bodies put into a sloop and thereafter thrown overboard and to the best of his knowledge the men so killed were Scotsmen". It was understood by the crew of *The Worcester* to have been Captain Drummond's ship. If these confessions were true, they put the fate of *The Speedy Return* and its crew beyond doubt.

After Green's execution all the crew were reprieved at Royal Will, and released whether they confessed or not. When he reached England, Haines retracted his first confession and made a further two: it appears a consistency in confessions was not one of his qualities. Some of the crew claimed they had been subjected to pressure and bribes which, if they had told their counsel of the matter, would certainly have been raised in the course of the evidence by any competent counsel and, if proved, would have been fatal to the prosecution case. One of the far-fetched stories of inducement to confess, already mentioned, was from Taylor – one of the crew – who claimed he was examined twenty times by the Privy Council and by the Lord Advocate. He claimed the Marquis of Annandale told him that, if he confessed, he would get a pardon – which the Marquis showed him – he would be looked after, and he should get the first commission that fell vacant in the Queen's Guard. It would be interesting to know if Queen Anne had been consulted on the possible addition of a convicted pirate to her Guard. Witnesses, it was said, were suborned, the confessions got by threats of torture. No such suggestions were ever made by the defence in the course of the trial that unwarranted pressure had been applied to anyone.

THE JURY

The many criticisms of this trial ignore the details of Scottish criminal procedure relating to jurors and witnesses. In 1705, Scots criminal law

---

[50] Temple, *Tragedy* (n 13) pp 254–57.

was actively and elaborately concerned to secure impartiality of jurors, honesty of witnesses and the extent of the evidence which the court could competently hear.

Temple calls the Green jury "a packed" jury, but he makes no mention of the then Scottish practice for citing jurors and for jury selection. To Sir George MacKenzie, assizers (jurors) were partly judges and partly witnesses.[51] Scottish practice in the seventeenth century favoured jurors who knew something of the accused and of the facts. In the seventeenth century, trials were often adjourned because there was no one on the jury list who "knows the verity". Scots practice in a case of this kind would regard ship's captains, as jurors, to be the jurors most likely to understand and appreciate evidence relating to all things nautical. Important here is that no one involved in that trial took any exception to the composition of that jury. The Scottish practice was for a list of forty-five names, made by the clerk of court, from whom the jury would be named. The individual jurors were selected by the court. They were then presented five by five to the panels, who were asked if they had any objection on cause shown to any of them, and, if so, what that objection was. There was no peremptory challenge of jurors at that time, but each accused had been served with a list of potential jurors fifteen days before the trial diet and they had, therefore, the opportunity to investigate any potential juror. If they had any objection as, for example, that the man had expressed desire for revenge or had expressed a view on the outcome of the case, and if such an objection were admitted or proved, that juror would be excused.[52] In the trial of Captain Green, at the very start of the trial, not a single juror, when his name was presented to each accused and his counsel, was objected to: this does not suggest a prejudiced jury.

WITNESSES

Scots practice required from each witness that he be solemnly sworn and "purged of partial counsel" such as favour and affection, or undue zeal for one party.[53] The crux of Temple's miscarriage of justice claim is that the Crown witnesses were lying. He describes their evidence as "tittle tattle, bearing grudges, perjury, perjurers acting from a wicked spirit of revenge".[54] In particular he says this of Ferdinando, Francisco and May. At the trial, however, there was no real challenge of any of the prosecution

---

[51] G Mackenzie, *The Laws and Customs of Scotland in Matters Criminal* (1678; repr 2012, Stair Society vol 59 (O F Robinson (ed)) paras 2.23.2 and 2.23.6.

[52] Hume, *Commentaries* (n 1) vol II, pp 308–09: "This has at all times been our invariable practice."

[53] Hume, *Commentaries* (n 1) vol II, p 377.

[54] Temple, *Tragedy* (n 13).

witnesses and, according to the trial report, it was never suggested to any of the witnesses that they were mistaken, had motives to lie, or were lying. Such an omission could be fatal to the defence in the eyes of a jury. There was defence objection taken to Ferdinando and Francisco that they were heathen and to Anne Seaton that she was a female, but these objections were repelled. Not one of these witnesses was objected to on the grounds of malice, bias, grudge, relationship and the like grounds, on which a juror, like a witness, could be excluded.

There is no suggestion from the defence that May's evidence of Madder's conversation was wrong; if it was wrong, in what respects; and what motive he had for saying what he did. None of the evidence of incriminating statements made by Green's crew was the subject of any cross questions.

THE DEFENCE

The defence team here had the reputation of being a distinguished one and certainly all its members were experienced advocates familiar with Scots criminal law: this, however, was not a trial where these qualities were displayed. There was no suggestion in their conduct of the defence that they had prepared a defence on the facts alleged here, and knew and took all the options open to them – admittedly a difficult duty when they had canvassed no defence except a plea of not guilty. Temple, writing on the absence of speeches from the defence, says that "without any direct knowledge of the defence which Green's competent counsel collected", the English public did not know what their defence here was: in this they were and are certainly not alone.[55]

The duties incumbent on defence counsel in the seventeenth and eighteenth centuries are familiar. These were to "resume the defence of the panel" that "the assize may judge by the deponar's countenance, gestures, assurance how far he should be believed", and that advocates are to be present that they may interrogate upon emergents. Even then it was accepted their interrogation could be vigorous. Again, according to MacKenzie,[56] the advocates "are accustomed to much freedom, and are oftentimes transported by the heat of opposition, and zeal to their client". Of the seven defence counsel here, there is no record in the trial of any of them indulging in any zeal for their client in cross-examining witnesses and, in particular, those witnesses whom Sir Richard Temple accuses of "tittle tattle" and of seeking revenge for some grudge against Green.

---

[55] Temple (n 13) pp 243–44.
[56] Mackenzie, *Matters Criminal* (n 51) para 2.20.2.

Scots law at the time had provision for an accused's defence where he alleged an exculpation or an extenuation of his guilt. If a panel claimed he had a positive defence like alibi, self-defence or coercion – much used in piracy cases – he was entitled to seek a precept of exculpation: a separate process before a judge in which the judge heard the evidence of the defence and, if he found the defence established, that ended the prosecutor's case. This procedure, however, was not open to an accused where his defence was that no crime had been committed – as appears to have been the import of the unsuccessful precepts of exculpation lodged on behalf of the accused here. If no relevant defence was stated and the accused's position was a plea of *not guilty* then the trial proceeded, with the prosecutor seeking to prove his libel in the normal way and with the defence cross-examining the Crown witnesses.[57]

The evidence of the first three witnesses (Ferdinando, May and Francisco) was recorded in the reports without division into examination-in-chief and cross-examination. Cross-examination was competent and was often bitter. Temple's explanation of the reports is that the witnesses were cross-examined "apparently during their examination-in-chief, not after it". Certainly, in the reports of each of the three vital witnesses, after what is clearly their evidence-in-chief, they answer questions directed at particular details in the witnesses' recollection. This is especially the case with Ferdinando and May. But in the reports of their evidence under examination-in-chief and in cross, there is no suggestion of the questioner trying to destroy, discredit or undermine the witnesses. This is another omission in the conduct of the defence: if Temple is correct there was ample material to justify having taken such a course.

Temple's comments on the evidence of these first three witnesses are scathing but I fear are unsupported by the evidence of the trial. Temple describes the evidence of Charles May, the surgeon, as "malignant, revengeful, unscrupulous – twisting innocent happenings into an accusation of piracy".[58] Of Antonio Ferdinando, it is claimed he utilised tales about pirates current upon the Malabar coast to concoct an allegation of piracy against *The Worcester* crew. Francisco, another Indian, is accused

---

[57] The crew members against whom the prosecutor withdrew the charges because they were not present when the pirate attack took place, as well as the crew members who claimed they were coerced to join the piracy, would have been entitled to a precept of exculpation in respect of their alibi. Such precepts, however, were confined to a very narrow field. In particular, they did not admit any defence that was contrary to the averments of the libel. Here, the decision of the Scots Privy Council that piracy, robbery and murder had taken place, as narrated in the libel, excluded any defence which sought to claim the opposite. The import of the precepts of exculpation, tabled on behalf of the panels and suggesting there had been no such crime as the prosecution alleged, was inevitably dismissed.

[58] Temple (n 13) p 10.

of backing Ferdinando's story out of petty spite and revenge for injuries he had received.[59] If these men were so lying or could be suspected of doing so, the failure of the defence to challenge each of them when they were, as they undoubtedly were, purged of malice, a process which could be confrontational. It is strange moreover that none of this emerged in the course of the Privy Council's four-month judicial investigation.

If the indifferent performance of the defence counsel was remarkable, so was their number. There was never any suggestion here that there was a conflict of interest between any of the accused which would have justified a separate or more limited representation. Any cross-examinations there were, were on behalf of all of the accused and it is difficult to see how seven counsel, notwithstanding the lengthy contribution on relevancy which they made early in the proceedings, can be justified in being involved in this trial from start to finish.

It is said that after Green's execution the defence counsel "were in ill odour and left Edinburgh for a while". Temple says they did so for their own safety; but their mute performance at the trial, I suggest, would hardly produce that public reaction. Perhaps their leaving Edinburgh was to distance themselves from what was an unprofessional performance and to escape from their brethren's gossip, not least about how they charged their fees, how they were paid and how many of them were required for the conduct of business.

The only contemporary written comment on the trial favourable to the Scots came from the Englishman, Daniel Defoe, the versatile and inquisitive journalist. His comments go a long way to rebut English criticisms of the trial. "Scotland lies under much scandal in this account," wrote Defoe, "which as to the methods of public justice, I think she does not deserve ... It is most certain," he concluded, that "the folly and imprudence of the men hanged them to say no more". He refers to their coming to Scotland and,

> [T]he men falling out among themselves and being open instruments of detecting what no one ever could have charged them with. These and more concurring circumstances which were observed by the most curious, and some which were noted upon the trial seemed to jump together so visibly ... nor was this the sense of the few, but I generally believed of the whole nation, I mean of considering [ie thoughtful] people, and such as usually notice such things and particularly of many who cried out the loudest when it was too late ... when the conviction of such circumstances was in the mind of people it is no wonder the men were found guilty by the jury and I persuade myself they themselves would have done the same. If they were innocent, as now alleged, yet as they were condemned by a due Court of Law, tried and executed by the common forms

---

59 Temple (n 13) p 10.

of justice in that country and in the same manner by which their own subjects were tried and executed, the fault must lie in the witnesses and the jury that condemned them.[60]

POSTSCRIPTS

There are two important postscripts to this trial, one of the utmost significance.

Robert Drury's journal (1729)

Drury was probably an ex-pirate returned to England. He claimed that as a boy of fourteen he was wrecked on the coast of Madagascar. He had been a sailor on the East Indiaman on which John Benbow, son of the Admiral,[61] was fourth mate. There, Drury claimed he found one Captain Drummond, a Scotsman whose ship had been pirated, holding high office under a native king. During his fifteen years on the island, Drummond was active in local politics – like a condottiere of Renaissance Italy to a native ruler – until he was killed by natives. "But they told me one piece of remarkable news. They said this Captain Drummond was the same man for whose murder and that of his crews, one Captain Green, commander of an English ship, was hanged in Scotland." Green, however, was never convicted of murder, still less the murder of Captain Drummond. Green was hanged after having been found guilty of piracy and robbery.

But this information is highly suspect. The last edition of Drury's journal was published in 1890,[62] edited with notes by Captain Passfield Oliver who effectively demolishes any claim Drury ever had to accuracy or reliability. His conclusion is that Drury himself was a pirate who came back to London with what he called his memories; his journal was edited by Defoe, or some associate, from material stolen from a French history of Madagascar published in 1661.

Alexander Hamilton

The last word, I think, on this whole matter lies with another Scottish merchant adventurer, Captain Alexander Hamilton, who first went to Bombay in 1688. He became a merchant of status, influence and experience: the Sultan of Johor was his friend. He fought pirates, he commanded an East India Company fleet and he traded extensively. He was a man

---

[60]   Defoe (n 3).
[61]   Also John Benbow: see J B Hattendorf, "Benbow, John (1653?–1702)" *Oxford DNB* (2004–).
[62]   P Oliver (ed) *Madagascar; or Robert Drury's Journal, during fifteen years captivity on that Island* (1890).

everyone held in the highest regard. In 1727, he was another sailor home from sea and published his *A New Account of the East Indies* which can, I think, be relied on from the very status of its author, as Drury's journal could never be.

I quote the passages in his account which concern Captain Green:[63]

The unfortunate Captain Green, who was afterwards hanged in Scotland, came on board of my Ship at Sun-set, very much overtaken with Drink, and several of his Men in the same Condition [at Colecut, 1703]. He told me, that he had some small Arms, Powder, Shot and Glass-ware to dispose of, and asked me if I would take them off his Hands at a very reasonable Rate. ... He told me, that the Arms and Ammunition were what was left of a large Quantity that he had brought from England, but had been at Don Mascherenas and Madagascar, and had disposed of the rest to good Advantage, among the Pirates. ...

I told him, that, in Prudence, he ought to keep these as Secrets, lest he might be brought into trouble about them. He made but little Account of my Advice and so departed.

About ten in the night, his chief Mate, Mr Mather, came on board of my Ship and seemed to be very melancholy. ... He burst out in Tears, and told me, he was afraid that he was undone. ... that they had acted such Things in their Voyage that would certainly bring them to Shame and Punishment, if they should come to light; and he was assured that such a Company of Drunkards as their Crew was composed of, could keep no Secret. ... I told him ...that I had heard at Coilan, that they had not acted prudently nor honestly in relation to some Moors Ships they had visited and plundered, and in sinking a sloop with ten or twelve Europeans in her, offCoilan. ... Next day, I went ashore, and met Captain Green and his Supercargo, Mr Callant, who had sailed a Voyage from Surat to Sindy with me. Before Dinner-time they were both drunk, and Callant told me, that he did not doubt of making the greatest Voyage that ever was made from England on so small a Stock as 500 pounds. ...

In the evening, their Surgeon accosted me in my Walk along the Sea side, and asked if I wanted a Surgeon. ... He said he wanted to stay in India, for his Life was uneasy on board of his Ship; that tho' the Captain was civil enough, yet Mr Mather was unkind, and had treated him with Blows for asking a pertinent Question at some wounded Men, who were hurt in the Engagement they had with the Sloop. I heard too much to be contented with their Conduct, and so I shunned their Conversation for the little Time I staid at Colecut. Whether Captain Green and Mr Mather had Justice impartially in their Process and Sentence, I know not. I have heard of as great Innocents condemned to Death, as they were.

CONCLUSION

That Edinburgh jury on 14 March 1705 were confident of their verdict: so confident, indeed, were they, that they not only reached it, they gave

---

[63] A Hamilton, *A new account of the East Indies, being the observations and remarks of Capt. Alexander Hamilton, who spent his time there from the year 1688 to 1723* (1727) vol I, pp 317–20.

their reasons for reaching it. Scotland has had very few jury trials where the prosecution could be described as harsh and oppressive: the trial of Captain Green and his crew was certainly not one of them.

Observing Criminal Trials

S J Summers

At an open day at Glasgow School of Law almost twenty years ago, two presentations were of particular importance in setting the study of law at Glasgow apart from that at the law schools of the other Scottish universities. The first involved the Glasgow arm of the William J Brennan Death Penalty Project co-ordinated by Dr Patricia Lucie,[1] and the second concerned the European Human Rights Project run by Professor Jim Murdoch and John Brown.[2] In the age of rankings and in the year of the Research Excellence Framework ("REF"),[3] it is interesting to reflect on the fact that the decision where to study law might not just be influenced by the research rating of the school or the likelihood of securing a job but might also be swayed by innovative projects and what they represent: recognition of the dynamic, contingent character of law and acknowledgment of the fact that law can only fully be understood if it is examined as a practice. I was fortunate enough to be afforded the opportunity to participate in the Strasbourg project and the experience proved to be of considerable inspiration, highlighting the importance of taking seriously the law's application and not just the black letter law itself.

This contribution, celebrating 300 years of the teaching of law at Glasgow,[4] takes its inspiration from these projects and aims to illustrate the importance of studying the application of the law by considering the issue of trial rights in criminal proceedings in the light of a trial observation project currently running in Switzerland.[5] Most academic criminal lawyers would likely consider themselves observers of the law, but their preoccupation is

---

[1] See P Lucie, "Justice William Brennan Jr: 'Constitutional visions take five votes'" 12 (1997) 12 Denning LJ 5.

[2] The "Strasbourg Project" is now in its twenty-first year and Jim Murdoch has been awarded, *inter alia*, the Pro Merito medal of the Council of Europe (the highest distinction granted by the Secretary General to individuals or organisations in recognition of their commitment to the Council of Europe's values and work), the Slaughter and May Partnership Award for innovation in the teaching and learning of law, and a University of Glasgow Teaching Excellence Award.

[3] The REF will be completed in 2014. It replaced the Research Assessment Exercise which was introduced by the Thatcher Government in 1986 in order to determine the allocation of funding to UK universities.

[4] And indeed the recent appointment of James Chalmers, as the first criminal lawyer to hold the post, to the Regius Chair at the University of Glasgow!

[5] See *http://www.rwi.uzh.ch/lehreforschung/alphabetisch/summers/trialobservation_en.html*.

largely with appellate decisions and general theories. A good grasp of the manner in which the criminal law is applied at first instance is, however, of considerable importance to our understanding of the law. It is perhaps no coincidence that two of the most influential books on Scots criminal law, Sir Gerald Gordon's *The Criminal Law of Scotland*[6] and Baron David Hume's *Commentaries on the Law of Scotland Respecting Crimes*,[7] were written by authors with considerable knowledge of criminal trials at first instance.[8] It will be argued here that observing the ways in which trial rights are applied in criminal proceedings at first instance provides a tangible basis on which to evaluate the law's claim to respect fairness in criminal cases. It also allows for consideration of whether theorising about fair trials, in the absence of an assessment of the manner in which trial rights are applied in practice, could be said to result in the perpetuation of myths about the weight of defence rights and misplaced confidence in the capacity of defence rights to uphold the legitimacy of the proceedings.

THE CASE FOR TRIAL OBSERVATION

In 1999, while working on my final year dissertation at the School of Law, Professor Lindsay Farmer suggested that I read a book written by Doreen McBarnet entitled *Conviction: Law, the State and the Construction of Justice*.[9] The book detailed research that Professor McBarnet had conducted by observing criminal trials at Glasgow Sheriff Court. She was concerned in particular with the question whether due process guarantees could be said to limit the powers of police and prosecution and if so how this could be squared, *inter alia*, with the fact that the vast majority of trials resulted in a conviction.[10] Her study concluded that due process and crime control – far from being polar opposites as suggested in earlier influential writings[11] – were not just closely linked but that due process guarantees could actually be seen to be for crime control.[12] Some commentators have suggested that due process guarantees at trial are of limited use in restraining the

---

[6] G H Gordon, *The Criminal Law of Scotland* (3rd edn by M G A Christie, 2 vols, 2000 and 2001), first published in 1967.

[7] D Hume, *Commentaries on the Law of Scotland, respecting Crimes* (4th edn by B R Bell, 1844).

[8] Both Gerald Gordon and David Hume studied law at Glasgow University.

[9] D McBarnet, *Conviction: Law, the State and the Construction of Justice* (1981). This book was based on McBarnet's PhD thesis, *Decision-Making in Magistrates' Courts: Law, Procedure and Construction of Conviction* (1980) completed at the University of Glasgow, and available at *http://theses.gla.ac.uk/2044/*.

[10] McBarnet, *Conviction* (n 9) p 2 noting that in 1978 more than 90 per cent of cases in Scotland resulted in a conviction.

[11] See in particular H L Packer, "Two models of the criminal process" (1964) 113 U of Pennsylvania LR 1; H L Packer, *The Limits of the Criminal Sanction* (1968).

[12] McBarnet, *Conviction* (n 9) p 156.

state authorities because the prosecution's case is essentially constructed before the trial and at this stage in the proceedings defence rights have less purchase.[13] Deficiencies in the pre-trial have considerable potential to undermine the fairness of the trial, which does much of the work of guaranteeing the legitimacy of the proceedings. Any account of fairness which does not take sufficient notice of the potential for under-regulation of the pre-trial to undermine the fairness of the trial will be incomplete. This does not mean, though, that it is necessary to develop a specific understanding of the fairness of the pre-trial, only that it is essential to keep in mind the potential for activities during the pre-trial to impact on the fairness of the trial.[14] In observing trials at first instance, the deficiencies of the earlier stages in the proceedings are often quite apparent.

In spite of the recognition of the limits of relying on due process rights, it might be said that little has changed since McBarnet's study, except perhaps that the individual rights of the accused have become even more firmly entrenched as the principal, or indeed perhaps the sole, means of guaranteeing the fairness of the trial.[15] The due process guarantees set out in article 6 of the ECHR have achieved so much recognition that some countries, including the UK and Switzerland, have even advocated taking measures to limit the powers of the European Court of Human Rights (ECtHR).[16] The concept of procedural fairness is now acknowledged across Europe to be the principal means of guaranteeing the legitimacy both of the criminal proceedings and of the state's mandate to punish individuals for criminal wrongs. The dominance of article 6 of the ECHR in establishing the legitimacy of the proceedings means that defence rights have become central to our modern understanding of fairness. The "fairness" of criminal proceedings is measured in terms of individual rights and procedural

---

[13] See eg M McConville, A Sanders and R Leng, *The Case for the Prosecution: Police Suspects and the Construction of Criminality* (1991).

[14] See also R A Duff, L Farmer, S Marshall and V Tadros, "Introduction: towards a normative theory of the criminal trial", in Duff and others (eds), *The Trial on Trial, Volume One: Truth and Due Process* (2004) p 1 at 11: "Exactly what kind of investigative and pre-trial process is acceptable, it seems to us, depends upon the nature of the criminal trial and what it attempts to achieve rather than the other way round."

[15] Some commentators have suggested that it is a mistake to focus only on fairness, see eg R A Duff, L Farmer, S Marshall and V Tadros, *The Trial on Trial, Volume Three: Towards a Normative Theory of the Criminal Trial* (2007) p 108: "Perhaps it is a mistake to focus so much on the idea of fairness, as if this were the only, or only non-truth-related, value relevant to the trial and its procedures, so that the question is always whether a given procedure or provision is fair."

[16] See the leaked draft of the UK's proposal to tighten up the admissibility criteria (draft Brighton declaration) available at: *http://www.guardian.co.uk/law/interactive/2012/feb/ 28/ echr-reform-uk-draft*. The final version of the Brighton Declaration is available at *http://hub.coe. int/20120419-brighton-declaration*. For discussion see J Jackson and S Summers, "Confrontation with Strasbourg: UK and Swiss Approaches to criminal evidence" [2013] Crim LR 115.

safeguards. But this theoretical notion of fairness tells us little about the practice of law or about the significance of this understanding of fairness in practice. In particular, the potential for defence rights to constrain the prosecuting and investigating authorities is seldom paid much attention. Much has been written on doctrinal and normative notions of procedural fairness. But there is comparatively little empirical data not just on the manner in which criminal proceedings are actually conducted but also on the way in which trial rights are actually applied in practice.

This lack of empirical evidence is problematic for a number of reasons, not least because this dominant understanding of fairness is underpinned by a number of assumptions which have not been adequately examined. Various issues which go to the very essence of this definition of fairness remain unanswered. These include the perception that defence rights are extremely strong and that this necessitates that they be balanced not just against the rights of other parties in the process, most notably victims, but also against other interests, such as efficiency and crime control. It is also commonly assumed that individual rights can be uniformly applied, irrespective of the procedural environment. The implication is that as long as the accused can exercise their participatory rights, then the trial will be fair. But this fails to take into account the importance of the procedural context in which the rights are exercised.

Such assumptions, however, rest on a significant inference. It is generally assumed that individuals know of and choose to exercise his or her defence rights. But what if individuals do not exercise their trial rights? And what if the various other participants in the criminal process (judges, prosecutors, defence counsel) do not actively ensure that individuals are in fact exercising these rights? This obviously has significant implications for any understanding of fairness based on individual rights. Is the question whether the accused actually exercises his or her trial rights of relevance to this notion of fairness? In other words is the theoretical opportunity to exercise defence rights sufficient to do justice to this procedural notion of fairness? If the theoretical possibility for the defence to exercise its rights were to be considered sufficient to guarantee the fairness of the proceedings, then the extent of the exercise of defence rights at trial might be considered unimportant. The proceedings would be fair irrespective of whether the individual exercised his or her rights or not. On the other hand, if fairness is more than simply the availability of individual rights, then the failure to exercise these rights could be said to undermine, perhaps fatally, the fairness of the process. Observing trials at first instance represents one way of gauging whether accused persons are exercising their defence rights. Before considering how trial rights are applied in practice, it is useful to consider this issue in theory and in the context of the principle of fairness.

CAN A TRIAL BE CONSIDERED FAIR IF THE ACCUSED DOES NOT EXERCISE HIS OR HER PROCEDURAL RIGHTS?

The definition of fairness in criminal proceedings is well established. A fair trial is a public, speedy process presided over by an independent and impartial authority at which the defence has the opportunity to be informed of the case against it and to present its case in conditions which are not materially different from those afforded to the prosecution.[17] In this regard the concepts of fairness and unfairness are broadly symmetrical. The violation of one of the aspects of the right to a fair trial will automatically violate the right to a fair trial. According to Trechsel, if any of the various guarantees set out in article 6 of the ECHR are not respected, then the trial cannot be regarded as fair.[18] A violation of the equality of arms principle, for instance, will automatically mean that the trial was not fair, even if it had been conducted speedily, in public and adjudicated by an independent and impartial judge.[19] Further, even if none of the constitutive elements of the right to a fair trial has been violated, the ECtHR has on occasion found a violation of article 6 of the ECHR on the basis that the fairness of the trial "as a whole" had not been respected.[20]

In addressing the question whether fairness demands that the accused person exercise all of his or her trial rights, a distinction is commonly made in theory between situations in which the accused was aware of his or her rights and chose, for whatever reason, not to exercise them and those cases in which the accused was unaware of his or her rights and thus was not able to exercise them. It is useful to consider these two scenarios separately.

Waiver of trial rights

The opportunity to waive trial rights is recognised by most jurisdictions. It is worth noting at the outset that an accused may well be entitled to opt out of participating in a contested trial altogether. The accused may

---

[17] S Trechsel, *Human Rights in Criminal Proceedings* (2005); J Jackson and S Summers, *The Internationalisation of Criminal Evidence* (2012) ch 4.

[18] Trechsel (n 17) p 86.

[19] Although this might depend on the accused being able to show quantifiable unfairness flowing from the procedural inequality. Contrast *Lanz v Austria*, no 24430/94, 31 January 2002 at para 58 ("As regards the contents of submissions filed by the prosecution, the Court recalls further that the principle of the equality of arms does not depend on further, quantifiable unfairness flowing from a procedural inequality. It is a matter for the defence to assess whether a submission deserves a reaction. It is therefore unfair for the prosecution to make submissions to a court without the knowledge of the defence.") and Trechsel (n 17) who argues that the defence must demonstrate some prejudice arising from the inequality.

[20] *Barberà, Messengué and Jabardo v Spain*, 6 December 1988, Series A no 146 at para 89.

confess or refrain from contesting a punishment order or fine issued by the investigating or prosecuting authorities with the consequence that no trial as such takes place. The ECtHR has acknowledged that such practices are legitimate and in *Deweer* famously noted that "the right to court, which is a constituent element of the right to a fair trial, is no more absolute in criminal than in civil matters".[21] It held that by agreeing to a settlement in the pre-trial, the accused had "waived his right to have his case dealt with by a tribunal" and that this kind of waiver had "undeniable advantages for the individual concerned as well as for the administration of justice" and thus did not violate the ECHR.[22] It did note, however, that "in a democratic society too great an importance attaches to the 'right to a court' ... for its benefit to be forfeited solely by reason of the fact that an individual is a party to a settlement reached in the course of a procedure ancillary to court proceedings".[23] Consequently it held that any allegation of a violation of article 6 ECHR in this regard had to be subject to "particularly careful review" particularly as regards ensuring the waiver was issued in the absence of any constraint.[24]

Assuming that a contested trial takes place, the question arises as to whether and to what extent the accused is entitled to waive his or her rights. There are many reasons why an accused person or the defence might decide not to exercise certain defence rights. In addition, the possibility of waiving various rights might be seen as a necessary corollary of the important principle that an accused person cannot be compelled to incriminate him or herself or to actively participate in the proceedings. Determining whether and under what circumstances such a waiver might be considered valid is a much-discussed issue. Some commentators have rejected altogether the contention that an accused is entitled to waive the fairness of the trial. Judge Loucaides, for instance, has argued that "human rights are conferred on the individual in the public interest in order to effectuate a policy of protecting him from the omnipotence of the State and of establishing a certain public order in Europe. They are not private personal rights than can be negotiated, compromised, waived or released by an individual".[25] Consequently he has argued that it is impossible to reconcile the right of waiver with the obligation under article 1 of the ECHR to "secure to

---

[21] *Deweer v Belgium*, 27 February 1980, Series A no 35 at para 49.

[22] Referring to the Commission's report in *X v Republic of Germany* App no 1197/61, report of 5 March 1962, Yearbook of the Convention, vol 5 at paras 55–56.

[23] *Deweer v Belgium* at para 49.

[24] See here A Donatsch, "Der Strafbefehl, sowie ähnliche Verfahrenserledigung mit Einsprachemöglichkeit, insbesondere aus dem Gesichtswinkel von Art 6 EMRK" (1994) 112 Schweizerische Zeitschrift für Strafrecht 317.

[25] See eg L Loucaides, "Questions of fair trial under the European Convention on Human Rights" (2003) 3 HRLR 27 at 48–49.

everyone within their jurisdictions the rights and freedoms defined ... in the Convention".[26]

This position has not been accepted by the ECtHR. It has recognised the right of the accused to waive at least some of his or her rights, but has made such waiver subject to limitations.[27] According to the ECtHR: "neither the letter nor the spirit of article 6 of the Convention prevents a person from waiving of his own free will, either expressly or tacitly, the entitlement to the guarantees of a fair trial, including the right to examine or have examined witnesses testifying against him".[28] In order to satisfy the requirement that the waiver is an expression of a person's "free will", the ECtHR has held that "the waiver of the right must be a knowing, voluntary and intelligent act, done with sufficient awareness of the relevant circumstances. Before an accused can be said to have implicitly, through his conduct, waived an important right under article 6, it must be shown that he could reasonably have foreseen what the consequences of his conduct would be".[29] In *Damir Subgatullin*, for instance, the ECtHR rejected the government's contention that the applicant's decision to leave the country constituted a waiver of his right to confront material witnesses. It held that "the right to confront witnesses, being a fundamental right among those which constitute the notion of fair trial, is an example of the rights which require the special protection of the knowing and intelligent waiver standard".[30] It held that it was "not satisfied that sufficient safeguards were in place in the present case for it to be considered that 'the applicant had decided to relinquish his right'".[31] There was no reason to conclude that the applicant "should have been fully aware that by leaving Uzbekistan he was abandoning his right to confront witnesses, or, for that matter, that he understood the nature of that right and could reasonably have foreseen what the consequences of his conduct would be".[32]

It seems clear that for the purposes of article 6 of the ECHR an accused is, as a general rule, entitled to waive the various aspects of the right to

---

[26] Loucaides (n 25). For criticism, see Trechsel, *Human Rights in Criminal Proceedings* (n 17) p 124.

[27] See eg *De Wilde, Ooms and Versyp v Belgium*, 18 June 1971, Series A no 12 at para 65, where the ECtHR suggests that a person cannot consent to be unlawfully detained in contravention of art 5 ECHR.

[28] *Damir Sibgatullin v Russia*, no 1413/05, 24 April 2012, para 46, citing *Hermi v Italy [GC]*, no 118114/02, ECHR 2006-XII at para 73 with further references, and *Vozhigov v Russia*, no 5953/02, 26 April 2007 at para 57.

[29] See eg *Talat Tunç v Turkey*, no 32432/96, 27 March 2007 at para 59, and *Jones v United Kingdom* (dec), no 30900/02, 9 September 2003.

[30] *Damir Sibgatullin* at para 48.

[31] *Damir Sibgatullin* at para 48.

[32] *Damir Sibgatullin* at para 48, citing *Bonev v Bulgaria*, no 60018/00, 8 June 2006 at para 40 with further references; and *Bocos-Cuesta v Netherlands*, no 54789/00, 10 November 2005 at para 66.

be heard (to speak in his or her defence, to question witnesses etc).[33] It is equally evident that the primary responsibility is on the accused to exercise his or her rights. Having said that, the test set out by the ECtHR places certain responsibilities on the state authorities to ensure that the accused, in waiving the trial rights, was aware of the procedural consequences of the waiver. In *Nefedov*, for instance, the applicant complained that the national authorities had failed to ensure his and his counsel's presence at the appeal hearing.[34] The government, meanwhile, argued that neither the applicant nor his lawyer had requested that they be able to attend the hearing and that the state could not be held responsible for the negligence of the lawyer appointed by the accused. The ECtHR held that the fact that the accused did not specifically ask to attend the appeal hearing could not be regarded as an express waiver. It noted in the context of a possible implicit waiver by the applicant of his right to participate in the appeal hearing, that "even assuming that it was a part of the lawyer's duty to inform the applicant about the peculiarities of appeal procedure", the presiding judge, "being the ultimate guardian of the fairness of the proceedings", could not be absolved of his or her responsibility "to explain to a defendant his procedural rights and obligations and secure their effective exercise".[35] In the absence of "clear and comprehensible instructions from the trial judge as to the manner in which a defendant's appearance before the appeal court could be secured", the defendant could not have been expected "to appreciate that the failure to make a special request to ensure his participation in the appeal hearing would result in his appeal being examined in his absence".[36] This underlines the fact that although the principal responsibility is on the accused person to assert his or her rights, this does not absolve the judicial or investigation authorities from taking steps to ensure that the accused person is able to enforce these rights.

This is connected to the requirements also set out by the ECtHR that any waiver must not run counter to any important public interest, that it must be established in an unequivocal manner and that it must be accompanied by "minimum guarantees commensurate to the waiver's importance".[37] This emphasises the fact that the public, and not just the accused person, has a

---

[33] See eg *Sejdovic v Italy* [GC], no 56581/00, ECHR 2006 at para 86; *Talat Tunç v Turkey* (n 29) at para 59; *Jones v United Kingdom* (n 29); *Paskal v Ukraine*, no 24652/04, judgment of 15 September 2011, para 77. One problematic issue concerns the waiver of the right to counsel; this is considered below.

[34] *Nefedov v Russia*, no 40962/04, 13 March 2012.

[35] Paragraph 44.

[36] *Nefedov* at para 44, referring to *Kononov v Russia*, no 41938/04, 27 January 2011 at paras 40–44.

[37] *Damir Sibgatullin v Russia* (n 28) citing *Blake v United Kingdom*, no 68890/01, para 127, 26 September 2006 at para 46.

vested interest in the fairness of the trial. While the accused person clearly has a considerable personal interest in the fairness of the proceedings, in some situations this interest alone might not be sufficient to guarantee that the fairness of the trial is upheld. This is well illustrated by reference to the public trial requirement, not least because the accused person may well have little interest in a public trial.[38] It is debatable therefore whether in such circumstances it is satisfactory to rely on the assumption that the accused person will exercise his or her right to ensure that the public trial requirement is upheld. Equally, the accused may well be unperturbed about the fact that the judge does not appear impartial (particularly if he or she is biased in favour of the accused), but this may nevertheless be of considerable public interest, and indeed concern, to those interested in the administration of justice. This illustrates quite clearly too the weakness of any notion of fairness which relies too strongly on the accused exercising his or her individual rights.

Whereas it is clear that an accused is entitled to waive various rights, including the right to be heard, it is questionable whether it makes sense for the accused to be able to waive the circumstances in which his or her right to be heard is to be exercised. This has been recognised by the United States Supreme Court which has held, for instance, that a defendant was not entitled to prospectively waive the right to a speedy trial as the requirement served to protect both the accused and the public interest.[39] The ECtHR has appeared to struggle with such issues. In the context of the independence and impartiality of the judge, for instance, it refused, in various early cases, to be drawn on whether the accused could waive the right to an impartial judge;[40] in more recent cases, however, it appears to have tacitly accepted this possibility.[41] In other areas, however, it has applied a stricter test and imposed obligations on the judicial authorities to intervene to protect the fairness of the proceedings, even in cases in which defence counsel expressly waived certain rights. In *Cuscani*, for instance, the ECtHR suggested that the right to an interpreter could not be waived by the accused and his or her counsel, even expressly, as the court was under an obligation to uphold the fairness of the proceedings. In this case the applicant complained that he had not been provided with an interpreter at trial and thus had been unable to understand the proceedings properly. It had been clear at trial

---

[38]   Trechsel, *Human Rights in Criminal Proceedings* (n 17) p 109.

[39]   *Zedner v United States* 547 US 489 (2006). See too eg *Håkansson and Sturesson v Sweden* (1991) 13 EHRR 523.

[40]   *Pfeiffer and Plankl v Austria*, judgment of 25 February 1992, Series A no 227 at para 39: "Thus even supposing that the rights in question can be waived by a defendant, the circumstances surrounding the applicant's decision deprived it of any validity from the point of view of the Convention."

[41]   See eg *Golubović v Croatia*, no 43947/10, 27 November 2012.

that the accused had had trouble understanding the proceedings, but his counsel had insisted that the trial could proceed. The ECtHR held, in finding that the trial had not been fair, that the trial judge had been aware of the applicant's inability to understand the proceedings but had allowed himself "to be persuaded by the applicant's counsel's confidence in his ability to 'make do and mend'".[42] It noted that while "the conduct of the defence [was] essentially a matter between the defendant and his counsel … the ultimate guardian of the fairness of the proceedings was the trial judge".[43] This judgment emphasises the public interest in the fairness of the proceedings and the obligations on the state authorities to ensure that the rights of the accused are upheld. It also draws attention to the fact that the right to an interpreter is not just important in the context of the right to be heard but is also "an essential pre-requisite to the proper functioning of the administration of justice".[44] This dual character of the right explains why additional obligations are placed on the authorities to examine the impact of a waiver on the part of the defence on the right to a fair trial.

It could be argued that it is not necessary that a contested trial take place but, if it does, then it must satisfy the requirements of fairness. It seems sensible in this regard to make a distinction between the right to be heard and the procedural environment in which these rights are to be exercised. Whereas the accused should be entitled to waive the various aspects of the right to be heard, if he or she accepts a contested trial, the state will be under an obligation to ensure that the accused can exercise his or her right to be heard in a particular procedural environment: at a speedy and public trial presided over by an independent and impartial judge.

In short, the decision of the accused person not to exercise trial rights is generally compatible with the notion of fairness in article 6 of the ECHR, providing the accused is aware of the procedural consequences of such a waiver and that the public interest in a fair trial is not compromised.

Ignorance of trial rights

One problem for a rights-based approach to fairness is ensuring that the accused is actually aware of and able to exercise these rights. A number of potential obstacles exist which may serve to prevent an accused person from exercising his or her rights including unfamiliarity with the language of the court, mental health problems or even the simple inability to come to grips with the legal and procedural environment.[45] As we have seen, knowledge

---

[42] *Cuscani v United Kingdom*, no 32771/96, 24 September 2002 at para 38.

[43] *Cuscani* at para 39.

[44] Trechsel, *Human Rights in Criminal Proceedings* (n 17) p 329.

[45] See eg R J Medalie, L Zeitz and P Alexander, "Custodial police interrogation in our nation's capital: the attempt to implement *Miranda*" (1968) 66 Mich LR 1337.

of the rights, and indeed of the procedural consequences of not exercising these rights, is a prerequisite to a valid waiver. If, however, an accused person does not exercise his or her trial rights because he or she is unaware of these rights, can the trial be said to be fair?

Fairness demands that the accused person be afforded "access to justice". Access to justice is in turn contingent on the accused being aware of his or her rights. It is quite obvious that an accused person will be able to exercise his or her rights in an effective and practical manner only if he or she is aware of these rights.[46] One obvious means of resolving doubts about whether the accused is aware of his or her rights is to compel the state authorities to ensure that the accused person can be assisted by legal counsel. This involves removing procedural barriers to lawyers having access to accused persons and participating in hearings, particularly at an early stage in the proceedings. Providing access to counsel not only ensures that the accused is aware of his or her rights but also serves to uphold the principle of equality of arms. This has been recognised in Strasbourg, and the ECtHR has afforded increasing weight to the importance of ensuring that the accused has access to counsel. Restrictions on the assistance of counsel at the beginning of the proceedings, which were commonplace across Europe, have been lifted following the ground-breaking judgment in *Salduz*.[47]

But even in the absence of specific procedural restrictions on the right to counsel, there are various ways in which the accused can, in practice, be dissuaded from employing the services of a lawyer. The most common of these is to invoke the issue of payment of legal costs. Ensuring that those who do not have sufficient financial means have access to legal aid is of crucial importance to the access to justice requirement.[48] Although the obligation to inform the accused of the right to counsel is now firmly established, the situation with regard to being informed about the right to legal aid counsel at the beginning of the proceedings is far less clear.[49] This is largely a consequence of the blurry nature of the tests in most jurisdictions, which in many cases will make it very difficult for the investigating authorities to establish whether the accused is in fact entitled

---

[46] *Airey v Ireland*, judgment of 9 October 1979, Series A no 32.

[47] *Salduz v Turkey* (GC), no 36391/02, 27 November 2008.

[48] *Granger v United Kingdom*, March 1990, Series A no 174; *Maxwell v United Kingdom*, 28 October 1994, Series A no 300-C; *Artico v Italy*, 13 May 1980, Series A no 37.

[49] It should be noted that the right to be informed about "any entitlement to free legal aid" is included in the EU Directive on the right to information in criminal proceedings, Directive 2012/13/ EU, 22 May 2012 art 1(b). It is notable in this regard that a recent EU proposal to establish minimum rules on legal aid proved so controversial that it was removed from the proposed Directive on the right of access to a lawyer in criminal proceeding. See further C Morgan, "Where are we now with EU procedural rights?" [2012] EHRLR 427.

to legal aid. This issue is inevitably connected to the matter of waiver. An accused who is under the impression that he or she will have to pay for counsel is much more likely to waive the right to counsel altogether.

It could be argued that in view of the importance of defence counsel as a counterbalance to the prosecutor, the accused person should never be able to waive the right to counsel. In the absence of counsel, the procedural imbalance would be such that equality of arms could not be achieved. In other words, the assistance of counsel might be considered to serve an "important public interest".[50] As we have seen, the accused is, as a general rule, entitled to waive the right to counsel,[51] albeit that this is subject to various limitations; in some situations fairness will require that the state authorities take steps to ensure that the accused is afforded the assistance of counsel.[52] Imposing a requirement on every accused person to appoint counsel, however, would be problematic.[53]

In assessing the validity of the waiver of the right to counsel, it is necessary to balance the freedom of the accused in determining how to conduct his or her defence with the public interest in ensuring that the conditions of the trial are such as to allow a fair trial to take place. One solution to this problem is to impose a requirement that an accused person is entitled to waive the right to counsel only after she or he has had the opportunity to take legal advice.[54] This was the position taken by Lord Kerr in his dissenting opinion in *McGowan (Procurator Fiscal) v B*.[55] In rejecting the suggestion of the majority that right to counsel

---

[50] *Håkansson and Sturesson v Sweden* (n 39) para 66; *Sejdovic v Italy* (n 33) at para 86.

[51] The ECtHR has refused to accept a waiver in the context of various accused persons *Panovits v Cyprus*, no 4268/04, 11 December 2008.

[52] *Panovits v Cyprus* at para 66.

[53] See J Chalmers and F Leverick, "'Substantial and radical change': a new dawn for Scottish criminal procedure?" (2012) 75 MLR 837 at 847, commenting that "it would be offensive to notions of freedom of choice and personal autonomy to force assistance upon someone who does not want it".

[54] The UKSC has recognised that where there is reason to believe that the suspect does not understand the right that is being waived, he or she may require legal advice before there can be a valid waiver. See eg *McGowan v B* [2011] UKSC 54, 2012 SC (UKSC) 182, reversing *Jude v HM Advocate* [2011] HCJAC 46, 2011 JC 252 and remitting the question whether the Lord Advocate's reliance at the trial of the respondent upon evidence of answers that the respondent gave during his police interview was compatible with his rights under art 6(1) and 6(3)(c) in circumstances where the respondent was informed of his art 6 rights of access to legal advice and he indicated he did not wish to exercise such rights without having received advice from a lawyer. It is also interesting to note that the EU Directive on the right of access to legal advice makes the acceptance of a waiver contingent on the accused having "received prior legal advice on the consequences of the waiver" or otherwise obtaining full knowledge of the consequences: art 9(1)(a) of the Proposal for a Directive on the right of access to a lawyer in criminal proceedings and on the right to communicate upon arrest, Brussels, COM (2011) 326/3.

[55] At paras 105–107.

was necessary to protect the suspect from coercion, he argued instead that access to counsel was necessary to enable the accused to actively pursue his defence rights at the investigation stage in order to ensure true equality of arms. He argued that it was for the prosecuting authorities to establish that the waiver was valid and that in doing so they were required to show that the suspect had been informed of his or her right to counsel, that he or she was aware of the circumstances in which it could be provided and appreciated the consequences of failing to have the assistance of a lawyer.[56] One simple way of ensuring this was to make sure that the accused person was advised by a lawyer as to whether or not to waive the right to legal assistance.

Fairness in the sense of article 6 of the ECHR requires that those accused of criminal offences are aware of their defence rights. Ignorance of these rights will fatally undermine the fairness of the trial.

Trial rights, knowledge and waiver

The importance of an accused person being aware of and able to exercise his or her defence rights is recognised in theory as being of considerable importance. A criminal trial may be fair if the accused chooses not to exercise his or her rights, but only if this decision is deemed to be taken in the awareness of the procedural consequences of the waiver and if it is compatible with the public interest in the fairness of the proceedings. As we have seen, the primary responsibility for exercising trial rights lies with the accused, although the authorities may, in certain situations, be required to take action in order to ensure that these rights can be implemented effectively. For the most part, the authorities can avoid being held responsible for an accused's failure to exercise his or her rights by ensuring that he or she is afforded the assistance of defence counsel. It is useful now to turn to consider the manner in which trial rights are applied in practice by examining some early findings of the trial observation project currently underway in Switzerland.

TRIAL RIGHTS IN PRACTICE

Trial observation project

The trial observation project, inspired by McBarnet's project, is a large empirical study of criminal trials in four Swiss cities: Basel, Bern, Geneva and Zurich. Each jurisdiction has a distinct procedural tradition, due in large part to the fact that criminal procedure law was, until recently, regulated at the cantonal level. The Federal Code of Criminal Procedure

---

[56] At paras 103 and 108.

which came into force in 2011 has resulted in procedural uniformity across Switzerland, but the cantons have retained responsibility for the organisation of their justice systems and considerable cultural and organisational differences remain. The trial observation project involves the simultaneous, systematic observation of criminal proceedings in the various jurisdictions over a two-year period in order to collect data on the manner in which criminal proceedings are conducted and in particular on the way in which the fair trial rights as set out in article 6 of the ECHR are implemented in practice. In addition data is being collected on whether fair trial concerns were raised during the proceedings, by whom and how they were dealt with by the court. The four principal trials observers are responsible for monitoring the trials, noting how often fair trial matters are mentioned and for assessing both the trial violations which are mentioned by the various participants in the court proceedings and those which are witnessed by the observer but not discussed in court. In addition, interview-administered surveys are conducted with defendants, prosecutors and defence counsel at the end of the proceedings in order to collect information on perceptions of fairness and to gather data which is difficult to obtain by observation alone.

Preliminary findings

Early data from the trial observation project[57] suggests that, as in McBarnet's study, the rate of convictions is extremely high. Around 95 per cent of the cases observed over a one-year period resulted in a conviction.[58] As regards the issue of knowledge of trial rights and access to counsel, it is notable that the accused was represented by counsel at trial in the majority of cases. The accused did not have the assistance of a lawyer at trial in about 20 per cent of all cases and in most of these cases the prosecutor was similarly absent.[59] In a large number of cases, despite changes to the law post *Salduz*, the accused – for various reasons – did not have access to counsel from the very beginning of the proceedings.

In spite of the broad access to counsel, perhaps one of the most interesting early indications to emerge from the study is that fair trial

---

[57] The data collection phase of the project is scheduled to run until the end of 2014. These early findings concern data collected between November 2012 and October 2013.

[58] This figure includes cases in which the accused was found guilty on any of the charges set out in the complaint.

[59] The prosecutor is only required to be present at trial if he or she has requested a custodial sentence of more than one year: see art 337 of the Swiss Federal Code of Criminal Procedure. On this matter see S Summers, "Presence, absence, dominance: the role of the prosecutor in Switzerland", in A Cavallo and others (eds), *Liber Amicorum für Andreas Donatsch* (2012) p 517.

violations at trial are rarely mentioned by defence counsel and, less surprisingly, almost never mentioned by the prosecutor. In fact, accused persons were significantly more likely to refer to fair trial violations than defence counsel. Surprisingly, in the majority of cases and in relation to a wide variety of violations, early data suggest that the judge is by far the most likely person in the proceedings to refer to potential fair trial violations. There are various reasons which might be put forward to explain the lack of activity on the part of defence counsel. One explanation might be that defence counsel are wary of mentioning fair trial violations for tactical reasons or for fear of antagonising the court. Another reason might be that they are aware that raising fair trial matters rarely has an impact on the verdict or the sentence. This is reflected in the situation in practice. In the vast majority of cases, an allegation that one of the fair trial standards had been violated had little impact on the case. A notable exception in this regard concerns violations of the right to a speedy trial. This is the only violation which is regularly referred to by defence counsel; it is also the only violation which regularly has an impact on the verdict or the sentence in that is will usually result in a sentence reduction.

It might be argued that the relative scarcity of allegations of fair trial violations is an indication that trials are actually quite fair. This does not appear to be supported by the findings of the trial observation team. The relative unimportance of defence rights as a subject of concern at trial contrasts with a number of systematic violations of trial rights witnessed by the observation team, which are rarely mentioned in practice. In the context of the right to interpretation, for instance, in 83 per cent of cases significant parts of the proceedings (such as the pleadings of the prosecutor or communication between the court and lawyers) were not translated, despite a translator being present. In a large number of cases the prosecutor was absent, thereby calling into question the impartiality of the judge.[60] In the majority of cases in one of the jurisdictions witnesses were almost never heard by the court, which relied instead on written transcripts produced during pre-trial hearings conducted by the prosecution.

The data collection phase of the project is still underway, but these early findings nevertheless give rise to the question whether ensuring that the accused is aware of his or her rights is sufficient to ensure that these rights are effectively implemented in practice. Even providing an accused with the assistance of counsel does not guarantee that the fair trial rights are applied in practice.

---

[60] On this matter see the judgment in *Ozerov v Russia*, no 64692/01, 18 May 2010.

LAW AS A PRACTICE: TRIAL RIGHTS, KNOWLEDGE AND WAIVER

The definition of fairness set out by Strasbourg is based on individual rights and is dependent on the accused actually exercising his or her rights. Waiver is deemed to be compatible with fairness, providing that the waiver is voluntary and well informed. Ignorance of trial rights represents a real problem for this notion of fairness. Knowledge of trial rights is essential to these rights being exercised in practice. Access to counsel is considered to be of crucial importance to ensuring that the accused can implement his or her trial rights. It is problematic however to put all the work of implementing rights on the accused; the state authorities are under various obligations to ensure that the rights of the accused are enforced. This is of particular relevance in the context of the procedural environment in which the accused can exercise the defence rights. The state should be under an obligation to ensure that the trial is public, speedy and supervised by an independent and impartial judge.

Trial rights appear to be significantly less important in practice than in theory. Defence counsel frequently appear unaware of, or unwilling to refer to, trial rights. Only very rarely will a reference to trial rights have an impact on the verdict or the sentence. This raises questions about the concept of procedural fairness in article 6 of the ECHR. Whereas, in theory, fairness is measured by procedural opportunities, there are indications that in practice other issues, notably perceived accuracy of outcome, might be considered to be more important. Trial rights are of critical importance to guaranteeing the legitimacy of criminal proceedings; for this reason it is essential that there be scrutiny of the manner in which they are applied. If trial rights are not being applied then fairness, far from providing legitimacy, may in fact serve to mask the unfairness of the proceedings.

Consideration of the manner in which the law is applied is of considerable importance to a comprehensive understanding of the law, not least because in practice the law has considerable scope to compensate for change in order to protect the status quo.[61] In this regard, projects such as the Strasbourg project at the School of Law, which draw students' attention to the manner in which the law is applied, are of crucial importance.

---

[61] W Stuntz, "The uneasy relationship between criminal procedure and criminal justice" (1997) 107 Yale LJ 1.